YOUNG SPIRITU

The Early Life Of

James Thompson:

(Future Radical Priest And Fervent Animal Activist)

Dedication:

With Gratitude To THE GOOD SHEPHERD
for the memory of a silver-haired, deformed, lady
with sparkling eyes - My Mother.

Also To:

Doreen, My Helpmeet & Ever Constant, Ray Of Sunshine

A catalogue record of this book is available
from the British Library.

ISBN 0-9523022-3-3

2005 © James Thompson

Ty Coch Publishing
Peace Haven, Fron Park Rd
Holywell. Clwyd CH8 7UY

Tel: 01352 - 712368

Contents

BY WAY OF INTRODUCTION	4
NURTURED IN BONNIE SCOTLAND	8
A BRIEF TASTE OF SHROPSHIRE	22
INTO 'GOD'S OWN COUNTRY'	29
JOBS START IN A FUME IMPREGNATED PROJECTION BOX	37
SPIRITUALLY I PASS FROM DEATH TO LIFE	53
DUCKED CONFIRMED AND DISILLUSIONED	63
GOD MAKES ME A PREACHER	78
A STUDENT OF GLASGOW'S BIBLE TRAINING INSTITUTE	86
I MEET A PLYMOUTH BROTHER	96
THROWN OUT AFTER ONE TERM!	106
A NOSTALGIC TRIP IN TO THE PAST	116
ROME, JEHOVAH, OR SIMPLY 'CHAPEL'	120
AN, IDYLLICALLY WELSH, POST ROUND	133
AMONGST DEAR ULSTER'S PRODDY DOGS & PAPISTS	143
WHICH IS IT TO BE? YOU CAN'T BE BOTH!	155
A NEWCASTLE PROTEST & THEN OFF TO LONDON	162
ACCEPTED AS A KENSITITE, AND THEN ENGAGED	168
A FICKLE FIANCÉE & A FANATICAL FRIEND	176
VARIED EXPERIENCES UPON TYNESIDE	184
A PASTOR TO PAUPERS COMES TO MY AID	199
PRIDE BEFORE A FALL: EXPERIENCED AND WITNESSED	208
THANKS TO YORKSHIRE, I'M A BAPTIST MINISTER!	215
A HEART RENDERING DECISION TO MAKE	226
WE ELOPE, BUT OH TO WHERE?	233
TRAILING THE STREETS OF LONDON	241
FRUSTRATING WORK & A FRUSTRATED LANDLADY	251
TWO MEN OF INFLUENCE TRACK US DOWN	258
BREATHTAKING DAYS CULMINATE IN SCOTIA'S CAPITAL	263
OUTDOING ROGUES AT THEIR OWN GAME	272
THE MARRIAGE OF THE YEAR	281
IN CONCLUSION	285
ACKNOWLEDGEMENTS	287
SUBSEQUENT NOTES ON THE AUTHOR	288

By Way Of Introduction

I believe in a Divine Presence, which can come to folk today as it did in far off Bible times. I believe it comes to sensitive creatures whose lives often seem insecure and fraught with danger. I see an easy answer why the fisher folk in Scotland are so deeply religious; why the people in troubled Ulster share a similar experience; and why the past miners in Wales were so devoutly spiritual. Yes, there is indeed a divine seed, which germinates when it finds conducive soil.

The trouble follows when those, with such an experience, begin to equate it either with isolated biblical passages or sectarian dogmas. Then it is that those accepting identical teaching are viewed as 'the faithful', 'the orthodox, 'the born again', 'the elect', while others become 'the lost', 'the heretics', 'the reprobates' or 'the goats.' For myself, I've come to believe in a Faith wider than any creedal formula or denominational confession; in a Saviour closer by far than any churches sacrament; and in a salvation as inclusive as the ark in Noah's day rather than the 'exclusive to human' one of today's Christendom. But while, awaiting this future age, I meanwhile follow the morality of the friend of sinners and I hold nothing in common with those whose moral priorities lead them to pick out gnats as they swallow camels.

What I've learned to appreciate today, apart from what I've learned directly from the book of books and the luck of life, is the simple result of having accepted much and rejected much of the teaching of a host of conflicting denominations; and I've been a minister of no less than five of them. Yes, and I'm actually thankful for the experience each one gave me. Way back in early years - about which this present volume is concerned - I was, as one cleric commented, 'fast becoming a spiritual tramp.' Well, whatever lack of character that term may happen to convey I'm sure you'll agree with me that it's preferable to being a 'conditioned ecclesiastical clone' or just one more 'pea from a denominational pod.' But what is the good of a unique past unless others are to benefit a little by it? Hence the purpose of the pages that follow.

A decade or two ago the friendly Bishop Darwent of Aberdeen was eager to send two of his clergy on an 'in service' refresher course; one of the fellows had to give back word and I was asked to take his place. The venue was the old theological college off Coates Gardens, the Haymarket area of Edinburgh; a district which I hadn't resided in since the spring of 1954. Indeed, little would those attending the seminar with me have dreamed of my past associations with that very area. They had been unique indeed. Yet, unless it were his very double, it would not be the first time to meet a now elderly priest by the name of Strachan, a cleric of great stamina and an ex-tutor of the college there. He was the type who appeared to remain the same with the passing of time. He could not now be expected to remember me. Yet, I remembered him clearly from no less than thirty-five years previous. He was so keen to go ahead and marry us when I, and my first wife to be, approached him within the grandiose Cathedral church of St. Mary's.

Ah yes, and my recollections of that elite Church of Scotland in Palmerston Place opposite, where the minister had decided, last minute, 'to call off' marrying us. 'And could anyone blame him considering the publicity the elopement had caused'? Piries Hotel, where thirty-five years previous we'd spent most of our days for residential qualifications to be married under Scottish law, was once again frequented. Andrew, a fellow priest, and I went no further inside than to the public bar.

The weird, sinister, old flat above the bank in West Maitland Street was 'still standing.' It still seemed sinister even though the flickering and hissing gas bracket at the foot of the stairs along the passage entrance had been replaced by electric. Indeed, it was all coming back into focus again through the decades now gone.

That seminar was largely on changing family patterns. Well, I suppose I held a more traditional outlook as to what marriage should be about than most of them there. They spoke about cohabitation becoming the norm. Well, I'd cohabited myself and now I was leaning if anything against it. They were arguing for the acceptability of divorce where there were grounds of incompatibility. I was arguing that marriage should be until death us do part. Yet, I was divorced and remarried myself. It all seemed quite inconsistent but then I dare say much of my life has been very inconsistent. The Almighty, however, can teach via our inconsistencies and knocks. He can use them for a purpose. I've learned to believe that each knock can be a knock forward in the school of life. Each, stumbling block can become a stepping-stone. Indeed, each set back is a potential springboard. It's taken the maturity of the years to prove all this and that, which follows, is the religious story of my early life of years that were quite immature. Those, however, who have depth of insight will look beyond the surface shallowness of outer events and perceive a young struggling soul beneath it all. The chapters in this volume lead up to my first acquaintance with Edinburgh and its Haymarket locality. Some day chapters may follow - even more unique still! - which lead to recent times.

That 'In Service' visit to the Capital's Haymarket vicinity prompted me, in the midst of an extremely busy life, to get pen to paper so as to compile, at a more leisurely stage, as authentic a record as possible; the only exception being that a minute number of names have undergone slight change. This has been to avoid any one sided criticism of others, be they here or – please God! – in Heaven.. May such a volume be the means of encouraging some who've been denied what the world might call a good basic education? May others learn from my early misdemeanours and the pride of youth. And may the spiritually smug of each extreme learn a little of a Good Shepherd's love whose arms have always been more embracing than their own.

The author at seven

Nurtured In Bonnie Scotland

On the fourth day of February, in the year 1930, I was born at Brunel Terrace, Westmorland Road, Newcastle-upon-Tyne, and a week or two later I was christened at the Parish Church of St. Aidan, Benwell, an adjoining parish.

At the age of two, mother and father were separated, and through the influence of my Grandfather, Mother was able to procure for herself, my brother and myself, a humble courtyard cottage in the Scottish border town of Coldstream, in Berwickshire. We stayed in this town until I was no more than in my eighth year. I can naturally remember very little about those far off years but, concerning religion, I do remember that the majority of folk attended a place of worship on Sundays, the Sabbath, as they termed it. Most attended the Parish Kirk, others a daughter Kirk, while only a minority attended the small Episcopal Church. The latter was dedicated to St Mary and All Souls. Some referred to it as 'the tin tab', and others quite wrongfully as 'English'.

I vaguely recollect, *at pre-school age* looking out of the door of a humble dwelling, situated between stables, while a frightened cow approached and appeared anxious to come inside. This was followed by an agitated farmer yelling towards it, waving a stick around it, and most profusely apologising to my Mum for the inconvenience this frightened creature was causing. When it couldn't get in front ways, it changed positions and appeared as if to be entering bottom first, while retreating from the prodding and cajoling of the distraught farmhand outside.

For some reason – even though I was so very young – I knew the frantic creature to be a lady of the animal kingdom and, somehow, felt that it should have been treated with the respect one owes to the female gender, of which I knew my own precious Mum to be. If the memory serves me correctly, the poor creature had possibly broken away from the herd, to end up in this private estate. Yes, expansive grounds, in a secluded corner of which one could enter a unique pet cemetery; all part of the exquisite 'Leaze Estate' wherein a late Lady Marchbanks had once doted over her dogs and horses, as well as her ferial cats for which she'd constructed a - now deserted – cattery.

As for *the earliest school experience* remembered, it referred to the very first day! The memory of being attired in School uniform - which felt uncomfortably on the big size! - is dwarfed by the thought of what happened to the school cap itself. This had the emblem of a salmon embroidered above the nib. Indeed, it related to the Tweed: a river that flowed along the side of the delightful town. On arrival, I remember being told to place my cap on a peg in a room that was adjacent to the classroom. A classroom surrounded by hangings with pictures upon them, such as that of a dog, and the words beneath ROVER LOVES ME AND I LOVE ROVER. However, on returning to the cloakroom at 'break up time' I'd difficulty locating my cap, and then noticed it on a shelf nearby. Quite bewildered, I lifted it by the nib, but was unable to place it on my head because of its weight. Then – horrors of horrors! – on looking within, I discovered that someone had 'pooed' into it. Indeed, in utter bewilderment I walked back in to the class and, looking up to the teacher, said: "Look what someone has done to my new cap!". And – as if to add insult to injury, she burst out in to spontaneous laughter. As for myself, I didn't think it was funny, and though she then endeavoured to pull herself together and show me some pity, it all came about as false. Worse still, she called for another teacher who appeared to have real difficulty in not laughing. They, just didn't comprehend how I was feeling about my cap.

Mrs Skinner – for that was this infant teacher's name – then took this newly prized headgear away and brought it back minus 'the plonker', She then wrapped it in a newspaper for me to take home, along with a letter of explanation for Mum. And - if the memory serves me well – she got the culprit to apologise and told him always to raise his hand whenever he wanted a 'Number One' or – as in this case – 'a number Two'. Indeed, it seemed as if he had no idea what lavatories were for!

On reaching home, Mum's face lifted up with radiance. She'd offered to meet me at the school, but I wanted to come home by myself. As her eye's sparkled with love she said: "Is this what you've made at school?" Well, I said nothing; just held my head down as she unravelled what could have looked like an old time wrapping of fish and chips. What else followed, I cannot remember; only that dear Mum forked out, within the next couple of days, more money for another school cap.

It was a veritable 'child's paradise' living in such countrified, though somewhat weird, surroundings as that of The Leaze. Yes, a vast area of private recreation in which my brother and I lived with our Mum; and in which we were warned, through her uncle (the factor) to keep well indoors, and never to venture out whenever a nearby chase was due! Indeed, the most we ever experienced of blood 'sports' was the shrill sound of a hunter's horn; and soon the Uncle would call and give the 'all clear' for us venturing out to resume our play.

A far less pleasant memory was when Mum allowed my brother – four years older than myself – to go out with a half cousin his own age; but Mum insisted, much to their annoyance, that I tag along with them. Well, obviously, my presence was not appreciated. Having sauntered along a path alongside of a fast flowing dam (which incidentally provided water for the town), we came towards a bower that stood near what was nicknamed 'the bottomless pool'. It was, indeed, a ghostly spot and when I dragged behind and began to cry as a spoilt younger brother, the half cousin took advantage of my open mouth, asked me to open it wider, and threw, what seemed a large pebble into it. Unfortunately for her, I gulped it down, and the pain that followed as it slowly made its way downward was not to be forgotten. Their attitude changed from one of fun, to fear as well as pity; and when I promised not to split on what had transpired or where we'd been, the half cousin proved nice to me ever after. However, I do remember how Mum, Granddad and Grandma had been deeply disturbed by 'a blood curdling rite' that had recently occurred to this youngster, for she'd been accepted into the hunting fraternity. Granddad – a proud quarter master sergeant and no sentimentalist – was horrified to learn that the heart had been ripped from a newly caught fox, and that its warm blood had been splattered over the girl's face as part of her initiation. His words were to the effect: "This macabre and sinister kind of thing can turn a child's mind forever! What on earth was up with her parents to agree to it? Their heads need knocking together to drum some sense into them!"

Indeed, the atmosphere of those grounds made me aware of spiritual encroachments. Were they not occasionally heard through an unexpected rustle of leaves, a breeze that gave movement to trees; the sound of nearby roaring water in a dam; or equally felt through the utter silence of a stagnant pool, alongside of which an antiquated bower leaned as though ready to submerge into it? If these were not enough to eerily attract the curiosity of an infant, there was an ice house built in to the side of a bush covered hillock, the door of which one wanted to open and yet was too terrified to approach. Then, quite near to it - in the vicinity of a looming unoccupied mansion - stood a circular open building of Pagan style and occult orientation. It was simply known as 'the temple', and for some unknown reason Mum told us always to keep well away from it.

Little wonder, that on moving to a more salubrious dwelling – the gatehouse at the estate's top entrance – that odd things seemed to occur! Indeed, at nights, when tucked in bed, the curtains would occasionally appear to move and patterns on the wallpaper would start to come alive. A gleaming face would appear to stare, having got through the window. The tick of the clock on the mantelpiece, above the fireplace, would become louder and almost lifelike. And then, one would suddenly awaken in a panic of sheer terror, with Mum soothing one's brow and saying: "Don't worry Jim. Everything is OK. It's just been a horrid, nasty dream! Go back to sleep again. I'm at your side." Indeed, my brother Colin may have felt less secure still. He had to sleep in a recess within the wall of the living room; isolated from it at night by a heavily draped curtain.

One thing was obvious to us all: the secluded world in which we dwelt – far removed from the populace of the town - was vibrant with life, both visible in the form of birds and beasts, and equally invisible in the form of 'other worldly' presences. Indeed, no one appeared more aware of the latter than a Romany Gipsy who came to the door selling clothes pegs. I squeezed my way forwards to be at the side of Mum, and as this bronze skinned lady looked down, she was overcome by emotion: "What a lovely boy... He's been sent to you from Heaven... Why! Look he has the face of an angel... God bless you pet. God bless you!"

Interspersed with such words of commendation that a young mind could hardly object to, she looked up at Mum. "Wont you by some more pegs, lady?" Naturally, I exceedingly liked this caller at our door. As for Mum, she could ill afford to buy more pegs than she needed. Yet she was perturbed, more than once, to be told that evil forces surrounded the place: "They're out to get you dear lady; and one person nearby is very jealous of you. She's out to do you great harm, but she'll not succeed. Buy more pegs lady, and I'll tell you more!" Mum declined, and the Romany courteously went on her way. This left Mum frequently regretting that she had not bought another lot of pegs, even though she didn't need them!

Mum was in certain respects quite superstitious and – though she quite detested cats because of the way they preyed upon birds - one, which frequently came to our door, was an exception. We named it Ginger; and whenever I was out playing in close proximity to the lodge, Ginger would be sat opposite. Mum said its eyes were constantly fixed upon me, and whenever anyone came near, Ginger would encircle me and look quite fierce towards them. "Jim! That cat never takes its eyes off you. It seems to be guarding you" she would affirm

Sunday brought its own problems. I well remember my dislike of having to dress up in uncomfortable Sunday clothes, and being forbidden to play on a Sunday afternoon because the latter could be regard by Mum's aunt as profaning the Sabbath. This was the day when the Parish Kirk was usually frequented. I can still remember the depressing feeling while sat there to undergo the ordeal of a long sermon delivered in a sanctimonious tone. I can still visualise shadows from possible lamps, the dark woodwork, the seemingly high pulpit occupied by an austere looking cleric arrayed in black except for preaching bands and hood. I can even remember how during his long and lengthy prayers I was forbidden to fidget. I noticed that Mother seemed to enjoy many services even to the point of occasionally shedding tears through what must have touched her. The Minister of Coldstream, to give him his recognised title, seemed a kindly gentleman, understanding and loving, and the Church officials, the Pillars, were always prepared to give us a welcome.

I remember one dreadfully wet afternoon. The sky was dark and the wind was howling. A number of people including the parish minister were sheltering under the trees outside the gates of our home: referred to as 'The Lodge' They were no doubt waiting for the weather to brighten so as to continue their country stroll because people enjoyed walking in those days. As they were drenched by the sudden downfall Mother made it clear that, at least, the Minister and his wife should be invited in, necessitating a quick tidy round and the best crockery being brought out for possible use. I know that my brother and I did not want such an intrusion but it was made very clear that, to have left the Minister and his wife in the rain, could have led to severe criticism of us throughout the town. The Cloth had to be respected.

'The Lodge where we lived'

The Revd. 'Paddy' Brown was very grateful to accept our hospitality. He was very prominent with his bushy eyebrows and big brimmed hat. His wife and he were the perfect lady and gentleman of the Parish. He spoke lovingly to us and understandingly to my Mother. We were well drilled to refer to him as Sir at the end of every sentence. On their departure Mother implied how nice and thoughtful they had expressed themselves. "Nevertheless, they only hob nob to the wealthy," we were told. Mother made it clear that she had little respect beneath the surface for a particular brand of Scottish cleric. I see them now, down the years, frock coats, lace cuffs, wide brimmed hats blowing in the breeze. I recollect a scuffle to move away unobtrusively in the opposite direction so as not to face the embarrassment of a head-on encounter.

The Parish Church of Coldstream had also a daughter Kirk termed 'The West Church,' which received a new minister, young and fresh from Theological College, or as the Scottish termed it, Divinity Hall. A man, who is young and pastorally less experienced, might not always see eye to eye with the cleric of mature years. I only remember the rumour, true or false, that rivalry between centres of worship was no doubt felt. Acquiring a racing car and exceeding the speed limit of those days would be enough to make oneself the idol of the young worshippers, as well as to receive the disdain of the elderly Scot who expected a standard more in keeping with the cloth. The young minister would either ignore me, or just pass me by with a quizzical grin. Who could blame him? I was too young and small to be noticed. My brother, Colin, was three years older, and Mr. Reid was truly loved by my brother and his pals.

Quite vividly there comes to my mind, perhaps, the first Movie I'd ever seen. This was in the West Church. It was a silent movie taken by the minister himself from in the mission field. I remember seeing little, coloured children looking so cute and having a wonderful time bathing in a large pool while throwing water over each other. The only other cinema shows were those of a secular kind - the visit of the travelling cinema once a year to the Town Hall. In our own home there was a toy cinematograph, worked by a handle and illuminated by a flat shaped battery. We screened upon a white sheet 'Felix the cat' and ' Mickey Mouse.'

The mother Kirk was privileged to have secured, as the organist, a talented man of the town who had acquired a doctorate in music. This well loved musician was eager to build up the Kirk's choir. Time plays tricks on far off days, yet the audition I attended was something that deeply hurt my young pride. I vaguely remember a keyboard to which different coloured lights were attached illuminating notes of the tonic solfa. Provided you knew the scale, you would probably sing in tune with the music to be practised. For myself, I was proved thoroughly illiterate and it was made plain that my presence could be served better elsewhere. I must have been very sensitive as this was to be the first and last choir rehearsal in which I ever took part. Well! certainly until I was a priest thirty years later and in charge of one!

There were those very pleasant Sunday occasions when Mother decided, for a change, we should walk a little further to a place of worship through the town centre which apart from bells, would be as silent as a cemetery. There, at the beginning of a country lane, the Episcopal Church stood. The clergyman nicknamed 'Daddy' Swinton was always ready to welcome us. He must have been of a 'High Church' outlook a marked contrast, indeed, to the austerity and drab solemnity of the other churches within the vicinity. This 'Rector' was revered for his saintliness. From aristocratic background he fulfilled the role of an Episcopal priest as well as private chaplain to the Earl of Hume. I recollect him as humble and gentle. His small, rather poor looking Church had plain jam jars on each windowsill, which sometimes contained wild flowers. I used to think it funny because this minister wore a long black dress to his ankles and yet he was a man. What amused me more was that, in one part of the service, he entered a side door and shortly afterwards reappeared dressed differently. I could hardly be expected to know the meaning of vestments and of ceremonial, but I well remember the loveliness of the atmosphere I, as a youngster, experienced in that hallowed building. Christianity is often caught more than taught.

'at the beginning of a country lane'

On many Sunday afternoons, and especially for some reason do I associate it with the colder months, my dear brother, Colin, and I would spend time in the isolated cottage where we lived pretending that we were at Church. Colin would pretend that he was a Parish Minister while I took on the role of organist. Teaspoons were put in a row under a book at the side of the table and I made out they were the organ keys. My brother would put on back to front his navy blue school gabardine; held cut out pieces of cardboard and made a collar, with preaching bands hung down from the same. With the aid of a combined Bible and Church Hymnary we would then take it in turns to play Church. This was all very enjoyable until my great aunt learned of how we were passing such time on Sundays: "Och, I'm no too happy about this. It is wicked!" Time and time again, as a reaction to how she had reacted more than once, we would reiterate her well intentioned words: "Yee monee do that on the Sabbath."

Only one other religious experience comes to mind concerning Coldstream and it was of a fair haired, saintly looking man coming to the door and asking Mother if she would listen to the recording of a sermon on a gramophone record. Mother being wary to ask him in, the stranger then placed his 'windup portable' on the well-worn doorstep, which had now formed a shallow pool because it had just stopped raining. Poor Mother, in her embarrassment, had no choice but to listen to this sermon. Afterwards, on refusing to purchase a book, she was presented with a beautifully bound one entitled, 'Enemies.' Another publication, a smaller one, entitled 'Is Hell Hot?' was also presented. The incident quite moved Mother, and it was to impress me many years later when I learned that the stranger had been a Jehovah's Witness!

Such are my spiritual experiences as I recall them years ago in Coldstream, the border town, where youngsters may still stand in the centre of the bridge spanning the Tweed; putting one foot in Scotland and the other in England at the spot where the immortal words of Robbie Burns are to be found:

Oh Scotia! My Dear, My Native Soil!
For whom my warmest wish to Heaven is sent,
Long may thy hardy sons of rustic toil
Be blest with health, and peace, and sweet content.

The River still flows; as does the memorable Leeth and I often wonder if youngsters who cannot swim, still make rafts and sail upon them, or ever get stuck in the bogs and marshes. Does the old mill vibrate with the grinding of machinery and can you still sneak through a long arch below, to the door where you can hear the rushing of water and the rumble of a massive wheel; a door you wanted to open and yet were terrified of doing so? Do youngsters still talk to tramps or 'respectable' strangers and then end up running for their lives? Is the travelling Fair one, which steals away little children; or the gipsy with pegs and lace, one a mother must always patronize for fear of the peddler casting an evil spell on her family? Life is full of danger and excitement to the young child; yet one's Guardian Angel is surely watching overhead when so many odds are against you.

So many of us fail to appreciate the influence a mother's prayers can have over her children. Few can appreciate the truth behind No. 116 in the Alexander Hymn Book: 'Mother's Prayer.' I know this, I owe more to my Mother kneeling with me at the side of the bed and teaching me 'Gentle Jesus' than she could ever have realised. There is equal gratitude because of the Bible stories she read from one of those children's books containing those lovely lithographic pictures appended. The book contained a hymn, which she would sing to me, 'I think when I read that sweet story of old.' These old books had an atmosphere about them, which the modern publications are unable to convey. The engraved pictures they contained plus the beauty of their binding is a grim reflection on the press of the present time. Prayers, hymns and songs such as, 'Be a man. Be a man':

> *So you want to know my laddie*
> *What I would have you be*
> *When the whole wide world's your playground*
> *And you're big and strong like me*
> *To fight and face life's battles*
> *Win them - if you can -*
> *But first of all my laddie, 'be a Man, be a Man!*

Sad that a mother was left to sing such a song, but she had high hopes for her offspring. She sang them with many a tear in her eye. And whatever is noble in her younger son today is largely due to her dedication then. Hers was the added task of seeking to compensate for our Dad's absence. Alas! her view of fatherhood and manliness was far removed from what fate later had in store! Godly counsel; and later, the recitation of poems such as Rudyard Kipling's 'If'. These things; these hallowed memories I owe to my Mother, and to my God my thanks for my Mother.

If many viewed this youngster with curly hair and jammy fingers as a little angel others saw a different side to his nature. Though only eight years old I was truly far from angelic, and it was obvious from tears shed by Mother that the gossip was out. The small tuck-shop, run by a highly respected bachelor with the name of Hume, was the target for my first childhood prank. He spoke to me in such a condescending childlike way that I thought he was silly, and I was determined to take the Mickey out of him. The opportunity could no longer be shelved. One day, with the advent of a new type of child's confectionery called 'Yankee Chews', I walked up to the counter, pulled a silly face and said, "Yankee chew". The gentleman behind the counter immediately began to fill a bag with this weird selection. Holding them over the counter, he found them remaining in his possession as an impudent youngster put out his tongue, raised his fingers to both ears, and uttered, "Yankee chew to you". He then ran out of the shop as fast as his legs would take him. The humiliating experience was in having to return to the shop a few days later, escorted by Mother, to apologise to the shopkeeper whom I'd looked upon as being daft.

Soon a bigger prank was indulged in: that of knocking at doors, pulling a face and running away. Each time it was indulged in the experience seemed to get greater, particularly when threatened by those who through advancing age couldn't run. They merely threatened with either shaking a fist or a poker - and it was usually accompanied with them pulling a funny face. The unfortunate thing about it all was that, round about the same time, some other children had thrown a stone through a window and I was viewed as the likely culprit.

The terrifying ordeal of a visit by the stern police superintendent, Rettie, was to be followed by the worse ordeal next day at school when 'called for' by the headmaster. I'd always been considered a teachers pet, receiving toys from them at the end of the year, but now I was to meet someone quite different in The Master of Coldstream School. A large leather belt, cut into tails, was taken down and laid on his desk before my very eyes. He uttered that it was very seldom used but that, on this occasion, he thought he would use it - and this was after I'd answered his previous question in which I'd stated I'd be grateful if he didn't! I think I literally quaked before him until after minutes, which seemed hours, he said he was going to be exceptionally lenient for once; no mercy would be spared if I ever entered his study again. My subsequent hatred towards him was to last many years as he'd been such a contrast to the lady teachers. His warning, however, had done the trick for never again did I indulge in prankish tricks. Yes, the memories of Mr. Jamieson's study, plus the worse ordeal of the sports day, were to leave indelible marks on one's life. The latter was public and held in the park: to come last in the race, and be howled at by spectators - especially a fat lady pointing the finger at me! - because of the inability to run fast enough was a horrific experience.

The ordeal in the master's study was a deterrent to a young rascal: the latter was the beginning of a school career resulting in hatred towards physical education and games which culminated many years later in truancy and also resorting to prayer that rain would occur when P.T. or games were soon to begin. Indeed, it seemed uncanny how often such prayers seemed to be answered.

Omar Khayam wrote

> *The moving finger writes, and having writ. moves on.*
> *Not all thy piety, nor wit, shall lure it back to cancel half a line*
> *Nor all thy tears wash out one word of it*

The implication is not confined to words but deeds as well. There are childhood escapades, which are purely mischievous, but there are others, which are not. These latter may be forgotten for many years; yet, when they return with some trick of the memory, one's conscience is cut to the core. One is the memory of having waited along a country lane until a frail old lady with curvature of the spine passed by. She would be walking along with a jug of milk and then I would jump out from behind a tree and deposit a dirty stone in it. This happened on more than one occasion. The last time she began to cry. Fortunately for her a gentleman came to her aid who made it clear to me, in a kind and understanding way, the wrong I was doing. Such memories could add support to the doctrine of original sin. Evil can undoubtedly influence the eight year old: for it is not as some would affirm, an age of innocence. The picture of that aged soul, poor and helpless at the hands of a young rascal still haunts me. I hope she'll have forgiven me, and by the Grace of God I'll give her my public apologies in Heaven some day.

Fortunately, even the dumb creation can help to bring out goodness in children. For there was not only Ginger - the cat that never entered our home! - yet kept turning up, as if from nowhere, to guard me; but we also acquired a domestic pet: a wire-haired fox terrier called Pat. One day – having taken her for a walk within the secluded grounds - she came pounding back to me with a baby rabbit, literally, sat squealing from beneath her teeth.

Our cherished pet probably thought I should have been pleased with the present she'd brought me! But then, looking up to me - and with a sense of deep reluctance – she allowed me to open her mouth and release the little creature which scuttled away, apparently non the worse for its ordeal: And then, to one's delight, I looked across the grass to spy mummy rabbit watching on with much emotion from outside her burrow. Indeed, her babe hopped up to her side, and they both hopped off very happily together!

Indeed, it seemed as if the environment then changed into a wonderful glow and that nature had become vibrant with song. I sense I danced my way home to the Lodge, accompanied by Pat whom I loved now even more than before. I sensed – in my young childhood way - that she'd scored a true moral victory! And when I narrated to Mum what had happened her eyes sparkled with pride, just like they did whenever one brought her wild violets, daisies or even dandelions!

This lovely mum wrote the following poem, as a submission to the Coldtream School Magazine. It was later republished in a national; but with no reference to her, the one who'd created it:

Each morning at my doorway a little Robin comes,
And chirps so sweet and pretty, as though to ask for crumbs,
Then flies away in to a tree, to whistle back its thanks to me

A Brief Taste Of Shropshire

Some folk, it appears, are born in one particular place and live there all their lives. Although they seem to see little more than their own town or village they remain quite happy. Fate is a strange thing for others are continually moving into new places and environments. One's 'Coldstream School class photo' for 1937 contains these prophetic lines beneath it:

> *One ship sails east, and one sails west,*
> *while the self same breezes blow.*
> *Tis the set of the sails, and not the gales,*
> *that send them where they go.*

Well, in 1938, we were to figuratively set sail; and – whereas my first recollection of Coldsream school had been one of disgust at discovering my soiled cap! - the last memory was one of delight. The three teachers, whom I'd been taught by, each presented me with a large and, apparently, expensive toy. Indeed Mrs Skinner, Miss McClure and Miss Dunbar had been wonderfully caring teachers. They now seemed emotionally moved; and having presented me with their separate gifts, they then told me to be always proud of one's Scottish heritage when down in England

We subsequently left Coldstream and travelled way down into Shropshire, to live in the town of Dawley. Our new address would be 211 Doseley Road. This was certainly a contrast to beautiful Scotland. Yet it had its compensations: along the single track railway embankment, facing the front door, the beautifully coloured green and brass railway engines of the G.W.R. pushed or else pulled their brown and cream coaches. At night it seemed even more exciting when the sparks, and occasionally flames, would flare out of the loco's chimney.

There were, however, many disadvantages now that we were living in England. I had, for instance, to attend a school where the education was markedly inferior and where the headmaster was grumpy and stern. The first day I was at school he gave my brother and me a severe dressing down because we'd walked across the hall when the practice was to walk round it. Yet, how were we to know when we'd never been told? I knew little about armies, but he reflected a baser side of Granddad who'd been a quarter master sergeant and – much to Grandma's protests – repeatedly derived pleasure on narrating how he'd dressed down young conscripts, making them quake in their shoes. As for this headmaster, he must have had a split personality: a few hours earlier he'd been so pleasant while explaining about the school to Mother!

This old establishment smelled in one quarter because it was illuminated by gas. I now presumed that half the pilot lights or mantles must have been faulty. The other smell was from the vicinity of the toilets. They were little better than primitive and had a smell peculiar to those frequented by children in old schools. I associate that ugly school with fog as well as darkness. Spiritually, all that could be said in its favour was that I there learned to sing Grace, not only before, but also after the two breaks we had each day to drink a bottle of milk.

At the side of the school was a dingy, old hill. I remember running up it, and then stopping as fast as I could when black, stagnant water confronted me. So many of the hills in that area were flat when you reached the top of them and the traces of old mine workings, now flooded, were everywhere to be seen. Well, did the title of the school seem most appropriate, 'Pool Hill'? Not only had I to enter the bleak building each school day (Doseley Road was at the bottom of the school hill), but my bedroom looked up and outwards towards this prison like edifice. "If only Mother would let me go to the Church School - up the main road," - I repeated to myself. The teachers and the children appeared truly happy there while discipline seemed almost nil. The decision of my parents, however, was final: "Church schools are always inferior. They spend far too much time teaching religion!"

I was soon to make new friends, having left my one and only school chum, Billy Kinghorn, in Coldstream. Indeed, we'd been inseparable buddies until Mother found us one day walking down a garden proudly displaying our 'manhood' to the world. Poor Billy was told to run along home and I was made to believe I'd done something terribly wrong. To touch 'down there' could lead to death! The thought of it, plus that look of horror on Mum's face, would haunt me down the years.

Hardly had I returned home from my first day at this grotesque Shropshire school when the letterbox rattled. Three girls outside were pushing through notes: "Do you love me? Will you be my sweetheart? Can I take you to the pictures? and "You talk funny!" Yes, a marked Scottish accent must certainly have sounded strange to young girls of a West Midland lilt. Before long I was frequenting the Saturday matinees at The Royal Cinema with two of these girls, one on each side, enjoying the adventures of the singing cowboy, Gene Autry. If Cathy was nice I thought a trifle more of Kathleen and well remember holding hands while watching 'The Adventures of Tom Sawyer'. It seemed as if Kathleen meant to me what Becky Thatcher meant to Tom!

Picture houses were a new fascination for me, and there was a less ornate one than The Royal in Dawley. It was called The Cosy. The building was of corrugated iron, with a multitude of plain bulbs over the entrance, and stuck out in the open was the cash desk. I remember how the sound always seemed muffled and how the music at the interval frequently warbled to 'The Umbrella Song' or 'Blueberry Hill', while outside the chug, chugging of the engine round the back was perpetual. It kept the electric generated. Indeed, a most humorous experience took place during a thunderstorm: The proprietor, who warmly welcomed his young patrons, came down the aisle during the time a heavy vibration of rain was heard on the roof. He was soon dishing out several umbrellas, each to a person occupying a place above which some rain was seeping through. Yes, the show always seemed to go on, except when, during the screening of 'A yank at Oxford; a fire broke out which destroyed the whole screen!

As the first evening, after school, had resulted in my making three new friends, the very first evening in our new home was to result in my becoming a Sunday School scholar. No sooner had the furniture van left than the Minister called. He was given the strange title of 'Vicar'. This man was very jovial and witty, contrasting to past clerics encountered in that he was also 'fond of the bottle'. My Dad felt, at first, that they had much in common. So Colin and I were sent off to Sunday School largely in return for his kind visit. However, as Mother and Father did not present themselves at Church he soon made a return visit. Much to Mother's embarrassment he was kept at the door. Alas, on yet another occasion, for he was very persistent, we conveyed the impression that we were out so as not to answer. Though incredibly young I can still remember how guilty Mother appeared in putting on such an act so as to appease Dad. Her face was red like beetroot and she felt as if she'd done a seemingly dreadful thing. She had always attended Church in Scotland, however Dad made it clear that going to Church was not his cup of tea. To keep the peace Mother broke our weekly tradition and up to her dying day, thirty-nine years later, it would never be resumed. Whenever the Vicar saw us he would enquire eagerly after our parents. We sensed he could be extremely stern, but seemingly only with adults. At Sunday School it was always a happy occasion when he addressed us. He would tell us funny stories, have us all in tucks of laughter, and this was often interspersed with telling us of Jesus.

It was either at Easter or Whitsuntide when new clothes were worn for the first time and this was to attend Church. Grey, or possibly white, hair-like shirt material would chafe my neck, yet I could still turn sideways and experience the feelings of a love, young and pure as the dawn, towards a friend or two adorned with gorgeous new bonnets, and beneath them a big, open smile. They were from humbler homes than ours. Yet those little lasses with open roguish faces were singing with gusto from their hymnbooks. They must have been close, indeed, to the Saviour's Heart!

Weekdays, of course, had their compensations in that you could clothe yourself more comfortably and be less concerned about getting dirty. One could play in a derelict shed nearby or crawl and hide, with playmates amongst the many sewerage pipes newly made in a factory near by. It was in such pipes that I had my first experience of claustrophobia, through pushing my way through several stacks of pipes only to find myself unable to retrace the procedure. If those pipes had rolled during such ventures then my end would have come; but such was not to be. On this terrifying occasion I eventually crawled through all the stacks, and came out safe at the other end. If such an experience sticks in my mind because of its accompanying sense of panic and helplessness the experience following remains because of my compassion towards what a dumb and helpless animal must have endured.

Between my new friend Gordon's house and our own, there lived a railway worker whose daily habit on returning from work was to make a great deal of fuss over his dog - and then take a lead - and give it a merciless beating. My schoolmates and I were appalled at this kind of thing. Mother eagerly informed Dad, but then, after talking it out, it transpired that both agreed not to get involved. There might well have been a reason for his behaviour but, in any case, it was none of our business to interfere and one would hardly wish to cross swords with such a character. Strangely, he came across as most polite and agreeable, and appeared happy for children to be present! The verdict from adults was unanimous: 'don't put your nose where its not invited'

Our stay in Shropshire must have lasted barely eighteen months. My brother and Mother disliked each day there. They reminisced about Coldstream and the beauty of Scotland, but such beauty never bothered me. For myself, the Doseley area had its own compensations: to visit the remains of a brick factory, within a hollow, to play within its kilns in summer and to return in the winter months to the same spot only to find it temporarily submerged by a stagnant lake upon which, for some unknown reason, floated a swan, was to experience a fascination all of its own. To stand round the top of old flooded mine workings surrounded by scrub land and, on one occasion, find amongst the blackened bracken the skin of a snake, were occasions which cast an eerie yet intriguing fascination over a young mind. To have played in a derelict builders' shed, accompanied with young friends, and to have received a merciless thrashing from Dad for disobeying his orders are factors not likely to be forgotten.

Dawley had its less pleasant experiences for me; apart from receiving on several occasions a merciless thrashing from Dad I also remember walking past the Church school on the ascent, which culminated in the shopping centre. All of a sudden, a group of children swamped on me from their play yard. They'd rushed across the road, encircled me, and were now dancing around me in war like fashion until I was truly rigid with fear. Then, as if out of the blue, a kind looking teacher appeared. He told them they were not acting as Christians. He made them apologise and saw I was all right. From that moment the ringleader became a friend. 'If only I could go to their school!' I said to myself; 'They're so happy together and they want me as one of them'. My parents would have none of it.

Indeed, it was on that very spot, during school holidays, I witnessed something else, which is indelibly embedded on the mind. A little Scotch terrier had been run over by a car. Blood was pouring from its nose and a dear old lady had picked it up in her arms and was crying her heart out. I, with my young friend Kathleen, wanted to cry with her but somehow the tears just wouldn't come. If ever praying entered my mind it must certainly have done so on that occasion, but then the only prayer I knew was that which formed the first verse of a children's hymn: 'Gentle Jesus, meek and mild' I no doubt added a request specially for her at the end of that verse, but of this I can't be sure. I do remember one thing. She said she'd no one else in the world - only that little dog. It was all she had to live for. She told a grown-up nearby that she'd lost her husband in what must have been the Great War.

Mother was a true lady in every sense of the word but Dad was far from being a gentleman. Young newly weds had moved in to the semi. adjoining us and were deeply besotted with each other. The fellow would sing to his beloved outside their open window, sometimes with flowers in his hand. But when it persisted late on, Dad - losing sleep necessary for an early rise in the morning – said, "I'll cure them once and for all!" Stout in stature, he lowered his trousers in the presence of Mum; shoved his bare bottom out of their bedroom window and gave a resounding fart before closing it. The young couple from the garden beneath never cooed to each other after that occasion; but my dear Mother could never lift her eyes to look at them again. She now longed, more than ever, to leave the district.

And this was accelerated further when Mum and I visited a dentist in nearby Wellington. "Is this your address?" he asked her. When Mum said it was, he replied: "Then you must be the wife of that burly, uncouth Scotsman who hasn't paid for dentures I made him well over a year ago!"

The day we left Shropshire was one not easily forgotten. Perhaps the forces of evil had literally come to a head because it was the very day that the Second World War was declared. We were proud to own a radio of our own which was a press button model, and I vaguely remember Mr. Chamberlain announcing over it that Britain was at war: This was of great interest to me because I'd saluted Mr. Charnberlain outside the Hirstle at Coldstream.

My parents seemed devastated and so did the neighbours. Yet, I sensed war might be exciting. If it was a sad day for the Nation then it was equally sad to me, but certainly not because of Mr. Chamberlain's announcement. Though no more than nine and a half years of age this was the day when I would have to say farewell to my childhood sweetheart forever. Soon the open lorry was loaded with all our furniture and Colin would have to squat amongst it for the long journey that lay ahead. I was being squashed between the driver's mate and my Mum. All that was left now was for me to collect our gorgeous fox terrier, Pat, from the arms of young Kathleen who'd turned up to see me off.

My memory still vividly recalls that beautiful young lass sitting on the garden wall with a distant and puzzled look in her eyes. She had pushed notes through our letterbox a year and a half previously, on the day of our arrival in order to say, 'Will you be my sweetheart?' The journey commenced. It was the longest and dreariest I was ever to experience: the destination was to be where the most formative years of my life would be spent.

Into 'God's Own Country'

Different counties have their own environmental characteristics. As the furniture lorry moved through Cheshire I well remember the wide, straight roads with white railings and the large number of houses built in black and white Tudor style. Through Cheshire the lorry passed into Flintshire. We were now in yet another country! Our new home, which Father had previously acquired for us, would surely be convenient for his work. It was a semi-detached house on the Mecca Estate in Greenfield, on the side of the main coast road and opposite Courtaulds' factory. The houses were similar in structure to Corporation properties and, as one or two neighbours seemed roughish, Mother decided the environment could have been better and allowed only a minimum of furniture to be removed from the lorry. The next day a house of a more congenial nature would have to be found. Indeed, the last straw for Mother came on learning from one of the neighbours that the former occupant had taken his own life within it. In desperation poor Dad spent that very evening seeking alternative accommodation for us. Fortunately for him his efforts were amply rewarded. Early the next day the sleeping material was reloaded on to the removal lorry and we made our way upwards to that picturesque town of Holywell. The vicinity was Pen Y Maes, which means 'Top of the Meadow', and it was considered a good class district in which to live. Snobbery is obnoxious. A few who lived in Sundawn Avenue appeared to feel superior to those who lived in the nearby Coronation Estate opposite. Yet, they were anxious to receive recognition from those who lived in more elaborate homes to our rear. It was that kind of petty snobbery amongst adults, which was later reflected amongst children; between those who passed for the Grammar School towards others (like myself) who failed.

I soon made friends with a school chum, Peter, who lived a couple of doors away. His delightful parents, although practising Spiritualists, frequented the Congregational Tabernacle. On being asked by their son if I could accompany him to Sunday School, Mother and Father proved a little hesitant - as they were Church of England and proud of it! But what was more, Dad said that 'Tabernacle' sounded Jewish! And one had little sympathy with them. "Didn't they crucify Christ and wasn't Fagan a Jew?" asked Dad. There was possibly little more love for a Jew in Britain at the beginning of the war than in Germany, and before long both German and Jewish shops would have their windows broken. Well, be that as it may, Peter's parents eventually persuaded mine that the 'Tabernacle' was far from Jewish; it was in fact Congregational (whatever that meant). The place was seemingly respectable and so the next Sunday I was received as a scholar. What good Sunday School did for me I fail to understand, but it allowed Mum and Dad to have an 'assumed' nap in bed. The atmosphere in that Sunday School appeared cold and dead. Usually the lesson that was given appeared meaningless; nevertheless, the first minister I encountered there seemed to my childhood mind loving and caring. But, alas, even to a ten year old, he seemed to be under the authority of a local mill owner who was the Superintendent of the Sunday School. He, like similar 'good' men, was of the type who saw to it that the shops, cinema and the local train were not permitted to operate on Sundays. Consequently, Sundays always seemed inhibiting and depressing. Yet, be that as it may, I was still glad that my parents had allowed me to attend the Tabernacle rather than join the Parish Church Sunday School where, it was implied, some of the 'riff raff' were sent. Yes, I sensed the Congregational Chapel catered for a more genteel and select group! Mum and Dad said it was because many of the pupil's parents worked at the Chapel Secretary's Mill, and that they knew on which side their bread and butter was spread.

Only on one occasion in the Tabernacle can I recall when Sunday School proved a special blessing. This was when a young couple specifically requested that their child be christened during the Sunday School assembly in the afternoon, rather than in the morning service. A visiting minister, void of all clerical attire, held the child in his arms throughout the length of his address. "Whoever receiveth one of these little ones, "he said, "the same receiveth Jesus." The child never once cried but repeatedly smiled up at him. Before he'd finished speaking it would seem that tears were discernible in the eyes of very many, and I was terrified lest I burst openly into crying. An idyllic peace had come over that Sunday School and it seemed as if Jesus had entered to join us. This minister was the first Preacher I'd ever encountered who seemed to be in direct and unmistakable contact with God and though I was probably only eleven or twelve years of age, I could never forget him!

The Sunday School trip was an annual event, but for me a first and a last timer. The destination wasn't far. It was just another outing to nearby Rhyl. Tea, sandwiches and a bun were provided on reaching the Congregational Church hall there. After, what seemed a lengthy speech given by our superintendent, we were asked to give a very loud applause because the local chapel had freely loaned us their premises. We then dispersed, later to reassemble at a fixed time outside the Railway Station ready for the return journey home. Being far from familiar with Rhyl, and my friend having disappeared from sight, I remember walking alongside the Minister and the Superintendent until pulled up. The latter said that I must clear off as they had important business to do and I couldn't accompany them. I hadn't meant to stay with them, but what really hurt was the way I was told I wasn't wanted. It seemed to hurt so deeply.

The most inspiring spiritual influence, during those formative school years, came from the unlikeliest of places. It was the school in Holywell itself. This is all the more remarkable because no one living ever more detested school than I did. I was constantly being criticised in front of the class, and frequently by the headmaster himself. It was repeated in no uncertain terms that I was 'thick', 'daft' and 'stupid'. The contrast, however, came in my twelfth year. It was then that I came under the authority of Ieauan Williams, who was a lover of nature, a practising Quaker and indeed, to my childlike mind, a living saint. He sought to instil into his backward pupils - his class comprised those who'd failed to pass for the Grammar School! - a love for the outdoor life and the animal kingdom. The 'true' exploits of the redskin chieftain, Grey Owl, were read to us in serial fashion, and each episode was eagerly awaited. The same teacher told us that we must never steal apples and, whenever we wanted fruit, we could go and help ourselves to as much as we required from his own orchard.

The hearts of other pupils, as well as myself, went out to him in sympathy when the headmaster, in front of a full class, reprimanded him openly for spending too much time on the Scripture lesson when it was now well into time for teaching Maths. It was only Ieauan's enthusiasm over sport, and especially football, which prevented him from being perfect in my eyes. As I couldn't run properly I concocted a story about having a weak heart. This excuse worked for so long and when after several weeks it failed to work, I then began to pray secretly in sheer desperation. I prayed for rain when the appropriate lesson came near. Indeed, so marvellously did many of these secret prayers seem to work, that the warmest of days sometimes changed into showers that were sufficient to call off the event, and I began to sense that I was not unheard. There was a spiritual Being who knew the sweat and agony I was undergoing as the clock approached the dreaded time. He came frequently to my rescue and, when He didn't, I stood quaking on the field wanting to die. And one time I nearly did: a cricket ball hit my head; knocked me off balance; and I was commanded to get off the pitch as a liability.

'No one living ever more detested school than I' (back row in white)

The last year at school found me in Gomer Williams's class. Gomer was a marked contrast in every way to Ieauan even though they bore the same surname. Gomer was renowned for flying into a rage under the slightest bit of provocation. He was always good at reaching his mark whenever he threw the blackboard eraser at anyone and I was quite a common object. It wasn't that I was particularly mischievous or troublesome, but chiefly because I was bored with most subjects taught and merely awaited the ringing of the bell so as to get home. The only subjects I had any flare for were Art and English composition. Gomer knew this and, sensing I was quite artistic, had me using English periods finishing off a painting, which depicted a man sawing a log. Indeed, he spoke about the possibility of having it framed and entered in a competition. Well, regrettably a secret ink battle brought a speedy end to this creation: A piece of soaked blotting paper descended on it from the other side of the room. I there and then received a heavy 'clout' from Gomer because I'd merely "sat back and allowed it to happen."

Gomer was now becoming so unbearable that I resolved on a new means of release from the schools harsh discipline as well as sport: truancy! Having been excused from school several times due to a 'running ear' – and Mum hadn't always furnished me with a written letter to hand in – I considered it a good alibi with which to con the headmaster. Indeed, the experience was truly exhilarating, particularly when Mr Evans (for that was his name) actually believed each story I told him. And, indeed, the more often I succeeded at truancy the more often I was determined to repeat it. Unfortunately one young rascal – many years later a church official! - sensed what I was up to and encouraged me to go ahead one morning and do it: 'just once more'. The ordeal that followed after 4pm proved most embarrassing. Mother asked for a detailed explanation as to what lessons I'd been taught which resulted in a whole list of lies. And the next day I appeared before the uniformed truant-catcher: the 'Head of the Gestapo', along with Mr. Evans who, rather than use the familiar cane, seemed a little more friendly and willng to listen.

My fourteenth birthday couldn't have arrived quickly enough and, when this head- teacher now sought to persuade me to stay on voluntarily for another year and in Gomer's class, he didn't stand a chance. "It is nothing short of criminal to see you going out in to the world as you are", he said. But his pleading was in vain. As for Gomer, he was basically a good man. In fact I was to learn later that his father had been the local Baptist Minister and Gomer was not only treasurer of the Chapel but also a very gifted and eloquent lay preacher. It is hard to believe, at this stage, that four or five years later he would be publicly commending me from the Deacon's pew – the set fawr – for conducting a whole service in front of a large congregation. Indeed, in later years I actually sought to make allowances for his erratic behaviour because I learned that the name Gomer was that of a biblical harlot – the unfaithful wife of Hosea! Yet, such a name in Wales is not uncommon.

Through living in Holywell one had ample opportunity, particularly during the holidays, to witness the annual processions of hundreds of pilgrims to the well of St. Winefride. Most of these pilgrims seemed to come from the rougher parts of Merseyside and others, if accent was anything to go by, from as far away as Southern Ireland. Many of these pilgrims gave me the impression of being either Italian or Spanish. The black scarves over the heads of so many hard skinned women still seems quite vivid, while the many houses round the vicinity of the well gave an impression of being dusty and dark, and the inhabitants not a little dowdy. Pictures of the Sacred Heart with a red light flickering could be perceived through the window or the open doors. So could a statue of Mary with a blue light close by, or else it might be a dusty crucifix minus a limb, or a weird drawing of the crown of thorns with damp marks upon it. These were the kind of things that stuck in one's mind at an impressionable age. As were, indeed, peering eyes through thick glasses while gnarled, hard worn hands fumbled at beads while the mouths mumbled something that didn't make sense. At a later stage it would convey the marks of piety but in my young years it conveyed something quite different.

Those processions through the streets were most colourful and often quite moving, but as the years passed I looked upon those 'sermons' in the open air as in a style reminiscent of oppressed agitators fighting for rights, and quite removed from the love and warmth of those heard in chapel and to a lesser extent in church. The religious festivities in the open were without doubt extremely colourful and bright but, when they were superseded by the sound of piano accordions playing jigs, it was time for us to be in our homes as these feast days would usually terminate in drunkenness within the vicinity on an unprecedented scale, and caring parents would call their children in.

Yes, this 'Lourdes Of Wales' was in those days, basically, a very select town. We'd been justly taught at school to be proud of it. Indeed, any youth loitering within shop doorways was liable to a clip on the ear from a local bobby's glove, and told to keep walking. I experienced it twice! The town's park – with a newly made stream flowing through the middle – was idyllic. As for the road above: it was associated with bigwigs, like magistrates and councillors. The latter were professional men and business entrepreneurs, whose capabilities were clear to all. Yes, and they were 'leading lights', within respective places of worship, whose contribution to the town was void of all expenses and a true labour of love! No wonder Treffynnon – to give the town its Welsh name – flourished, peacefully, during those latter years of World War Two!

Indeed, it was during this period that I often accompanied Mother to nearby Chester, and one Saturday afternoon seemed to have a lasting effect. After a visit round the Cathedral, and following confrontation with a few marbled mouthed clerics and choristers, we dined in a Kardomah coffeehouse nearby. Indeed, the aroma of freshly ground coffee coming from an escape pipe on the outside was intriguing. So, indeed, were the uniformed waitresses within. Complete with tray they courteously moved around the dark wooden partitions which partly separated one table from another. Everyone appeared courteous and kind, and Mother saw to it that I kept on my best behaviour.

Indeed, during such a privileged outing an elderly gentleman smiled across at Mother. He had at the side of him a violin case, and Mother in a soft voice assured me that this white headed gentleman with kindly eyes was quite probably someone of distinction. Kind glances were further exchanged and Mother, having asked him if he were a musician, found out that he was a professional violinist of some standing. In a rather shaky and yet most refined voice he said that he'd had the great honour to play before the late King George the Fifth. "Indeed, I've had the honour to play before various royal families throughout Europe" he said. We smiled and got on with our respective meals.

"What a lovely gentleman he is. You can see it on his face!" added mother quietly across our table. Then, a few moments passed and – on leaving – the elderly gentleman, clasping his case, came across to Mum. His eyes began to fill up and he said to her: "My greatest privilege has yet to come." "Oh!" responded Mother, "And what may that be?" With a voice full of emotion he softly replied: "I'm looking forward to the day when I play before the King Of Kings!"

Mother's eyes filled up as she smiled and nodded. I sense mine did a little bit! But on returning home and narrating her encounter to Dad, he blurted out: "You've met a blooming religious crank! You've met an absolute nutter!"

Jobs Start In A Fume Impregnated Projection Box

During the last year at school the 'head' had barged in to the classroom. "'Where are you, Thompson lad?" Then, on catching my eye at the back, blurted out: "you'll be pleased to know you got 3 out of 100 for your maths exam. And let me add: the 3 weren't because you got some right - because you didn't! - It was only for neatness". Somehow, I even sensed Gomer felt sorry for me. I could hardly wait to leave!

Once fourteen years of age, an opportunity I had eagerly sought presented itself. The Manager of the local picture palace, knowing my enthusiasm over cinematographs, agreed to give me a start as a trainee projectionist. His offer was gladly accepted even though my parents had strong misgivings. They sensed that such work would be far from healthy and the cinema was certainly not the best of its kind. Major Burns, the previous owner, having made a fortune from the army, had apparently converted the building at minimum expense from an old theatre into a cinema. It stood next to his other establishment The Old Boar's Head Pub. The Major, however, had recently died and a new proprietor by the name of Bayliss had purchased the cinema. His hobby appeared to be that of opening up picture houses within the various tourist centres of Wales, and he seemed very successful at it.

As far as self is concerned it need only be said that within three months I would be seeking work again as the Manager's attitude towards me had changed. The most decisive factor transpired during the screening of Waterloo Bridge when the film snapped no less than fifteen times during one performance. Three of these breakages occurred in front of the arc beam, resulting in three fires within the projection room and one - but for the quickness of the chief projectionist, who badly burned his hand - could have resulted in an inferno.

The second projectionist had been unwell at the time - the result of the two of us having fooled around a few days previous using a pulley as a lift. He had fallen from the hook of the pulley at the top of the fire escape to the yard below and was for a while confined to bed. I'd been doing his work in preparing the film, but seemingly with not too much success. As he returned to work I was booted out. Mother told me how ashamed she was of me, particularly as she'd been in the audience and had witnessed the many jeers as the film constantly broke. It seems almost incredible to believe that within that same short period of employment I'd inadvertently pulled the tab ropes off the pulleys at the commencement of another prominent feature film.

The Metro Goldwyn Mayer lion had just roared when the curtains at either side sagged down upon the screen and refused to open or even close. I was pretty hopeless on heights so the chief projectionist had the unenviable task, in the midst of a packed house, of propping up the ladders in the centre of the large screen, and of climbing to the top so as to pull these sagging 'tabs' fully open by hand. This necessitated several ascents and descents as they were extremely heavy, and he could only open them further to each side a little at a time. Indeed, I felt awfully uncomfortable for him as the sound of 'cat calls' could even be heard in the projection booth, which was considered sound proof. His name was Wild and he lived up to it on returning, via the back of the circle and through the door, into the projection department. As he came in one way I went out the other, and waited outside for a while until he'd cooled off. Then, 'on being sacked' by the manager, I had no hesitation in telling my friends about it all. Mother felt she could never live it down. "Never tell anyone what's happened", she said. "I truly dread to think what the neighbours might say, if they found out!"

Apart from toy cinematographs my only other hobby was one of printing with lino-cuts, so I called round to a local printer by the name of Arnold Williams. He was a delightful fellow who accepted me as an apprentice once he'd talked it over with my Mother. I stayed in his full-time employment at least two wonderful years. That printing establishment was a kind of meeting point where ministers of religion frequently met, and if I were a young rascal, the compositor was an elderly one! The repeating of four letter words in a quiet voice when sanctimonious clerics were around, was a sport indulged in. We just wanted to assess their reactions. One Chapel minister, who appeared more sanctimonious than the rest put together, carried a massive Bible with him. The poor fellow had a constant limp so Blackwell (the elderly compositor) and I assumed it was due to an ungodly practice.. With eyes that sparkled behind round steel specs and under a compositor's shield, the old compositor would lead me into close proximity, and repeating something naughty, would quizzically look for some shock reaction from such a pious preacher but it never transpired. The dear proprietor himself had little time for such clerics. "They're always wanting something on the cheap", he affirmed. "Believe it or not, getting money from some of these chapels is like getting blood out of a blooming stone!"

One minister alone impressed me in those formative years. As for the rest, I sensed their absence would only have been missed by the old women of their flock because they appeared very much as one of them. These older clerics usually spoke in the Welsh vernacular, many of them had more reputable degrees than any bishop; yet they appeared content with the pastorates of little Bethels scattered around the countryside. Yes, they were obviously good and humble men of God. Alas, they were comparable to many a traditional undertaker, pious but most unappealing to a young mind out to enjoy the sparkle of living.

The sole cleric to impress me was the young curate, a Mr. Daniel. On one occasion Old Blackwell quizzically asked him if he had any words of counsel to give to the establishment's young apprentice who was inclined to wander from the 'straight and narrow'. The Curate refused to look at me and affirmed in a sharp manner that young folk, like myself, were selfish through and through and hadn't as much as a thought for their Maker and their God. Indeed, such words hurt me to the core and particularly as he repeatedly ignored me when I sought his attention. Other ministers would usually speak, or raise their broad brimmed hat towards any who looked their way. But with this Curate it seemed you had to honour his God to acquire his friendship, so a month or two later I attended his mission church and found his whole attitude temporarily changing in my favour. Yes, it was temporal because, when I ceased to continue there, he ceased once more to acknowledge me. It seemed as if he walked exceedingly close to His Maker with a heavenly radiance. It was said by many that what he preached, he practised to the full.

'The Firm', as this printing establishment was styled, was a truly wonderful place. Arnold Williams and Old Blackwell were amongst the salt of the earth. The former treated me as if I were his very son. Although his code of morals would not have been by any stretch of imagination on a par with the many local preachers and chapel deacons who were regular customers, I sensed I knew, even then, with whom Jesus would have been happiest. He saw intense beauty in birds of all varieties as well as in both species! He idolised little children and was intensely fond of animals. He seemed so different to the many religious folk who often went around with a muck rake and a list of 'Thou shalt nots'. His consuming hobby was pigeons, and the locals nicknamed him the pigeon king. What is more, this dear soul would never turn away a vagrant from his premises. Old Tom was a typical example; he was like a human fixture alongside the coke stove. The hotter the stove got then the stronger became the stench. It was poor for business, and received the frown of not a few 'respectable chapel folk', but Arnold Williams tolerated Old Tom to the end, saving an old vagrant from the confines of the local workhouse.

As for old Blackwell, he appeared well past retiring age and had a slightly withered arm. His brother was a Congregational minister and he, himself, had occasionally helped out at a local chapel or two. Blackwell could indeed laugh with the world, yet he was always anxious to lift me to a higher standard and later he did all in his limited power to spur me on to reach spiritual heights.

The atmosphere of 'The Old Firm' haunts me still fifty-eight years later. At night I often sense I can hear again the sound of the large treadle press as the rollers slithered back and forth over the type. I visualise that wonderful little man, Blackwell, with pipe in his mouth, leaning over the many cases of type; of Old Tom sitting and reminiscing over a previous age while reclining on his special chair at the side of the stove. Then it would appear as if the sound of whistling approached the door once more and it was followed by the entry of the proprietor. His face radiant with outdoor activity after having fed his hens and pigeons, while his little dog, the worse for age, followed closely by his side.

All went remarkably well in that small printing establishment until, owing to expansion; a new employee came on the scene. He was old enough to be my father, yet far more tyrannical. Over fifty years ago teenagers were taught to respect their elders and to address them with courtesy. My mind, however, was to be opened, in a way it had never been opened before. It was to open my mind to a side of human nature which I'd never known before but would repeatedly encounter amongst certain adults whenever too timid or nervous to defend oneself against them...

To look forward to manhood merely to discover that many, who achieve it are the least worthy of respect can be quite a blow to any youngster who has been taught from childhood to look up to his 'betters'. To lie awake most of the night, truly frightened to return to work the next day, can play havoc with one's nervous system for the rest of one's life. No one who knows the world from experience can ever deny the depravity of so much human nature. In years just beginning to recover from Nazi atrocities one learned through first hand knowledge that certain folk, given the power that Adolf Hitler possessed, would have been infinitely worse than he.

Such temporary relief, from the assaults of those who are depraved, usually comes when the mind can literally stick no more and flares up *in defence. When I did this on two occasions within that wonderful establishment, Old Blackwell warmly commended me for proving myself at last to be a true man. Yes, but after a profuse apology from the culprit, 'the thin end of the wedge' would be felt in a few days. All this was new to me. Surely the man responsible for such victimisation was one on his own, I reasoned. So I decided to secure employment elsewhere, where the atmosphere proved most congenial.

The opportunity occurred in the town of Flint. At the top of Church Street, standing in all its splendour, was the smartest cinema of its kind for its size. It was named The Plaza and I associate it still with several things: a delightful odour of perfumed disinfectant, plush carpeting in to which one's feet literally sank, an auditorium surrounded by glorious pillars which, with the whole ceiling itself, was during intervals and ads. constantly changing colours. And, indeed, added to such qualities was a delightful young blonde, named Irene. She gave a gorgeous smile to certain favoured persons as she issued tickets from the ornate cash desk. Sometimes she smiled and gave me a kind of half wink. With bangles round her wrists, and perfumed to high heaven she was attractive and what was more she knew it. My new employer was the manager who ran the place as if we were one happy, caring, family. He was cultured and refined in every detail: the perfect gentleman, always ready to welcome his patrons and an absolute pleasure to work under.

There were three projectionists: Eddie who was a delightful eighteen year old, Trefor who was a seventeen year old, and myself. Trefor and I hit it off from the start. We often fooled around in the cinema sometimes quite irresponsibly. Occasionally, during the mornings, we would screen reels of old, golden film from the days of the silent movies. These reels were then being sold in toyshops for use on home projectors and they went back to the early twenties. Indeed, such screening on the latest cinema equipment, provided light and secret entertainment for the cleaners to watch as they worked away hard in the mornings. As for the lady in the shop outside, she would give us a buzz if she saw the manager coming up Church Street early in the morning rather than at noon when he normally began work. Often, with the cleaners, we would raise up the screen on the stage and with music blaring loud, stand in a line and perform a knees-up. In the afternoons, though under age, Trefor and I were often a little inebriated. On other occasions we would visit the Harbour Master at Mostyn Quayside -seeking possible employment on an old steam tramp, which carried iron ore. But we were not to be successful!

Each morning, as well as late evening, we would cycle home from the cinema to as far as Bagillt using the same pushbike. But, then, one day I learned to ride on my own -this was at first, round the Plaza. On that memorable day I later collided with the back of a horse and cart in Bagillt. I had obviously gone solo too soon and suffered the consequence of riding a bike, without brakes, and the necessary skills to take evasive action when confronted by the back of a cart and, even more frightening, a bus approaching on the other side. It was, when I came round, that I realised the bus driver was vexed because I received nothing but abuse from him. "Serves you right, you silly young fool!" he said. Meanwhile the fruiterer had rushed out of a shop to stop his horse and cart, the creature having trotted off into a sprightly gallop after the impact.

On many a morning while cycling through Bagillt we would pass the young Congregational Minister, Mr Latham, returning to Flint from pastoral duties at Bagillt. Indeed, we sometimes had the hilarious experience of passing the local Vicar who used a 'sit up and beg' style ladies cycle. I dare say the model was amply suited for his cassock. The cleric's head was always donned with a Cure D'Ar hat (a kind of round bowler with an exceptionally wide brim). As we waited for him to raise the hat we would just about burst our sides. We always saluted him, and with difficulty, refrained from laughter until he was well out of sound. The Reverend. Walters was truly a well respected and much loved cleric of the old school.

When the snow and ice returned, travelling to Flint and back twice daily - by cycle part of the way and due to the hill from Bagillt to Holywell, walking the remainder - had its disadvantages. It therefore, came as a welcome surprise when the new manager of the 'Prince of Wales' cinema in Holywell, from which I'd been fired three years previous, pleaded with my parents for me to return to a more remunerative post there. Though the manager of the Plaza did his utmost to keep me I nevertheless accepted the offer, but only to regret it later. This new manager of the Holywell picture house, though small in stature, was not without a large and generous heart. He took me on several 'hair raising' afternoons tearing round the countryside in an open sports car. Usually, when his office was open, it was observed that at least one usherette would be at his side; sometimes provocatively sat on his desk. In the presence of one of these young ladies he asked me: "Do you know what this is?" Then he endeavoured to blow up a Durex. Indeed, it was rumoured by others that occasionally tickets were having to be re-used or else ignored, as the replacement rolls hadn't arrived. Well, I only know that he was very generous with every penny he acquired.

I often visualise that spacious picture palace; the large queues discernible from the projection room window, the stifling heat from the arc lamps, the noise of those projectors -particularly the clicking as each film joint slipped through the mechanism, and each with the awful possibility of a breakage! To be viewing the screen only to feel the slight touch of something round your legs, and then to see yards of film entwined round your ankles, was another living nightmare experience one occasionally encountered. Through the mist of bygone years now, I see the chief operator puffing away at his Woodbines while above his head are the words 'Smoking strictly prohibited! I see him, in the rewind room, leaning over reels of highly inflammable nitrate film while large portions of ash are about to fall from his mouth. He was more fortunate than the projectionist at Buckley. That dear soul was burned to death and the Tivoli would have been burned to the ground, but for two young lasses passing by and noticing belching smoke.

Young Avril and Joyce returning from Sunday school at St John's rushed to the nearest police station; ran back with the Bobby and followed him in to the foyer until dense smoke met them at the foot of stairs leading to the circle. He told them to run off home while he made his way upwards. The next day the newspapers highlighted the tragedy and the Constables most heroic efforts. But it appeared the little girls were void of even a mention.

The Prince of Wales – towering over Holywell - was an eerie cinema, perhaps, because it retained much of the atmosphere of an old music hall. Preparing films on a Sunday evening was certainly the eeriest of all experiences, but it saved getting up for work on Monday mornings and an extra lie in bed meant a lot. On a Sunday night I would frequently climb up the fire escape on the outside of the building in order to enter the rewind room door. Once inside, while making up the programme on the bench, I would become extra conscious of a dark passage directly behind me. It led into the projection room and, then beyond it, out into the old circle. One could repeatedly hear noises in the distance while 'making up the programme' and humming was often a means of retaining sanity.

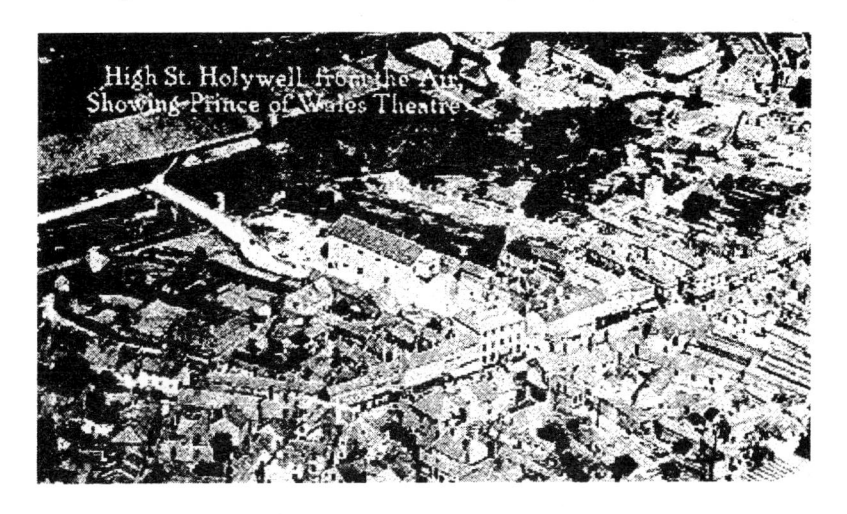

High St. Holywell from the Air Showing Prince of Wales Theatre

But then, I dare say, an equally frightening experience occurred each weeknight when left in the old cinema by myself at the end of the evening's performance. Most lights would be switched off before coming down from the back of the circle. Then, all other employees having left by the front entrance, it was my task to bolt the swing doors after them. With the light of a torch I would knock off the master switch and then grope into the large auditorium. It was then necessary to make one's way down towards the region of the massive red curtains, which surrounded a gold engraved proscenium. When I reached the side of the screen I had to descend the steps near the side of the now' unused orchestra stand. One was soon through a door below the stage and walking along a passage past dressing rooms, covered in cobwebs, which hadn't been used for years. Doors were sometimes ajar. The reflection of the torch would often light up an old fashioned mirror in which one sometimes saw oneself. If this were not enough on reaching the end of that passage, one was confronted with an opening where stairs lead up on to the disused stage, which contained ropes and old scenery. As a later employee once remarked, "you were wise if you kept your eyes from looking up the stairs, lest some ghost was to be seen standing at the top, gleaming down at you." Noises, on such occasions, were often heard. You interpreted it as nothing worse than a stray rat or a contraction of the central heating system. You dare not think otherwise! To open the final door that brought one out into the cool evening air was a nightly relief, and strangely enough, though far from being a Christian, I found myself praying each night to God. This was not in bed, nor out of any sense of love or loyalty to Him; but in sheer desperation during these nightly episodes when, after the close of each final performance, I groped my way through the darkness of an empty theatre which, uncannily, still felt as if it were full.

Incidentally, one of the most unusual cinemas visited as a youth was the so-called Super Regent in nearby Bagillt. Indeed, to enter it was to frequent a once stately chapel. The seats within it certainly appeared plush upstairs, but they were actually as hard as nails when sat upon. Yes, and whereas they were far from plush, the toilets were far from flush! This was hardly the proprietor's fault as mains sewerage had not at this stage been laid down in the region of this picture palace.

Should one choose to sit down stairs, just below the front of the balcony, the strong smell of Jays Fluid emanating from the toilets near the front of the auditorium appeared to hit the roof, and then to descend downwards.. The fact is, the toilets within the gents consisted of a bucket under the seat; and sometimes it was far from empty! Admittedly, a window above always appeared to be slightly ajar when the performance was on. This, no doubt accounted for the sole bit of illumination - a gas flame protruding through a damaged mantle! - flickering while one sought to transact a call of nature.

The last occasion I found myself needing to 'spend a penny' within this cinema is one that was strange to say the least. As a young teenager – no doubt undergoing a kind of busman's holiday! - I made my way down from the circle, and then forwards towards the right of the large screen. Indeed, to one's consternation, on this occasion it appeared as if the gas mantle had blown out in the breeze. Well, I fumbled towards the urinal trough but discovered it difficult to locate. 'Were they in the process of alterations?' I asked myself. It appeared as if some temporary tarpaulin sheet was now in front of me. So, quite desperate 'to go' I began to relieve myself against it. But then, quite uncannily, it began to waiver in the apparent breeze from the window. And then it was that oaths and curses followed which I would not like to repeat. To my utter horror I'd been stood behind another within that dark cubicle and had been urinating all over the back of his gabardine. He was hardly in the mood to accept an apology; and I was hardly inclined to offer it. Making a speedy exit, I ran up the side isle of the auditorium, and vacated the Super Regent - for the last time? Well, not quite!

Let me temporarily digress! No less than half a century on, and I returned to enter this same cinema which was now called The Focus. A budding entrepreneur had taken it over. "Delighted to meet you!" he said. "I'll take you up to the Projection Room. You may well recognise some parts of the equipment that are still in use". Doreen and I followed this most courteous and helpful fellow, up a dusty cast iron spiral staircase. There were two landings. On reaching the top one we found ourselves on the projection platform. The equipment was purring away alongside the crackling from the speaker. Indeed, it was nostalgic, indeed, to witness the fellow switching projectors in the twinkling of an eye. There and then, I considered it might well be an honour to help him as 'an old hand' now retired.

"Please feel free to enter the Circle and view the rest of the performance" he said: "It's on me! And feel free to return here at any time you wish." I sensed we were kindred spirits, and accepted his generous offer to enter that old, familiar Circle. Later, he entered it briefly himself and, for an unguarded moment, appeared to stare 'as if through me'. Did he sense that I was a cleric and, somehow, disapprove?

Months passed by and then a sense of deep guilt. I hadn't returned such kindness by a return visit! Subsequently, on two occasions I arrived around eight pm. 'Should I ascend the long spiral stairs - and apologise for not having called before'? Both times I prayed and then tossed a coin for Divine guidance. The answer both times was: No. The last, and third, time I preferred to use my own sound judgment. I got in our car from home and drove to profusely apologise for not having returned before -

though I had commended his enterprise in the readers views section of the Chester Chronicle: 'If a civic theatre in the vicinity could get financial augmentation from the local Council surely entrepreneur Peter Moore should!' - Alas, on arriving to meet him, the premises were shut and a police car was stationed outside.

Within weeks a high court judge would brand my 'new friend' as 'the most dangerous man ever to step foot in to Wales' - a serial killer who lured other men in to horrific torture and death. Tossing a coin, after prayer, hadn't been as stupid an idea as one might have thought! The good book says: 'In all your ways acknowledge Him and He will direct your paths'. I believe it now with all my heart, but fifty years previous – to an unregenerate young teenager - it would have been meaningless.

Mother had repeatedly stressed that I should seek a more congenial source of employment than that of working in a cinema, which she viewed as little better than working in a fairground. On several occasions the manager of a local gents outfitters had expressed sympathy at the unkind treatment I had previously received while in the printing occupation because of one individual's attitude. He assured me that many folk had more than one side to their nature: "they can be nice to converse with," he inferred, "but sheer demons to work under. Such a pity! " he said, "that there wasn't a vacancy in my shop. Your Mother would like that. I'll see what I can do for you!" Then, a week or two later this little man offered me employment. Mother was truly delighted, neither the Manager nor Chief Projectionist could persuade me to stay.

That first morning in the Gent's Outfitters proved a real eye opener. It was the first morning and the last. No sooner had the premises opened, than was I ordered to brush the floor vigorously from one end to the other. This new employer presumably failed to appreciate the way I held the brush. After much cursing and swearing he told me that, if I didn't get a move on, he would make my life Hell itself. Throughout the day the bullying went on and, in a sadistic fashion, I sensed he enjoyed every minute of it. Back at the printing office I looked up old Mr. Blackwell. "You've played right into his hands through telling him of your weakness", he said. "Stand up for yourself and tell him where to get off. Let him see you're a man!"

Mother showed little sympathy towards my attitude that evening, and affirmed that I would have to return to the shop the next day. She went on to say that the man was kind and courteous to her. She remonstrated that I return to work in the morning and apologise to him. She was a lady in every sense of the term, but was obviously very naive towards the different facets of human nature.

A few days later and I presented myself at the local labour exchange. Was indeed in the process of seeking unemployment benefit when, of all folk to walk in there, was the manager from the Gent's Outfitters. He remonstrated vehemently with the manager of the Labour Exchange not to give me benefit. "A job is still open at my shop", he affirmed, "and I want him back immediately." I need only add that I was exceedingly glad when the man behind the counter began to stick up for me, adding later that I would have been unwise to return to such a tyrant who was now possibly in trouble with his head office. Well, my period of unemployment lasted for but a short time. The war was hardly over and folk were being pushed into government work without much say in the matter. In a very short while I was amongst their ranks. Yes, I was soon travelling daily to Broughton, near Chester, working for DeHavilands' who had ceased making aeroplanes and were now involved in making prefabricated, portable houses.

I can still recollect catching that early morning bus 'for the workers' while the refined office staff, caught a later and much smarter vehicle. Indeed, the office staff strongly resented sharing a bus with the workers on the evening journey back and, when shortage of numbers demanded it, we were compelled to occupy the upstairs. The first fortnight found me working as a storekeeper's assistant, and while the workmen were often rough and uncouth, they were basically kind, genuine and thoughtful. Yet, for myself, I soon wished to aspire to something higher and, having pestered the Personnel Officer, was offered a post within the tool-room as an apprentice. The storekeepers considered this as a big step up the ladder and said I wouldn't want to know them. How sad! What was worse, the toolmakers parading around in their white jackets mostly appeared to have an inflated ego. My pride and persistence had got me into a post I would regret. Indeed, such conceit and rivalry as witnessed on a factory floor would put much later experiences of a University and Oxford college: out of the game!

In this new sphere of employment one was certainly not individually victimised for I was but one in a team. Every apprentice in that tool room was bullied. The keys would be thrown across at me, and then a toolbox containing an assortment of spanners. My own mate would wait with a smirk on his face as I fumbled.. He appeared delighted when I passed him a wrong tool rather than the right one. In the 'jig and tool' section of that tool room more conceit than ever was exhibited. The one 'in charge' insisted that the apprentices click their heels, salute and treat him as if he were a sergeant major. This broad accented and loud mouthed Scotsman, nicknamed 'Mac', enjoyed seeing any apprentice quaking in his presence. He actually thrived on it.

The kind folk in that tool room were amongst the grinders and the millers. Their work was considered more menial. Bullying the apprentices was not, however, the sole sideline of many of the toolmakers. One of these, who appeared to be so kind and caring, used to boast of seducing girls, often younger than his daughters. This was a prominent topic of conversation and nearly every sentence uttered included either an obscenity or a blasphemy. This was grownup manhood in reality. A marked contrast indeed to the song Mother had taught me to live up to when I reached adulthood:

To face and fight life's battles.
Win them if you can;
But first of all, my laddie,
Be a Man, Be a Man.'

If most of these toolmakers were men, then I would give far more respect to animals any day. The hours spent in that old aerodrome works at Broughton could never pass quickly enough, and if anyone there felt nervous and inadequate then none more so than myself. There was seemingly only about one way in which to be accepted and admired - to excel in dirty stories. Indeed, having tried it and received acclamation, I soon excelled as a narrator of mucky jokes. Then a better opportunity arose to assert my ego and this was because of an excessive appetite for food. A bet was held in the works' canteen amongst the workers, concerning myself and another apprentice as to who would eat the most lunchtime helpings. I won by eating thirteen dinners at one sitting; was hailed as the hero in the tool room and carried through part of the factory. Then the works doctor examined me to discover whether or not I had a tapeworm. But on discovering that I was merely a growing lad, who could do with putting on more weight, he provided me with a chit with which one could procure as many helpings from the canteen each day as one wished to stomach.

While in bed at night, and repeatedly in the earliest hours of the morning, I would awaken in a sweat, only to be wonderfully blest in discovering that one still had several hours in bed before having to arise and face the living nightmare ordeal of nine hours amongst such creatures. But then, when the time arrived and the bus had been boarded, the fear and depression accelerated on approaching the works. Soon I would be walking through the hanger doors, breathing in first the odour of paint spray, and then that of oil and metal filings. The factory siren would then sound and I considered us little better than slaves in a massive cage.

Satanic, spiritual forces, having burned themselves out in Germany, were still burning in Britain. It was the same power of darkness and the tools now were sometimes people I had occasion to rub shoulders with. The apostle Paul uttered no truer words than when he said, 'We fight not against flesh and blood but against principalities and powers, against the rulers of the darkness of this world and spiritual wickedness in high places.' Many times since those days I've objectively sought to analyse the situation then, to criticize myself and make allowances, but the conclusion has been the same. There is an evil realm perceptible to a sixth sense, which uses men as pawns and turns them into veritable demons. Thankfully, however, there is equally a realm perceptible to a seventh sense, and its task is to seek and turn others into saints and, within a few days, I was to become highly aware of it.

It was always a great relief to me when Saturday lunchtime arrived. I would often spend the afternoons in Chester and then, again, on Sundays with my friend Trefor when we would compare cinema performances in that city with those at the Plaza or the Prince of Wales. Nevertheless, fear, timidity and loneliness were constant shadows in my life. The harshness of the present led me to daydream about many years previous and to dwell on my childhood sweetheart Kathleen. I had known her -she was a year older than I - when I was no more than nine and a half years old. Yes, I was becoming a dreamer who fantasized because the real world was so utterly cruel.

Spiritually I Pass From Death To Life

On quite a few Sundays I travelled the hour's journey on the Crosville bus to the ancient city of Chester, deliberately going via Sealand so as not to pass Broughton and its works, the very mention of which created a heavy cloud of oppression resulting in a slight sweat and a gripping sense of fear. With, or without Trefor, I would usually visit the Odeon, the Tatler, the massive Gaumont Theatre or the Old Majestic beyond it. I would count the remaining hours of each swiftly passing weekend, determined to keep that detestable factory out of mind as well as sight. Every remaining hour of each Sunday evening counted and, when the cinemas had been frequented, the newer novelty of visiting an occasional pub was begun. Chester was not without its own form of nightlife for youth beginning to tread out, nervously and yet with daring. But then, one Sunday evening, something transpired which was 'out of this world'. While aimlessly meandering up an unknown side street I felt as if someone above knew the dreadful plight I was in: someone had come, not only to deliver me from it, but to introduce me into the fellowship of those who really cared for others.

Being now within close proximity to a rather secluded Presbyterian Church. I thought of my Church of Scotland days with Mother at Coldstream. More important still Grandma, whom I dearly loved, was as proud to be Presbyterian as she was to be Scottish. Mother, to please her Scottish parents, had been married within a Presbyterian Church. Well, I stood and looked across at that Church. I am certain in those days, that in no way would I have felt drawn towards the English Parish Churches as I associated them with foisty smells, aloofness and snobbery! On that April or May evening in 1947 however, I followed one or two folk who were walking along a short path, lined with shrubbery, towards a Church door, which was slightly ajar. The ringing of several bells from different vicinities merely drew me to this silent Nonconformists' building. There was a peace that intermingled with the sound of birds, and an awareness of something beyond one's five senses. And then, as if already planned, indeed, as if expecting me, the Minister came forward from within giving me a gracious clasp of the hand and such a loving look as to melt one's heart. With a soft, refined, Ulster accent he said: "Welcome home!" This tall, dark cleric, arrayed in Presbyterian attire, (cassock, gown, bands and hood) was so graciously humble in spite of being a double graduate of those days. There was no scrap of snobbery in him. Breeding and finesse were as prominent as his spiritual joy. A delightful family came forward to warmly welcome me and to share their pew. The worship that followed was dignified and reverent although the sermon went completely over my head and meant nothing. Then, at the close of the service, the hospitality given by the Minister was as warm as before it began. To see a young man coming to worship his Maker, and from such a distance as Holywell, was goodness in itself. "How good of you" were the words that kept ringing in my ear as I left that vicinity. 'Good' to worship my God. But why shouldn't I? I thought. As I left that holy place, somehow it seemed as if the sound had been turned up and birds were singing in harmony with me, I felt God was no longer a vague probability but, now, a very personal presence.

On reaching home at Holywell, Mother, Father and Brother were truly stunned to learn that I had preferred to attend Church than see a film. To have merely been in a church building might have been of less surprise because, as a family, we'd visited old Chester churches. Such precincts held the same fascination for us, as a family, as did the Castle, City Walls and Museum. The inability to view the Cathedral Cloisters fully, because 'worship' was commencing, had actually resulted in extreme embarrassment. While most visitors had hurried out we'd lingered. Consequently, hurrying round a corner, we nearly stumbled, head on, into a procession of plum voiced choristers and marble mouthed clerics who were waddling along. Yes, my parents had nothing but praise for my taking part in worship at St. Andrew's Presbyterian Church. But, alas, when the practice was repeated two Sundays following their attitude rapidly changed. Father just couldn't understand it but then my brother quite amused him by affirming that I'd obviously had a common religious experience 'seen the light' or 'been converted'. Dad laughed heartily at first. Then, in a subdued tone, spoke of certain swearing seamen he'd met whose lives had been changed from debauchery and drunkenness to sanity and saintliness because of a sudden spiritual experience.

Soon, religious talk became a source of embarrassment at the table and my family were content to affirm that they were respectable Church of England. Then, when I mentioned that they never went, I received a clip over the ear and was told that I was speedily heading towards a condition termed 'religious mania'. Dad swore he'd knock it out of me, and poor Mother became not a little concerned. As family opposition increased it seemed, as if, Christ became even more real. Was it not what He Himself had experienced and had prophesied for His children?

Mother, like Mary, loved her son dearly; but there was now a spiritual side of her son, which was outside her perception and to which she was a stranger. Yes, while walking the streets and lanes, and even at work, a tremendous sense of elation kept flowing through me. Indeed, during those early months one felt so in tune with God as to feel a power within to heal those who were sick. So much did I then feel as if I was 'walking on air' that I could see no difficulty whatever in believing that 'Enoch walked with God, and was not because God took him!' or that 'Elijah went up into Heaven in a whirlwind!' At this time particularly, it proved most difficult to contain one's feelings during worship as one considered the goodness and mercy of a God whose presence felt so intensely close. Hymns were now sung with meaning, as I was on a wavelength equivalent with that which inspired many of the authors to write them. If fire and water were scriptural symbols of God's Holy Spirit then 'Mild' electric sensations or, more so the heights and raptures of consummated sexual ecstasy could have been compared with the rapture I experienced for several months.

It was a wonderful day when the Reverend R. W. Lawson layed his hands upon me, confirming me into membership. It meant more than any subsequent laying on of hands would ever do - from a Pentecostal baptism in the Spirit to an Episcopal ordination to the priesthood. Of less importance by far, it meant that on the rare occasions when Communion was observed, I could place my card into the offertory plate, and during an additional service that followed, receive a cube of bread and a miniature glass of wine while knelt at the communion rail.

Before many weeks had lapsed, I expressed a wish to either train for the Presbyterian ministry or become one of its missionaries. The Minister seemed thrilled to hear it and spoke of a shortened course recently started for ex-service men. Later, however, he learnt that, because I was well under twenty-five, a degree in arts, followed by another in divinity was stipulated, and there was, regrettably, no way round it. The first preliminary step was to matriculate: - that was to pass the rough equivalent of seven O level G.C.E.'s all at the same time, with subjects such as maths. being compulsory. The dear Minister had every faith in my doing it. A retired Minister would even give me free tuition, but Mother didn't relish the thought of a weekly visit from a cleric. "Just imagine what your Dad might be like on returning from the Pub!" she said.. And she knew, as I did, that having left an elementary school at fourteen with three out of one hundred for maths. meant that I hadn't a cat in hell's chance of ever reaching the grade.

My brother, Colin, claimed no specific spiritual experience, but had, nevertheless, considered the possibility of a clerical career either High Anglican or possibly Roman. A booklet for ex-servicemen entitled, 'Training for the Church' proved a mine of information. Were all Church ministries as rigid and demanding in their training as the Presbyterian? Fortunately, they were not. Indeed, Baptist churches were completely autonomous, as were Congregationalist ones. This meant they could call whomever they wished as their pastor, even though a 'union' within each denomination was strong and stipulated its own form of academic training for those seeking benefit from its funds. Meanwhile, at least for a few months, I was proud to sample what Presbyterianism had to offer. But being unable to attend Sunday morning Worship in Chester - except by a long cycle journey - I now sampled morning worship in Holywell, sharing attendance between the Congregational Tabernacle where Sunday School days had been spent and what I discovered to be a small Presbyterian Church of Wales. Indeed, one's first Sunday morning at the latter was a strange, memorable and sad one.

I picked up courage and crept into the back pew of this smallish place of worship and quite marvelled at the simplicity of it all. It was a vast contrast to Chester, for the Welsh Presbyterians were much more simplified. Their buildings were much less ornate and, though there was a pulpit here, it was little more than a platform with a rail and at the side of it stood a harmonium. The Minister wore no distinctive attire and, on this occasion, not even a parson's collar. But, for his culture and style, one might have easily mistaken him for one of those many local preachers who attended the Tabernacle. It was hard to believe that this man, leading the worship, was the same gentleman as the young athletic cleric I'd noticed several years previous. Yet he carried the same name! This poor creature, in this low pulpit, was exceedingly round shouldered and the sweat was running off his forehead. He had entered the pulpit with great difficulty and then when halfway through the sermon, asked that he might be excused for sitting down to finish what he wished to say. This message was the only one I was privileged to hear from him, for the Revd. Levi Thomas was a dying man, yet his theme was on the closeness of God expressed through the beauty of nature. He spoke of the loveliness of flowers, and of birds as messengers sometimes sent from God!

At the close of worship there was no difficulty in leaving without, seemingly, being noticed. I had occupied the rear pew and, as for the Minister, he must have been too ill to have noticed a stranger. Two days later, however, I discovered that this was not so. While walking along Bagillt Street, past a row of old Welsh cottages, one became conscious of spluttering and banging from a car coming up from the rear, which seemed to be trailing me. I turned sideways to view an old, three-wheeled jalopy of the day – an ugly contraption between a car and a motorbike. It stopped and the perspex window was opened. Within the fume impregnated cab the occupant asked whether or not I'd been the young man in his congregation the previous Sunday morning. He said he'd been trailing me because he thought I was and just wanted me to know that I hadn't been unnoticed, that it was lovely to find a young man worshipping his Maker, and how sorry he'd been that he hadn't got down to the door in time to welcome me personally. I told him of my longing to enter full time Christian work. He said he would like to have helped me, but was moving away very soon, perhaps, for good. He appeared extremely sad.

Local gossip soon confirmed that the Revd. Levi Thomas had returned to South Wales to his mother's home where he spent the last days of his mortal life. He'd been a remarkable man, having moved out, or rejected a manse on acquainting himself with the plight of a young, frail widow who had been forced to take in washing in order to support herself and her child. Yes, he took up lodgings in a dark, old cottage, which was plain and bare. I know this was true because I was friendly with this delicate widow's most caring son. Through stable doors you descended onto a cobbled floor and, then, the smell of soot met you as you peered through the smoky atmosphere.

Such a step on the part of the Minister had not escaped criticism. Indeed, a leading elder of the congregation and former postmaster felt their pastor was largely to blame for his own breakdown. Nevertheless, his Minister was self-willed, or more appropriately 'God motivated' and, though the Presbyterian ministers were then the best paid of any clerics, it was rumoured that this one gave away his last penny to the needy of the district. Such self-denial undoubtedly had its price. As 'galloping consumption' ate its way through his body there was difficulty in getting around and he'd been given his jalopy as a gift from a poor yet grateful admirer.

From South Wales the Minister, knowing he was dying, wrote to his one and only flock apologising for not having lived as close to God as he might have done. At his memorial service more than one minister was so emotionally overcome as to break in to tears. More moving still, as the cortege made its way along the route a woman temporarily distracted the mourners. She'd been a non-believer. Overcome by grief, and completely dishevelled, she ran out of her cottage to cry out, "'What must I do to become a Christian like this good man here?" Yes, and if my memory serves me well, he was only forty-two. A verse in Genesis reads: 'There were giants in the land in those days'. Well, in the glorious land of my youth I came across one or two spiritual giants. He was one of them; and his memory is a blessing to one's soul.

Other churches of a Presbyterian order were also to be found in the vicinity. These were Welsh speaking; and as the teaching of the language at school had been restricted to those whose parents spoke it at home, the nearest I got to worshipping in the vernacular was outside Rehoboth chapel. The name biblically meant: 'there is still room', and judging by its size, it was indisputable. However, to 'pause for a breather' on cycling up the hill alongside this Chapel, when weeknight choir practice was in session, became a foretaste of Heaven. I hardly knew a word of Welsh, but the singing that came from within melted one's heart. Jesus presence drew close and - to use John Wesley's words - 'my heart was strangely warmed'. Their minister was a godly soul; and, obviously, so were these worshippers. Theirs was, demonstrably, the language of Heaven!

'my heart was strangely warmed'

Sunday evenings were always looked forward to as occasions for worshipping at Chester. I had previously made the journey for selfish pleasure and had now determined to use it to glorify God. Well, on one such occasion, on making one's way to St. Andrews, I chanced to pass the end of Grosvenor" Park Road. There, I was confronted with an open-air service, which was in full fettle. Folk had gathered in a circle and in the midst of them, was a young Minister, of small stature and with a broad collar. One moment he would be squeezing a concertina and the next addressing passers by who seemed unimpressed! He conveyed the impression to me of being amateurish which I had attributed to his youthfulness. Yet, I was to learn that he was around thirty. However, no sooner had the meeting come to a halt than a beeline was made towards me, "Are you saved? Do you know the Lord?" he asked. I told him that due to a wonderful experience having occurred several months previous I truly felt ready to meet God. He was not impressed "Feelings are not reliable," he affirmed. Then, taking a large Bible from under his arm and opening it, he quoted certain scripture passages. Then, as the time for the Service in the Chapel opposite was getting near, he led me into the building. It was a Baptist Church and he was the minister. I could become a 'true' 'born again' Christian if I would read and obey the declaration form within the back cover of a copy of the Gospel of John. Well, this I did there and then. I sensed he had clinched a deal.

What followed was a truly homely and informal type of service. As well as hymns, sung in joy, and often spurred on by the happy pastor himself, a clear and simple sermon was given from a high pulpit, which was the focal point of the building. The Pastor undoubtedly enjoyed his position there and a smile emanated from him. "Once again I have brought a young man into 'saving Faith' with the Lord", he said, and suddenly I realised that he was speaking about myself. While 'A Hearty Welcome to All' was displayed on the outside of the Church an even heartier welcome was delivered within. Yes, such folk meant real business for God. They were following in the steps of the disciples by going out into the highways to invite people in. Pastor Harry Whyte could truthfully have been nicknamed Happy Harry - his faith was a tonic.

Members of Grosvenor Park Baptist Church usually referred to one another as -brother or sister. They always seemed active and though they often had little time to listen, they always had time to utter a word from the Lord. A brusque handshake with an 'Every blessing, brother', was another phrase that would later become part of my vocabulary. The Bible would be as much a part of one's attire as a wallet or purse, and soon I would be seeing the relevance of selected Scriptural verses for each situation confronted in life. Perhaps of more relevance to me at the time, I learned that the tremendous spiritual experience I'd undergone several months previous was not unique. They, also, had experienced similar through following a Scriptural formula or A.B.C. of Salvation something I myself hadn't needed to do. It had just happened"

The Minister taught me a great deal in a short time. He soon convinced me that baptism was a scriptural need to be confined to believers and administered by immersion. He impressed me a great deal. but two spinsters he failed to impress. Basically, due to his use of words not grammatically quite accurate, the two dear spinsters would open up their dictionary in Church as well as their Bible. These two old dears made their practice quite conspicuous as they always enjoyed one of the more forward pews. They were not averse to looking round and, whenever, they looked up the book of wisdom one used a lorgnette! The Minister continued as confident as ever attired in his black jacket and pinstriped trousers. Notices were often lengthy, and when the new secretary once made a hash of them, the Minister – with a lovable Scottish firmness – interjected: "You must appreciate that our dear brother hasn't had the expertise in training that I have undergone. Allowances must surely be made!" Well, it was thoughtful of him.

Worship always seemed to go with a swing and the good book, at sermon time, would frequently get a good bashing. The Pastor was mature enough to consider it quite hilarious when a fellow minister, of more mature years, had called him to his face: 'a puffed up spiritual windbag'. Temperaments, as well as theology, differ considerably amongst ministers as they do amongst others. What a miserable world it would be if we were all alike! The Church needs the bright and breezy as well as the solemn and supposedly saintly.

Ducked Confirmed And Disillusioned

Several months later, having frequently joined in the worship of the Grosvenor Park Baptists, I was amongst the candidates awaiting baptismal immersion. The service was undoubtedly an impressive one and the most impressive of all services that Mother was to experience. The congregation was larger than usual and the candidates, who occupied pews to the front, were appropriately dressed. The ladies wore special gowns and the gent's a white shirt with grey trousers. Underneath the high pulpit, which occupied the central position, was the baptistery with stairs going down to it from each side. The Minister wore big waders, like a fisherman, over the top of which was a gown, leaded down at the hems, so as not to float on the surface of the water. At the close of the sermon he was the first to descend into the deep and then, with water around his waist, he beckoned each candidate who, after his or her word of testimony before the congregation, was to follow him down into the baptistery. For myself, I have never been fond of water and was sometimes criticised for a dirty neck and ears. However, the Pastor had reassured me that, when he swung me back into the pool, all I needed to do was to relax and then I would soon come to the surface. In actual fact the experience was about the nearest I ever came to the grave. As he pushed me in the chest, to make sure that I was totally immersed, all wind was pushed out of my lungs, resulting in receiving more water than was good for me. The anthem, which struck up as I came up spluttering (and the nearest I've been to choking), seemed most appropriate: 'Up from the grave He arose'. Yet, my ordeal wasn't as bad as another's.

I've always had a tendency to laugh at the most inappropriate times, and a weakness to see the lighter side in most solemn moments. It was so on that particular event, as amongst other candidates keen to express allegiance to the Lord, was a plump lady. The memory so easily plays tricks. I'm however, pretty sure that the official had left her 'to be done' last of all as, being a small man, he'd been a little apprehensive about things. I certainly remember this well endowed 'sister in the Lord' being swung back into the baptismal waters. There was not only a splash, but very regrettably a loud thud. He must have gauged her height wrongly because she hit the side. Being of that temperament, which makes much out of events, which others might seek to cover up, this poor soul made it obvious to the whole congregation what had happened to her head. Even the extra gusto of the choir, with 'Up from the grave He arose', was unable to drown her loud sobs. Dear, dear soul! She'd entered the waters with a gorgeous hairstyle. Now she stood, in a great commotion, literally howling towards the congregation with her hair: 'dead straight' while the little pastor, at her side, was trying to make the best of a bad job. Nevertheless, Mother felt the service, on the whole, had been most impressive, but when we later narrated the fete of the well-endowed lady, Dad just about burst his sides. My brother wondered how many Baptist pastors had been brought up on charges of manslaughter. "Are they insured for indemnity?" he asked, "because he needs to be sued!"

The fellowship, and the encouragement to 'go on in the Lord', given by the parents of the Minister's fiancée, will not be forgotten. They were a lovely couple whose other daughter became engaged to the new, rather timid Church Secretary. Indeed, though the congregation was usually far from brilliant, there was a warmth of fellowship, which I'd never witnessed before. They were obviously not without their differences, but there was a love, which transcended the barriers. Indeed, the home of those two dear spinsters, who carried a dictionary to Church as well as a Bible, is worthy of mention here.

I certainly considered myself privileged when the maiden ladies invited me to their sedate residence near the beautiful riverside. On this honoured occasion the manners I'd been taught at home were meticulously observed. The tea, already prepared, looked a most delightful one, though the assortment of cutlery, and the order in which I should use it, proved a trifle embarrassing. They reassured me, however, that the guest was always privileged to start eating first, and I sense they waited to observe. Hardly had I lifted a fork, when they suggested that their guest might like to 'offer grace' for them.. And then, following a surge of panic, the blunt knife I pressed upon a tomato resulted in its contents spurting across the well-arrayed cloth. Yet it was something they politely chose to ignore. Later however, when they passed me a bowl after the first course, they asked me to start as they had had sufficient. I considered this to be the sweet, for after all, dessertspoons were set out! I, there upon, took the bowl, which was possibly full of honey, stuck the dessertspoon within it and was about to consume the lot. But then the dish was swiftly snatched out of my hand and they offered to come to my assistance. One spoonful of honey was placed on the side of my small plate, and then bread, minus the crusts - which I hadn't noticed before - was passed over. No desert followed.

After high tea, it proved much more relaxing to recline in a comfortably upholstered chair and then the Pastor became the topic of conversation. His choice of large, though often wrong words was touched upon. As a young believer I needed to be aware of such shortcomings lest I should also fall into them. Nevertheless, their Pastor believed in 'The Word' from cover to cover and, if for no other reason than that, he was a minister of whom they were justly proud. The conversation then moved to the work of the 'One by one band'. The dear Miss Yardley's enlisted me into this movement and told me that, if each converted Christian succeeded in making no more than one convert, the Church would numerically double.

However, when two sisters wish to fulfil the role of a Mary to any guest, and neither wishes to be a Martha, you can imagine the outcome! It so happened that the one who entertained me did so without the approval of the other, who was 'encumbered about much washing!'. The result was that the hospitality and spiritual chat given by one was interspersed with the loud noise of crockery from the region of the kitchen given by the other. During the moments I was left to entertain myself and consider spiritual issues - a large Bible having been left in my lap - the sound of a terrific row reverberated, and added to it nothing less than the noise of breaking crockery. The din continued for quite some time before my eyes, focused on the Bible, were raised upwards because of a soft refined voice saying, "Do have one!"

I looked up to see a beautiful box placed in front of me. Being a self-indulgent young man – with a sweet tooth - one was keen to open the lid. On doing so I merely saw bits of paper screwed into rolls on top of which rested a pair of tweezers. "Do have one!" she repeated. I did, and on unravelling a roll of my choice, read thereon a verse of scripture. I was asked to apply it to myself and then replace it. Yes, it was a Christian's 'Precious Promise Box', the first I'd come across. In years to come a similar box would help me spiritually to grow through meditating on a different verse each day. But at that particular stage I sense I'd have preferred a chocolate with the coffee, which so graciously followed.

These ladies, so prim and proper, were undoubtedly devoted to Our Lord, yet they appeared to me as a hangover from the Victorian Era. They certainly appeared to 'know The Saviour' in a wonderful way, but quite paradoxically, they never radiated a smile. Like others whom I would later meet, theirs was a solemn brand of the Good News. Yet, that sole visit to their home proved a mine of information regarding what my future policy should be if I felt called towards the Ministry.

'The Baptist ministry, throughout the country, was divided between ministers who were affiliated to a union and those who were not. The union emphasised training which involved a highly critical approach to the whole Bible and many young men had lost their faith through pursuing such courses. "Could one absorb poison into one's system each day and not be poisoned?" asked one of the sisters. Indeed, the value of such a union might include a guaranteed basic wage and also an approved form of ordination, but it could very much be at the detriment of one's preaching and calling' The two ladies much more approved of those other ministers, some of whom had spent periods of time at one of several Bible colleges, their own Pastor being amongst them.

'These latter ministers lived by faith, as some congregations could not afford to be as generous as others. The Lord honoured men who stood for the truth of the Bible and preached for decisions. The Master blest such congregations who kept to the traditional pattern of each Church, under the guidance of the Spirit, conducting its own affairs. Indeed had not the great king of all preachers: Charles Haddon Spurgeon been one of them?'

The maiden ladies then went on to affirm that, whereas, the title 'Rev.' prefixed to a minister's name was always the practice within the union, that ministers outside of it often preferred the prefix 'Pastor' due to its biblical connotation and because the term reverend was only applicable to God's name. One of the dear sisters fumbled through her Bible. "What does the Book Of Job say?" she asked, and handed it to me to read. "I know not to give flattering titles to any man for in so doing my Maker would be sore displeased with me." I said. "There you have it", she replied. A pity our Minister has recently chosen to address himself as Reverend. instead of Pastor. "Have you noticed how he's recently altered the notice board?" said one to the other. "I don't think if Brother James enters the ministry that he will be carried away by such vanity," said the other. Then they both nodded approvingly as they turned towards me. And I preened in response.

Round about this time the need for pre-fabricated houses ceased, and the ex-aeroplane factory at Broughton was no longer needed. Work as an apprentice toolmaker, was drawing to its close and those foul mouthed, sadistic creatures, with whom by then I was well acquainted, would be on the dole. Yet, strangely enough, whereas I once cursed them I now began to pity their plight; particularly those wth a family.

On applying for reinstatement at the Plaza cinema in Flint, I was successful and my work resumed as a projectionist there. But this time things weren't quite the same. I was sharing the work with a bright young stranger because my two former friends were required to do their National Service, 0' how I missed them! When I'd applied to the R.A.F. I'd been rejected on medical grounds and classified C3. This was due to eyes and feet. The work in this small luxury cinema was again congenial and pleasant. In fact you seldom heard a swear word; never a blasphemy and smutty jokes were quite sparse. Unfortunately, interest in 'the things of God' so absorbed me that I couldn't confine them to the Lord's Day. On Wednesdays and Saturdays, between the matinee and evening performances, while sharing tea in the lounge with manager and commissionaire, I would continually touch upon spiritual issues. Although I'm sure I was morally no better than they were, I nevertheless found that they were becoming more and more embarrassed with the topic of such conversation. The Manager merely reiterated that the Quakers had much to teach and offer whereas the priests of the Church of England, if the Cathedral at Chester were anything to go by, were as superstitious as a gathering of witch doctors. Within a side chapel he'd found them robed to high heaven, burning candles, ringing bells and seeking to do some magic act over some pieces of bread while mumbling incantations. I deeply respected his views.

Sometimes, on leaving the cinema during the free time allowed between a matinee and an evening performance, I would go for a cycle ride in the direction of a delightful Church. On occasions I would dismount and pay a little visit inside. It was, one supposed, a church of basically foreign extraction. Locals referred to it as a Roman church and I associated it, at first, as primarily for the Italians and the many other foreigners who'd come over because of the war years. Well, the building was left open to encourage the faithful to visit it. I identified myself as amongst 'God's' faithful and began to visit it regularly in order to pray. Well, on no less than five occasions, when I was praying inside that beautiful building a young priest entered. He looked handsome and smart. While I was praying he began, in almost a military fashion, to walk up and down the length of the isle while reading from a book in his hands. Indeed, he almost clicked his heels whenever he swung round. He was meticulously reading prayers from this book, (it would be the Daily Office from his Breviary) and I longed to be given an opportunity to catch his attention so that, at a relevant time, I might ask him about his church and religion. It was obvious, however, that he was never in a frame of mind to be disturbed as he could not have failed to notice how very eagerly I sought to attract his attention.

I was to purchase from the back of this church a delightful little prayer book, which was cherished for many years. It contained such lovely pictures and there were loads of prayers in it too. After each prayer, within brackets, there was reference to a number of days. One was to learn much later that they were indulgences; that is the days depleted from Purgatory for each time the prayer was said. For every page I could read in this book, which I quite treasured, there was one I could not. It was in Latin. How clever these worshippers must be, I reasoned. They know two languages! Well, looking back, I only know that if the priest had been as identical in understanding as the one portrayed by Bing Crosby in 'Going My Way?' or Spencer Tracy in 'Boy's Town', (both these films had been screened round about this time!) I would have been a convert to the Roman Catholic Church for the rest of my days.

In order to stem growing opposition from Father, and particularly to please Mother who did her utmost to understand me, I was advised, after a visit to the local Parish Church in Holywell, to seek out the young curate and do the respectable thing, which they had both once done: get Confirmed!. Dad was pleased and so was my brother. Mother was truly relieved: "Get confirmed and stop talking all this religious nonsense," she said. "You're becoming a laughing stock to the neighbours!" Well, the Curate, the Reverend L. M. Daniel, was saintly and caring. All I needed to do was to see him for half an hour each week and in six weeks time I would be ready for Confirmation. Indeed, those meetings, though short, were enlightening. "People who are educated enough can never believe everything in the Bible," he affirmed. Yes, he was without doubt a Modernist, but as such, he still shared the experience of a spiritual conversion alongside me. Mr. Daniel's theology was in complete contrast to Pastor Whyte's. Yet he still shared each moment of his day with Our Lord! Spiritual radiance shone forth from him and yet he discarded the virgin birth and the physical resurrection of Jesus!. I'd learned from making his acquaintance, first of all in the printing establishment, that to win this man's friendship one had to respect his God, otherwise he was too busy to bother with you. His mind was fully in control over his body. He became an idol in my life and I longed to be like him.

Then, one afternoon, right out of the blue, a surprise visitor called - the previous idol. He'd come all the way from Chester to find out whether or not I was ill. I was not a little embarrassed in entering the house to find the Revd. Mr Lawson waiting to see me. Several months previous he'd received me into full membership of the Presbyterian Church. Since then I'd been immersed and had become a Baptist and now, within a month, would be an Anglican. This must be a record. My conscience, however, began to deeply trouble me for this man was the last person in the world I would ever have wanted to offend.

Sitting in our home, enjoying a cup of tea, Mr. Lawson seemed so sad to learn about my worshipping elsewhere. He expressed few words. That I had subjected myself to a believer's baptism, when I'd already been baptized as a child, had been totally unnecessary. He did not wish to discuss the matter further. No doubt he felt that I lacked the academic ability to discuss the matter in depth. He may well have been right. One thing was obvious. He was not impressed by my quoting isolated biblical texts. Mother seemed more interested in discovering how our guest was able to drink two cups of tea without leaving any sign of tea stain on the lip of the cup. "He is a gentleman and has marked breeding," she said, "He's not like the little upstart at the Baptists!" On this occasion Mother had taken care to bring out, from the cupboard, her finest crockery: a gift from her far off wedding day.

Walking Mr. Lawson back to the bus station found me on edge. Teatime was approaching. This was the time when the Curate might pass and possibly refer to my coming Confirmation. It would appear I'd been stringing along three ministers at the same time! Thankfully the Curate didn't pass by, but the Welsh Wesleyan Minister, busy as ever in his garden, seemed mildly surprised that a son of the Thompson family should be walking with a member of the cloth. In a roundabout style he would later in the week question me about this. And from that moment onwards, the Revd. William Price took deep interest in my spiritual progress. He too, while appreciating one's spiritual experience, was another to warn about the dangers of accepting everything in the Bible 'as gospel'. "The Bible is a good book, like Pilgrim's Progress; but the moral teaching of parts of it are quite barbaric", he affirmed. Such words again quite shocked me. Could he be one of those wolves Christ spoke of who come to you in sheep's clothing? Had not my brothers and sisters in Christ, worshipping at the Grosvenor Park Baptist Church, warned of these Modernist preachers who empty once thriving churches because they sow the seeds of biblical disbelief from the very pulpit itself?

The day of Confirmation eventually arrived but spiritually I found it sadly lacking to evangelical fellowship at Chester. Being grouped with several I'd known from far off school days, there appeared no spiritual interest in common. We had all seemingly gathered for a formality during which a Bishop would lay his hands upon us, after we'd approached him in two's; and then the Holy Spirit would flow from him into us! Well, I felt like a fish out of water! The Vicar - recently elevated to that lofty and coveted post of Rural Dean - appeared keen to please the Bishop; and the main concern was that everything went off to plan. Mother rather naughtily said his wife had purchased a new hat for the event, and was fussing round the Bishop's wife! Well, who knows? It was a great social occasion, not unlike a Vicarage garden fete: planned to impress.

The need to Matriculate again reared its ugly head, and this time for acceptance as a candidate for the 'Church in Wales's Ministry. Both Kelham and Mirfield monastic establishments existed in England and were able to accept candidates for the priesthood way below matric, But the Vicar of Holywell was Low Church, and possibly an Orangeman! He would hear none of it. Indeed, wait until turned twenty-eight, and two years would suffice at nearby St Deiniol's in Hawarden, said the Curate. But twenty-eight appeared as old age! His offer to then coach me for Matric. was short-lived as his valedictory service soon followed; and my unaided attempts, through a correspondence course with Wolsey Hall, Oxford, fizzled out within a year.

The Curate's valedictory service was indeed a sad one. He spoke of how God had used him chiefly amongst the young folk whose years were besought with so many problems. Mother felt he was speaking in his sermon with myself in mind, and I was pertinent to think likewise! During the recession of the choir at the close of the service he was so moved with sorrow that his fiancé, the Vicar's daughter, left a front pew, ascended the chancel and took hold of his arm to walk down the isle together. Not a few hearts were moved; I cried bitterly that night. Friends and acquaintances who were non-spiritual, on hearing of it, merely considered it odd that a Minister should in such a way become overcome with emotion.

I thank God for Holywell Parish Church, and usually associate it with the first Watch-Night service ever attended: just a handful in Church even in those far off days. Yet, in the darkness the Altar seemed so welcoming from a distance, and as the New Year came in, I sang for the first time: 'Lead us heavenly Father, lead us, o're the world's tempestuous sea.' Only a handful of worshippers were there, but then, there was also God. You could feel His presence and it brought tears to one's eyes; and, what was more, a bubbling up sensation of gratitude that one's heart could scarcely contain. On returning home in the early hours of that morning, passing so many who were under the influence of alcohol, one only wished that they could also experience such a Presence and share such spiritual elation.

Bitterness, associated with a person, can so easily creep into one's life too, particularly should one be audacious enough to feel more worthy of help than another. It so happened that a school chum, whom I remembered mostly because his dodgy jokes once usurped my own, had an Uncle who was a Canon. Well, although this old school pal had no wish or inclination to train for the Church, the Vicar visited his parents to encourage their son to consider the Ministry 'as a career'. He'd noticed that the young man's vocabulary was so eloquent, his reading in public most marked, and of course, his uncle was a prominent Canon and there may be hereditary connections. Well, my friend had no wish what so ever to pursue such a calling and clashed over the matter when pressure was put upon him.

This revelation was for myself 'the last straw' concerning the Vicar who neither appeared to understand a spiritual conversion or a spiritual calling. If he wouldn't help me in contacting places such as Mirfield or Kelham, then surely the Bishop himself would! After all, hadn't he just recently confirmed me?

Several weeks passed, and then one morning I packed sandwiches into the saddlebag, mounted my cycle and set off for the tiny city of St. Asaph. On arriving, and enquiring that afternoon as to the location of the Bishop's residence, one was amazed to find a rambling edifice situated in such exotic grounds. The term, Bishop's 'Palace', seemed most fitting;

though it hardly savoured of the humble Nazarene! At first I wondered if I should dare to casually call at such a place as no appointment had previously been made. Nevertheless, bishops were men of God, shepherds of The Lord's flock. He would no doubt welcome me with a firm handshake and with eyes squeezed in kindness say, "What can I do for you my son?" So the bell was pressed and I waited in anticipation. Then the door was opened and a lady who weighed me up and down, asked quite brusquely what I wanted. But not before a small sausage dog was yapping its way around one's feet, and then I was ushered into a room.

This Secretary, who had the appearance of a traditional 'school marm', seemed truly shocked that anyone should consider calling on the Bishop without an appointment. "I think you've come on a wasted journey," she affirmed. "This is very strange!" After further questioning she said she'd see whether he might give me two minutes of his time. Well, a considerable period elapsed before she returned to confirm her opinion. "He can't see you. After tea, he has a very heavy schedule!" Then, on leading me to the door, she again turned to view me up and down: "I may be wrong, but you do not come across to me as a fitting young man to consider ordination! Education and money to pay for lengthy college training is what is required" On opening the door she added: "I really think you should think of something else!" Then the door was firmly closed behind me. Admittedly, such a blow was slightly softened when days later a kind letter awaited me from a Revd. Charles (much later to become Bishop!) mentioning limited grants one could apply for, having first matriculated.

On a subsequent visit to the old printing establishment in Holywell I had hardly related my experience when the Vicar walked in himself. Although he was unknown to lose his temper it seemed as if I now saw another side of his nature. "You had no right to see the Bishop without going through me," he said. "What will the Bishop think? This could reflect very badly on myself!" I told him that I was more concerned about what God thought. Then Old Blackwell and Arnold Williams joined in to support me, and the Vicar, deep in thought, quietened down and left. The two printers told me they weren't bothered if the

Vicar never returned with anymore orders: "Integrity comes before custom every time, Jamie!" They felt I'd had a raw deal. Then Old Blackwell later took me to one side. "Haven't you ever thought of becoming an MP? You'd achieve much more for society ministering to a whole constituency than to a mere congregation. And what is more", he added: " you don't need to go to a university and theological college to become one. In fact, you don't even need a school certificate!"

Through having trained as a cinema projectionist one was in frequent demand to help out whenever a fellow projectionist was sick or on leave. And this was frequently undertaken in a part-time capacity as an evening 'step in' within the two leading picture palaces of the area. However, this had once resulted in a sharp and jagged edge of film causing a cut that was now festering in the middle finger of my left hand.. Not only was the hand becoming swollen but a lump was now appearing in the armpit. Indeed, my friends in the printing office, which I'd just visited, were adamant that I seek medical treatment without one moments delay. They very much feared for the safety of my arm.

Unfortunately, the doctors I'd learned to revere since childhood days were without a surgery that night, but there was one surgery that was open. It was that of a Dr Flutter. His residence was stately indeed. Money was obviously made from medicine! Within his surgery he first looked at my hand and then stared very coolly in to my face. "You've heard the saying kill or cure? Well this is what is involved here! Do you understand what I am saying?" "Yes" I replied. Then, after moisturizing and dabbing the palm of the hand, he lanced my middle finger from one side to the other.. And as if this were not enough, used a hook like tool to pull out more of the diseased flesh. Indeed, cutting with scissors what he had brought to the surface followed this. Then, watching my eyes continually – in a stoical manner – he repeated the process. I could not assess whether he was watching my face in case I was about to pass out at any moment; or whether he was watching the perspiration on my forehead. But I certainly felt he could have used some form of a local anaesthetic. Nevertheless, he did not ask me to return unless really necessary; seemed satisfied with what he had accomplished; and quite probably saved the arm from being amputated.

Little did I realise that within a few weeks I would meet this practitioner once more when I would again be at his mercy! A dentist of the district suggested that several of my teeth be extracted under gas. They were just about beyond saving; but as his drill was powered by foot pedalling – seeking to drill into the respective teeth with one hand on the drill, as one foot went up and down on the pedal wheel! – I considered losing one's teeth, in a state of temporary unconsciousness more preferable. Consequently, a few days later, in turning up at the Dentist's surgery, one was not only confronted by the courteous dentist but also by Dr Flutter. Indeed, he appeared to recognise me; walked to the appropriate cylinder, turned round and said: "I don't think there's enough gas with which to finish the job!" Then, after having discussed it with each other Dr Flutter looked towards me and said: "It's up to you. I'm happy to proceed if you want me to!". I acquiesced and soon, with mask clamped to the mouth, felt a choking sensation as I fought against the gas. My head buzzed until slumping in to the relief of unconsciousness and then a vivid dream occurred.

Like the sound of traffic moving past a window – coming and going – a hand seemed to travel towards me as if coming along a clothes line of white washing. And then it was that the most excruciating pain would transpire as a tooth was extracted from one's mouth. But then it would pass on as does the sound of traffic once it has past a window. However, the agony would be experienced all over again as the whishing sound again approached. The pain was intense. How much of this could my heart withstand? But then, again, the whishing noise would pass as if it had travelled past on a clothesline. This utter agony, while my fingers seemed dug in to the palms of the hands to withstand the intense pain, must have been experienced three times; possibly four, when I was then becoming aware of the surgery window. "He's coming round" uttered a startled voice. "He needs more gas!" And then it was that I slumped in to a slumber land sleep.

Later, on awakening, I was sent on my way by the courteous Dentist. Seemingly, Dr Flutter had already gone. Well, the night that followed became as frightening as the day that had preceded it. Congealed blood appeared to be building up within the throat and the thought of choking on it made one almost panic. As the Dentist only visited this High Street practice about once a week I made my way to the surgery of Dr Flutter. For some reason he'd moved it from alongside his stately home to part of a dilapidated mansion. A hall previously used for billeting troops during war years, under a commanding officer whom we locals had learned to revere and love. Without as much as looking in to my mouth Dr Flutter blurted out: "Go and see the Dentist. It's nothing whatever to do with me!" Then he closed the door forcefully behind himself.

Fortunately, that night I'd promised to help out for a few hours at the Plaza in Flint where the dear manager was most concerned. He phoned up the doctor who lived nearby and had me sent round to see him. The doctor was horrified: "He's not fit to be a vet, never mind call himself a doctor!" he said. "He's gone against all medical ethics and should be struck off! I'll plug your gums, and if this does not do the trick then I'll have to stitch them!' Thankfully, the latter procedure was not necessary and one had cause to be thankful again to the wonderful theatre manager. Yes, and to a lesser extent this Scottish doctor. He sent me a hefty bill! The manager was livid: "you must never pay it! He's used my fridge for months on end in which to store his surplus medical supplies. It hasn't cost him a penny. I did it as a gesture of good will. If he is not prepared to return a little kindness to one of my colleagues then he can go and store his medical supplies elsewhere!"

Sat in the fabulous lounge, Dick Waring turned to his uniformed commissionaire: "Blake, man! How mercenary minded can some folk sink?" Mr Blake clicked his heels: "Don't know Sir!" Then looking to me once the commissionaire had gone, Mr Waring said: "Don't think I'm hard on Blake. He's a military man and if I spoke to him as I spoke to you, he would be simply lost. He wouldn't know how to respond. He's been programmed, not to think for himself but to immediately obey a command. And I must say – Yee Gods! – it gets him out of difficulties!"

I later narrated my encounters with Dr Flutter to a school chum who lived a couple of doors away. His grandfather had been a doctor, and Gordon himself would one day aspire to be a psychiatrist. His words were to this effect: "O we know Dr Flutter … He has given me one or two old medical instruments and books on anatomy… What do you think about his fabulous house? Did you know that under the eaves; within the loft; he has cages to keep animals to experiment on?" To the response on my face my old school chum appeared astonished. "How else could they further their research?" I was fast becoming as disillusioned about medics as clerics! I simply knew that such 'academic coldness' to animals was a marked contrast indeed to dear Joey Brown in the Western I'd screened round about that time. He'd been cast in the role of a Wild West pastor who'd triumphantly led his congregation to oppose blood sports practised in his parish. Indeed, the film ended with the congregation lustily singing:

Holy, holy, holy, though the darkness hide Thee.
Though the eyes of sinful men Thy glory may not see.
Only Thou art holy. There is none beside thee
Perfect in power, in love and purity.

'Would to God that one day I might have the post and influence of such a preacher!' - I prayed. As for Dr Flutter, he was a cause of local gossip through trotting round with a caring gentleman's wife; both in traditional livery, crop in hand, and as if lord and lady to the manor born. Yet – rightly or wrongly – I learned that he was of extremely humble stock and against mounting odds had, nevertheless, more than 'made it'. He was a marked contrast to my own doctor; for a more humble, helpful and Christ like Irish Catholic I had yet to meet. Dr Hugh O'Connor, whenever he saw me his face appeared to light up. With a smile and a wave he would say: "Hello rascal!"

God Makes Me A Preacher

By this time I had started working as a junior postman at the Holywell Post Office. It was a job which one thoroughly enjoyed. In the evenings it was not only possible to help during busy periods in the printing office but, as already mentioned, to help out in both cinemas. Nevertheless, although they were always keen to procure my services, it would appear as if my consuming interest in spiritual factors didn't entirely endear me towards them. One's presence might have been at times an embarrassment or a conscience troubler. Be that as it may I could hardly blame the chief projectionist for flying off the handle when, at the Prince of Wales cinema, I allowed a bit of religious music into the midst of screening what might have been a Charlie Chang or Humphrey Bogart detective feature. I only know that, having brought from home a pile of Glen Miller recordings, I had inadvertently included a religious record amongst them. The outcome was that, when the interval arrived and the spotlight focussed on to the sexy young ice-cream sales girl, who was softly saying: "Ice-cream, sweets, cigarettes!" over the speakers came a male voice choir singing 'Abide with me!' Well, this appeared too much for Mr. Wild. He lived up to his name as much as when, on that occasion much earlier mentioned, the curtains had sagged before another packed house. As for the sporting manager, Mr. Clark, he had interpreted the record as one hilarious joke. My newly acquired zeal for the things of God was not appreciated: this was certainly not the place nor the time. The pickup arm was speedily lifted, on the non-sync as the chief rushed in from the Circle, and I dare say a Glen Miller record took its place.

I was, however, not the only relief projectionist in the area. On several occasions, sharing work with me at Flint's Plaza was a fellow who was a trifle older than myself. He had recently come home after having done a spell in the Merchant Navy. This fellow's Dad was the secretary of the small Baptist Chapel, which was to the left of the cinema next door. On informing him of my wasted journey to St. Asaph to see the Bishop, it was suggested that I come along to Chapel the following Sunday. "Dad is so eager to meet you!" he said, so the invitation was accepted. I was made extremely welcome and, what is more, was given the opportunity to try my hand at becoming a lay preacher. Yes, reading out a sermon of my own composition at a morning service when there would be hardly more than a dozen in the congregation. Mr. Isaac Williams, my friend's father, did all he could to encourage me. The sermon I read, on that momentous Sunday morning, was my own creation from the text, "Blessed are the meek for they shall inherit the earth." After having successfully delivered that first sermon the invitation was then extended to conduct the whole evening service a month later and possibly with only notes. That eagerly anticipated Sunday evening soon came round and the congregation happened to be larger than usual. But, before leaving the vestry so as to enter the pulpit, I was shown within a large frame on the wall: photos of past 'men of God', some of whom had occupied the same pulpit. I was reminded, in no uncertain terms, that in becoming a preacher one was following in the steps of a godly tradition. Isaac Williams, who was an intensely caring man, assured me that, as I entered that pulpit to speak for The Master, I would not be alone. "The Master Himself will be at your side", he said.

'the small Baptist chapel - to the left of the cinema'

I remember how, on coming forward from the preacher's chair and grasping the Bible-stand of the rounded pulpit, I was shocked to hear my own voice in the stillness. It seemed as if I would stammer and go to pieces. Then the words, 'you will not be alone', came to recall and, possibly of even more consequence, there in the back pew was Mother full of radiance, while next to her was a nearby neighbour, a Spiritualist. This gentleman was a truly devout soul for, though he had been shot through a lung in the great war as well as partly poisoned by mustard gas - indeed, though he was a chronic consumptive! - he'd travelled with Mother from Holywell especially to support me. It appeared that he was looking directly towards me and motioning me to go ahead while he was seemly conversing with spirit friends for my benefit. Suddenly, it seemed as if all nervousness departed. With Unexpected boldness and uncanny eloquence words needed for my prayers and sermon just flowed forth from my lips. I was truly 'carried along' with no effort on my part. God's Spirit seemed to permeate the building and the singing of the congregation - an act of worship in itself - was only what a Welsh chapel can ever create. The sermon's text, which God had placed on my heart, was the testimony of my very life; "One thing I know that whereas I was blind now I see."

That a new Preacher had been born was the topic of that evening's large congregation. Only one member had voiced displeasure; and this was quietly uttered in my ear. I'd quoted words from the book of Revelation: 'Whoever's names were not in the book of life would be cast in to the lake of fire!' "There is no lake of fire. Hell does not exist; and you had no right to mention it!" he whispered. And if looks could have killed then I would have been dead. Yet his snide remark was in the presence of others commending me as they passed out in to the night air. That solitary critic was a foretaste of those who criticize in a preacher what the majority commend; and haven't I met them!

A few weeks later and our dear, Spiritualist neighbour loaned me a book on 'How To Develop Mediumship In Seven Easy Lessons.' Mother forcefully dissuaded me from studying and practicing it as one of the daughters of his family had undergone a nervous breakdown. Nevertheless, a special invitation to address the Spiritualist Lyceum in Rhyl was accepted, and here it was that Mr. Nicholson's Wife was the clairvoyant

At the close of that first service in Flint's Baptist Tabernacle the Secretary had affirmed that I could well be following in the steps of a young preacher who'd lived half a century previous. For Charles Haddon Spurgeon, king of all preachers, had also started preaching as a teenager. Yes, and without the credentials of college training behind him! Indeed, so much was made of my preaching talent after the end of that first evening service that pride entered. And pride comes before a fall! Though the first evening service at the Tabernacle in Flint was amongst the best I have ever taken, the next service taken there would be the very worst! Several weeks later, upon standing up to preach, I was spiritually deserted. Words would not come, as I wanted them to, and those which did, were often grammatically incorrect. Yes, I was being taught by God's Holy Spirit - what any successful preacher forgets to his absolute peril! - that one must be emptied of self and solely reliant upon God.

I had indeed received spiritual life and vision; my calling, as a Preacher, had been confirmed by the Spirit's anointing, but there was a long way to go and the spiritual path was straight and narrow. Sunday evenings at the Tabernacle, once the congregation had dispersed, provided the opportunity to gather round a harmonium and sing some delightful hymns. The tears would run down the cheeks of the chapel Secretary who was also a gifted organist as we sang from the depths of our hearts versus such as:

> *How I praise Thee Blessed Master*
> *That Thy love lay hold on me*
> *Thou hast blest and filled, and cleansed me,*
> *That I might Thy channel be.*

He reminded me, again and again that we were indeed a privileged people to share such spiritual elation. The scriptures clearly affirmed,' he said, that 'many kings and rulers, will long to experience such things and yet be denied them.' And indeed, no matter how humble our lot in the eyes of others we are children of the Great King. Regrettably, I failed to follow much of that godly man's advice and consequently did not always walk as close to God as I should have done. I had no time for a mediocre middle path. Perhaps I wanted the fullness of both worlds. Whatever my ambitions I was intensely human and on one occasion, when a disturbed and yet sincere lay preacher shocked a Sunday morning's small congregation I revelled in it. The dear man, in fiery Welsh fervour, alluded to the lusts of the flesh. Well, that was acceptable! But when he hinted about his own temptation to masturbate, not only were the 'old dears' shocked and the young dears embarrassed but I was wanting to laugh out loud and couldn't wait until Monday to relate the episode to my workmates.. As for the saintly Church Secretary, who'd been sitting next to me, he'd been in a dilemma as to whether or not to call the service to an immediate halt. "What is he going to come out with next?" he whispered. "There are young girls present. Shall I tell him to stop?" "No. Not yet!" I replied, and waited with anticipation. Fortunately, little else followed. But the young lasses added after the close of worship. "We don't want him conducting our worship again. We think he's a dirty old man!"

Indeed, if my hankering after both worlds was not unknown to members of the congregation then the Secretary must have sensed it. In the vestry, above the fireplace, he pointed to a picture of the rich young ruler who came to Jesus, but refused to become His disciple because of love for riches. Yet even he appeared a wonderfully clean, upright man he said. "Yes, it is certainly necessary to be clean and pure in heart to follow Christ!" His words quite disturbed me. The title of that memorable picture was 'The Great Refusal'. Underneath were the words of scripture, 'But one thing thou lackest'. Just one thing could deter us from being a follower of The Master. Many, like the rich ruler, will have eternity in which to bemoan their refusal to surrender their one pet sin. This Chapel Secretary was full of spiritual wisdom; he certainly knew The Saviour and I sensed he knew me a good deal too.

After I'd fulfilled several more preaching appointments a letter was sent by this wonderful man to a clergyman who was strangely styled 'District Superintendent of the Baptist Union.' (The denomination had followed the world in forming a union so as to offer mutual support amongst its affiliated members.) Such a letter recommended me as a candidate for the Ministry and the reply was not unhelpful, all I needed to do was to undertake a course by correspondence, which included a University Certificate for proficiency in Religious Knowledge. And, after a period of three years I would be given the Pastorate of a church without having to undergo the heavy financial expense of college training. What is more, fulfilling the course meant that I would be financially safeguarded by the Union.

Well, I commenced the correspondence course conducted from Wolsey Hall, Oxford and found it highly critical of the contents of the Bible. The approach was destructive to the extreme, and when I mentioned it to the fellowship in Chester - where I'd been baptized by immersion - they were truly horrified. Had not the dear Miss Yardley's warned: "Can a person take poison in to his mouth and not be poisoned thereby?" Whereas Pastor Whyte's Bible studies made the Bible come to life, this correspondence course made its contents appear duller than the driest schoolbook. 'Were not the fruits of this Union's form of recognition, via higher criticism of the Word, reflected in chapels that were closing?' 'Their bona-fide ministers were giving their flock: stones for bread!' If Spurgeon, the greatest of all Baptist Ministers, had opposed the formation of a Union in the denomination, perhaps I should do likewise. Well, it was good rationalisation!

Then round about this period, my Father, who had been working in power stations far away from home, returned home ill. On seeing a local doctor, a question was put to Mother who had accompanied him, which she considered strange: "Who is your minister?" Within a couple of days Dad entered the local cottage hospital for tests and observations. Apparently, he had been rapidly losing weight and becoming uncannily weak. On returning from my morning post round a day or two later Mother suggested that I call at the hospital to ask when my Dad would be returning home. "Wait, are you Mr. Thompson's boy?" asked the Sister. Then, with a face as hard as flint or marble, went on: "You'd better go straight home and tell your Mother there is nothing we can do for your Dad. It's just a matter of time." It appeared as if a brick had hit my head, and I was momentarily frightened of fainting. 'To whom could I turn?' Mr. & Mrs. Nicholson were the salt of the earth. Thankfully, with the help of those Spiritualist neighbours, the sad news was broken to my Mother. She put on a brave face and she thought I'd got the story wrong and refused to think the worst until she'd visited the hospital herself. I felt disturbed, for had I not told my Dad that if he opposed me living for Jesus, then God would take his life from him? I felt stunned. Was I in any way to blame?

Just at that moment, like a bolt from out of the blue, light came into my darkened mind. "Thank God, " I cried, "there's Pastor Pomroy! ". He owned a small mission hall in a back street at Flint as well as a large hall in Chester. Indeed, I'd attended several of his meetings and, on one occasion, even got Mother to go. This converted miner, now in clerical attire, was termed a Pentecostal minister. At meetings attended he'd related the many hopeless cases who'd been fully restored under his ministry. But now, for some reason he appeared to be evading my request. Having, in desperation, phoned this white haired, kindly looking fellow whose words were interjected with praises to Jesus, he was 'worming out' of visiting my own dying Dad. I pleaded with him, but it was of no avail. Then finally, as an after thought, he suggested I bring along a handkerchief to his weeknight service so that the congregation and he could pray, and anoint it, in line with a New Testament practice. This, of course, I gladly did and then took it and placed it upon Dad's body. I felt I could never forgive that man of the cloth, but I must admit that a peace and serenity came over my Dad even though it became the peace of death. And he, who had become the biggest opponent to my Christian enthusiasm, was to die with a smile towards me saying, 'God bless you!' Perhaps he too had passed from death to life!

Left now with a widowed Mother I sensed that training for a worthwhile Ministry was definitely out. Yet such a wonderful Mother would have sacrificed her very last penny for either my brother or myself. When, within three months of such bereavement, an offer came for me to enter the Bible Training Institute at Glasgow on the sole condition that I pay the course fee at £50 per term, she actually pushed me to accept it. She was hard up, yet an insurance policy for fifty pounds could now be cashed in my name as I'd reached my eighteenth birthday "You may either use it to buy a cinematograph so as to become a travelling cinema, attending village halls" she said. "for I know this is something you've thought about a lot! Otherwise, go to this Bible college for one term!" I chose the latter at a time when I should have stayed at home, caring for her. It would be three months in an institute, which might well have been better termed an institution. But what a revelation!

A Student Of Glasgow's Bible Training Institute

My three months at B.T.I. Bothwell Street, Glasgow, were to seem an eternity as I'd never been away from home before even though well turned eighteen. The start of a new phase in my life and, one with far reaching consequences, had begun. Though an intelligence test was required of the new students, none seemed to fail it. Two references were adequate and, I sense of more importance, the fee paid in advance - the Lord's seal on one's calling! At least, that's how those folk running the Bible Training Institute interpreted it.

The sight of this large, ostentatious building, situated on a busy street, with the trams rattling along until the early hours of the morning, was quite impressive but it would prove a sore trial to one who was later homesick as well as unused to study during morning, afternoon and night. To learn the discipline of such prolonged studying when, more often than not, the central heating had to be turned off due to government restrictions was hardly easy. Indeed, food rationing certainly didn't improve the matter nor the low hygienic standards. Ah, but then all this was a true education in itself, plus much more; and for such reasons, in retrospect, I wouldn't have lost the opportunity for the world. To be sat in a dismal room with worn lino which appeared as cork; to have a light bulb minus even a shade; and the sole furnishings of the room a mere desk, chair, bed and book rack; seemed a come down from home. Then, when reprimanded by the young warden because I'd publicised discovering maggots on my bacon, my longing for home comforts became really strong.

Indeed, a shadow over all such circumstances was also the knowledge of Dad's not so distant decease. Nightmares were still experienced and, during them I heard the knocking of nails, witnessed them being driven into a coffin, then saw a leering face, coming and going, which assured me that I was to be its occupant. Such dreams had never troubled me previously. It seemed as if the strange environment had merely accelerated things. It was a relief to awaken in a cold sweat and to realise that such experiences had been no more than horrid tricks of the mind. However, I had no doubts of the Devil's intention to ruin my life at this period. The actual funeral of my dear Father I'd been unable to attend as, just prior to it, a feeling of intense faintness had sapped my energy. I felt aware of something unknown and panic grasped me to such a degree that I was unable to stand. 'Was I in some way responsible for my Dad's death?' 'Am I here in this Institute to do God's work or merely to evade working unconcernedly?' 'Shouldn't I be caring for Mother? ' Well, whatever guilt I then felt I realised that I must never let her down by allowing the course to prove itself too hard. Indeed, there were also those Christians in Holywell who would be anxious to know how I was faring and I dare not loose face with them. Yet, from the very first time I stepped foot into that large and eerie Victorian edifice a sense of loosing control seemed to heighten.

'that large and eerie Victorian edifice'

The very day of arrival still seems quite vivid: a broad accented Scotsman, but a true gentleman, escorted a few of us to an old lift which, he stated, was driven by water power. The gate into the shaft had to be opened even though the cage was not present. A rope, which hung the length of the shaft, though near at hand, had then to be pulled either for the cage to ascend or descend. "You must never stick your head out to look down the shaft," he said." One student, while doing so, failed to realise that the cage was quietly descending and it hurtled him to his grave. We cannot afford any more accidents like that!" We subsequently entered the contraption and began to glide upwards in silence as the pressure of the water increased in the lengthy pipe above the piston. Then, on reaching the top floor of this lofty dark, weird building, we were escorted to our individual rooms and later to be introduced to two senior students in there. Strangely enough these two came from a district in Yorkshire where five years later I would be a minister. We related our testimonies to each other and it was gratifying to know that the spiritual experience of conversion, which I'd undergone in a Church in Chester, was very similar to theirs.

As for the Principal of the B.T.I., he was a canny Scot approaching, if not past, retiring years. He affirmed belief in the Bible from cover to cover; held a professorship from the University; and held the honoured position of a moderator: - Moderator of the Original Secession Kirk; one of several denominations which so emphasised the sovereignty of God as to affirm that God chooses a few to be saved and has created the rest for damnation. A doctrinal interpretation of salvation which stands in marked contrast with the Salvationists, the Methodists and a whole host of others. Such Sovereign Grace Kirks are known for their austerity; sometimes their refusal to have either hymns or organ and yet they are not without a large following; especially in the Scottish Highlands.

Lectures started in full swing on the very first day of term, as sloth was sinful, and the time free from lectures, meals and prayers were largely taken up with re-writing lecture notes in a more legible style. Unfortunately, before the week was out, half of what I had scribbled I was unable to decipher and I sensed myself to be way behind many of the others. Practical work was undertaken on occasional afternoons and this I enjoyed to the full. Indeed much of it was spent on visiting the slums and the local lodging houses where the dregs of society existed and, on entering the doors of the latter, one's nose would meet with a putrid smell and one's ears with obscene remarks as one observed the rudest of gestures. But, in a sense, who could blame these men when often confronted with young spiritual prigs.

One house in the slums would leave an indelible mark on the mind indeed. Within a single roomed tenement, where sewerage from a faulty toilet above literally seeped down the wall, there lay a young woman of ghastly, white appearance. She was dying of consumption. Her child was still with her, cuddled up in the blankets. The stench of the room was vile and the poor young woman looked exceedingly frightened. She knew she was a consumptive and would soon die. Within a few days the authorities would step in and take her child out of her very arms. An older student, by whom I was accompanied, read to her from the Bible and I possibly prayed with her. We asked that she 'accept the Saviour.' I think the next time we called she told us that she had. She said she was no longer afraid and was ready to meet 'Him.' Our mission had proved successful. We promised to call back and see her later, but it was then that she told us that, should her husband return the worse for drink, as was usually the case, she wouldn't like to be responsible for our condition. He was a staunch Catholic and we sensed she was not a little frightened for either us or for herself.

Each tenement, I felt, had an odour, which was reminiscent of old, butchers shops where the droppings were absorbed amongst the sawdust on the floor or, perhaps, the odour came through being in close proximity to the Clyde. I haven't discovered the cause yet. Those stone spiral steps, where youngsters and older folk often urinated, were sinister places, if they were lit at all, it would be by a gas jet minus a mantle. One communal toilet on each landing, was the sole sanitation for the occupants of several single roomed tenements; and each room contained little more than a bed plus the fixtures of an old fashioned sink with a dripping tap. To resume lectures after such visits as these was often most laborious. How could one concentrate on a Pauline epistle being expounded when one couldn't eradicate the frightened little face of a young dying female out of ones mind? 'Poor soul, she would be better off in the next life than in this one.'

Around the lodging houses, amongst the dregs of society, one would find past members of the highest professions. Now they were using the meths. bottle instead of the whisky flagon, and many of them were in the last stages of T.B. Some were coughing their lungs out, while some of the more fortunate cursed them for the disturbance they couldn't help making. Indeed, it was then suggested that future visits round such places should involve us having a handkerchief lightly hung down over our mouths, lest we breath in more germs than were good for us. This we did, while the inmates were conspicuous for spitting into their bottles and putting the cork on, to trap in the germs. However, a few showed their contempt for us by spitting their consumptive sputum before us.

One weekend following, three of us were commissioned to Maybole Baptist Church, to hold a series of meetings there. The student, with whom I shared a bed, kept getting out during the night because there was blood in his mouth. A few days later he was sent home for good as consumption had been confirmed after he had been spitting up blood! Indeed, if such an episode were to mar his memory of that weekend, a much lighter one would mar my own. With the young people of the Church we'd gone out on an evening hike, singing hymns and choruses and getting to know each other quite well. I happened to like one of the lasses and on returning to college sent her a note to that effect. Consequently, word got back to the student body - that such frivolity as this was hardly becoming of a Bible institute. One or two strongly rebuked me for my action. Fortunately there were a few who felt that fascination for the opposite sex was not necessarily evil. I had merely acted a little unwisely.

As the colder months came in, the effort to study complete with coat on and hot water bottle beneath, seemed unendurable, but even in Glasgow's winter not every day is cold. So, for a means of exercise as well as for study, I occasionally took to briskly walking around the vicinity. A memorable occasion was visiting the Botanic Gardens, with an equal determination to learn the Hebrew alphabet in that single afternoon. This incident followed the first Hebrew lecture, which had taken place that morning. Being unaccustomed to study I determined there and then, not to give in, but master the alphabet, when suddenly I began to reel, felt extremely sick and revealed all the symptoms of a full blown anxiety attack. What had happened before Dad's funeral repeated itself more forcefully now. The regrettable thing is that it was to stay with me daily for several years and only to subside once I was married. A frequent feeling of death drawing in during the day and of impure thoughts and fantasies at night, with nocturnal emissions, made one feel very unworthy of a spiritual vocation. But even assurance from the college doctor, that my strong sexual nature was perfectly normal, failed to diminish my rising sense of guilt. I strongly sought at times to crucify the flesh and, if I'd known how to castrate myself, would gladly have done so (as had Origen, one of the early Church fathers) to the glory of God. Alas, other times I gave full vent to the flesh and then went through hell for days afterwards.

I sought deep spiritual fellowship with a Welsh colleague in the next room. He had a truly remarkable command of the larger words in the dictionary, and this proved a source of acceptable and justified humour. Being also deeply in love with a Blodwyn he expressed his feelings for her in deep, poetic style and on other occasions he would burst into singing hymns in the minor key. When the wind howled, he would say, with big staring eyes, that the Lord was possibly angry. I must confess that there was an odd side to his nature. It did feel a bit eerie when he was around. He had a habit of springing up when least expected, or of staring at you through the fanlight. He was a marked contrast to others who slapped you on the back and said, 'Hallelujah, Brother.'

One day a student of Pentecostal persuasion - literally, the thinnest person I've ever laid eyes on - came up to my side, squeezed my arm and said, "oh, aren't you skinny!" This began to make me feel that either the place or I must be bewitched, and what occurred a few days later confirmed it.

Being on the top floor, and away from any fire exit, I became convinced that such a building could soon become an inferno. I knew that several students were illegally using electric fires. One afternoon the thought of a fire out-break was not far from my mind when I actually began to smell what appeared to be burning wood. It seemed to rise from near the vicinity of that old lift shaft with the spiral stairs round it. On mentioning the matter to two senior students, they suggested it be ignored as possibly something had burnt in the basement kitchen. But later, a cloud was actually rising up the stairs and along the passage. A third student I approached supported me in setting off the alarm immediately. Before long the sound of fire engines could be heard making their way in and out of the traffic and above the trams. Indeed, a considerable fire had developed at the foot of the stairs and at the bottom of the lift shaft, but was speedily brought under control. The cause, they said, had been planks, which had lain against the side of the boiler for a considerable period of time.

The next day the Principal asked to see me in his flat. He'd heard via the pious young warden that I seemed to have things on my mind and assured me that my studies were average and satisfactory. He told me that, though I could only afford to pay for one term, he would from a special fund, meet the cost of my training for the full two years. He shook my hand and expressed deep gratitude because I'd set off the fire alarm. Perhaps I ought to have gone out of his study dancing with joy; but now I was worrying about money needed for clothes and pocket money to cover a whole two-year period.

The College, regrettably, had one more disadvantage for me. It not only had its own football team, but each student was fully expected to take part in it. My past, associated with being ridiculed at Coldstream by adults pointing the finger, and laughing as I came last in each public school race; of playing truant after a cricket ball had almost knocked me out at Holywell; and the problem of my hammer toes, all came rushing to the surface again. If not the memories, certainly those emotions surged back during the sound of student feet coming down the corridor, followed by strong persuasion from them that I must join in. Perspiration and personal prayer had not stopped the warden from sending them to collect me. However, this Bible course was far from free and, to their annoyance, I adamantly refused. But then my timidity was not helped when a week or two later the eccentric lecturer in New Testament Greek clipped me over the head for being so 'bloody dense!' He might have been partly right but how he retained his lectureship in such a fundamentalist, Bible orientated foundation, baffled most of the student body. They made him a top priority at a prayer meeting, as some believed he was possessed. The warden, an ex Baptist graduate and now a 'Plymouth Brother', would do nothing about reporting his rudeness but remonstrated on the many students who complained.

However, within this very active three months, which seemed to last an eternity, not all proved dismal and depressing for some extra good friends were made. This included the wonderful fellowship at Whiteinch Baptist Church, which became, during the whole term a spiritual home. The Pastor, the Rev. Philip Pont was an ex-student of All Nations Bible College. He had me spending most Sundays in the comfort of his home; while his Wife – rescued as a little girl from the sinking Titanic – proved a tower of strength. Like myself, her husband would end up a Scottish Episcopal priest!

Weeknights, when free from study, found me walking many miles, as I preferred my own company to anyone else's. I often walked along the back streets of Glasgow's busy thoroughfares looking eagerly for some religious gathering dotted here or there. On one such occasion I slipped into a disused Parish Kirk recently taken over by a religious splinter group. A gaudy notice board, which seemed very much out of place, conveyed the words: 'Bible Pattern Church.' The interior of the building was dark and solemn, yet the worship sought to be bright and uplifting. The old pulpit was dusty and unused. The Pastor, dressed in black, except for a white shirt and dazzling red tie, conducted the meeting from a boxwood type of platform. The Preacher certainly had gifts even if culture and English were not among them; he had convened a large sized congregation within a building, which the Presbyterians had been forced to close for lack of attendance. And then to learn that this Hot Gospel Pastor had done no more full-time training for the Ministry than three months at the College of which I was myself a student, gave me much encouragement.

The atmosphere, generated at this gospel service, seemed exciting and at one part weird. Past the shadows of the gas lamps one could see an old harmonium furnished with an ornate mirror. Seated in front of this was the player, a lady with a wide brimmed hat. From the latter: projected a long feather, curled at the end. The lady's hands glided up and down the keyboards to the singing of Sankey and Moody songs. And, as if such a setting were not a little eerie in itself, I noticed that those around me, who were praying, were often groaning, mumbling or seemingly hissing to themselves. Then suddenly a woman, who seemed to me to have gone into a fit, shook quite violently. She rushed to the front and began to speak with strange, repetitive guttural sounds. After she'd finished the Pastor, who appeared comparatively unemotional gave a coherent message. He was 'interpreting' for her. I couldn't help but wonder how genuine it all was: unlike the gibberish that had preceded it there was nothing repetitive in the interpretation. I was a little relieved when the service drew to a close. Not only had the whole worship appeared strange but there was an unpleasant smell within this dark, dusty, old Kirk; the grained and varnished doors had recently been painted a kind of pillar-box red.

On another evening, curiosity led me into a massive Church while a service was in progress. It was the first Roman Catholic service I'd ever attended. This building was possibly of marble, and had for me the associations of a massive vault. Though so very ornate the atmosphere was nevertheless deadly cold and, as the acoustics were so very poor, the priest's voice echoed as to be almost inarticulate. What was more, having a markedly foreign accent he made things worse. Indeed, whereas the preaching was the poorest I'd ever heard, the congregation appeared the poorest with whom I'd ever worshipped. As some of the latter passed me by in the shadows, I perceived that some were clutching black scarves round their heads. Others were mumbling as they fumbled with beads, and others would light candles before images while the thud of coppers in the offertory box echoed.

Making my way to the entrance I noticed how all types of people - and some looked far from angelic - pushed forward to dip their fingers into the same stoup of water, which was cloudy and a little green. I knew nothing about world religions and felt, for the first time, I was visiting some ornate temple comparable to those Paul might have come across on his three missionary journeys. The building was rich but the people seemed to be weary, oppressed and under a burden. I know that they made me feel sad. I eagerly returned to college to narrate my experience. They agreed fully and warned me to be extra careful.

I Meet A Plymouth Brother

Open-air meetings were always enjoyed. Not only did the students of the institute hold most successful meetings, but it seemed as if almost anyone was free to stand at a street corner and spout for all his worth. Consequently, a few eccentric folk availed themselves of the opportunity. One fellow, for example, would wait for our meeting to end and then quickly come forward before the crowds dispersed so as to tell the passers-by what Jesus meant to him. Once a large crowd of highly respectable folk had started listening, and the students of the BTI had left, a whole load of blasphemous and obscene remarks and comments would pour forth from his lips. Most students were convinced that the fellow was possessed, but it was truly exciting to wait around and watch the sudden reaction on the sanctimonious faces of those listening, especially when the vocabulary unexpectedly changed. To see old ladies, shocked to the core and almost collapsing out of horror, could just about split one's sides.

One evening, walking within the vicinity of St Enoch's station off Argyle Street, I came across another strange fellow. He belonged to a sect, which denounced sermons being added to Scripture as much as Christ denounced the traditions of the Pharisees being added to the Word of God. The poor fellow would only mutter verses of Scripture, trusting in God's Spirit to do the rest. The man was seemingly poor yet, in respect for the Scripture, he had placed his Anthony Eden - style hat upon the pavement in front of where he stood. Well, he must have been there for some time and seemed oblivious to the rain. He was certainly oblivious to the fact that his hat was now partly submerged in a pool of water. Nevertheless, he was honouring God, so I felt he should have a little moral support. I stood at his side and listened. I heard little from him except muffled utterances. Well, it so happened that I wasn't to be the only supporter for this lone prophet. I soon became conscious of a stocky, smallish gentleman of immaculate appearance. With his fine-rimmed spectacles, umbrella and kid gloves I might have assessed him to be a medical consultant of the old school. In a soft Irish accent, which conveyed marks of breeding, he stepped forth and asked whether or not I was a believer in the Lord Jesus. Had I actually been 'born again': It was obvious that, if I hadn't committed my life to Jesus, I would have been urged to do so there and then. As it was, he appeared 'over the moon' to make the acquaintance of a fellow believer. He went on to say that he worshipped with a group of the Lord's people who shunned a title and simply preferred to refer to each other as 'Brethren'. I wouldn't have dreamed then, through the providence of God, I would meet Victor Gilmore again nine active, exciting months later in Ulster where I was to meet more types of the Lord's people.

Because of wanderlust I decided one Sunday morning to skip worship at Whiteinch Baptist church. Curiosity had led me, the previous night, to scan the Saturday evening paper so as to discover what strange Sunday services were being advertised. 'The Church of God' in Glasgow was a title, which really intrigued me, and, as an added attraction it was located in the heart of the Gorbals - Glasgow's notoriously dangerous slum area where God would surely still be with me!

Immediately after breakfast I set off on foot. The sun was shining and being the Sabbath morning the trams were silent! I reached my destination. And there in view, at the corner of a weird old tenement block, was a corner shop with dark, heavy, curtains drawn and, between them and the window, a number of religious posters. The building inside was dark and musty. There were several odd chairs in rows and in front of them was a little rostrum, which was partly obscured by a big aspidistra, rising up from the communion table. Well, it seemed as if I were to be the only member of the congregation except for a young woman who sat with an open Bible. Then a youngish man, attired in a preacher's pinstripe suit, appeared. He introduced himself to me as the Pastor and, on learning of my connection with the BTI, seemed a little nervous and embarrassed. He led through the doorway an old lady who was totally blind. She was his mother who waited until her son had moved away and then eagerly informed me how good and sincere he was. Alas, that morning we were the only worshippers present and at the end of it the pastor was deeply apologetic for such a poor attendance. He had circulated the area with invitations and, on stating the expense of advertising each week in the Saturday editions of the Glasgow newspapers must have been 'running' at muh financial loss to himself; I felt very deep pity for him and inwardly wept.

On making my way out from the Gorbals, however, I laughed when I thought of how even the police would only patrol the district in pairs. Here I was on a bright Sunday morning with the rays of the sun shining through the dust of the streets down onto the pavements. Everything was peaceful and silent. Well, hardly had these thoughts passed through my mind when an empty beer bottle came hurtling down from a flat above, smashing into smithereens two or thee feet in front. I could easily have been killed! Indeed it was hard to believe that such wasn't a prank planned in some flat above. I thereupon increased the pace of my steps and was relieved to vacate the district.

Past timidity was being replaced by an evolving boldness. Did not the Scriptures say: 'The righteous are as bold as a lion?' The excitement of having dared to visit the Gorbals gave one a sense of achievement. A short time later my newfound colleague, Victor, accompanied me around similar outskirts, preaching the Word to the unconverted. We would find some spot on waste ground near a thoroughfare and then, after a prayer, warn those who came our way of the hell, which awaited them unless they came to terms with Jesus Christ. Although in one sense, we were both very sincere, one could see the humorous side in spouting to the passers-by because their reactions were so mixed.

On one occasion a minister stopped to listen to us and this so put us off track that I was pleased when he went. "You are witnessing as Paul and Peter had done, for the Master!" he said, then graciously smiled and moved on. To others we probably appeared as irresponsible dawdlers in a dodgy district. One evening in the old Tent Hall area, while preparing to proclaim the gospel, a gang of youths made their way in our direction. They wore flat caps and one of them was swinging a bicycle chain. It was well known that such gangs often attacked folk for the pure pleasure of thrusting chains at their faces or butting their victims with the nibs of their caps on which were sewn razor blades. We had to make an instant decision, so to avoid them sensing any fear in us we walked closer towards them as they came closer to us. But then on approaching a side ally we slowly moved in to it and then ran 'hell for leather'. From yet another ginnel we watched them pass by; they obviously hadn't focussed on us. The leader was swinging a bicycle chain for all his worth, and they all appeared in a state of stupor.

Incredible as it may seem, a few days later we felt the urge to visit a similar area to preach again in the open air and to distribute gospel tracts to passers-by. It was then that an oldish lady approached us. In a rough, broad accent, she asked: "Are ye two gentlemen completely out of your minds? Are you waiting to have your throats cut?" When we told her of our desire to proclaim Jesus she became most courteous, but advised us not to loiter but to move fast out of a district she'd been forced to live in.

One Saturday, Victor and I went off for the afternoon to Edinburgh. He not only paid our bus fare but also the cost of a full meal, one of many which were a contrast to those dished up in the Institute. Several days previous a shop selling clerical attire had attracted our attention and for a lark we each purchased a dog collar with the black bib attached. The outing to Edinburgh proved an eye opener. To have folk stepping off the pavement to make way for us; to have gentlemen raising their caps or hats to us; and to have ladies saying, 'Good day to you, your reverences,' really made one's day. Why, it transported me into the world of the cleric. 'What an exalted world this must be!' and all that was required was to smile back or say a 'God bless you' and their faces would light up with joy. Indeed, on the following Monday I showed the collar to two students. They dared me to don it near the entrance of the Institute. When I accepted their challenge they forcibly kept me outside when the Principal was due to arrive. Word passed round as fast as lightning and, though the Principal used another door that morning, news had reached him of my attire in time for college notices. He touched on it in quite a humorous manner, reassuring the students that I had not broken any law and was free to wear it. However, the wisdom of any student wearing one was questionable unless one could really hold his ground in argumentation for the Faith. For myself, I'd learned that the correct term was the 'Roman collar', and the only people with a legitimate claim were 'the religious' of that branch of Christendom!

The Apostolic Church in Glasgow was another denomination I visited. It proved the centre of much 'full throttle' evangelism. Pastor Turnbull created enough fervour and evangelism to make any bull turn! Attired in a broad collar, he clapped his hands and yelled out Hallelujahs while young ladies banged their tambourines and swung their hips to lively hymns. One hymn, with the chorus, 'Saved, saved, saved' had such rhythm that I nearly danced my way back to the Institute after the close of the meeting. This rhythm was so infectious that, with two emancipated students of a Salvation Army background, we began to jive with the use of the chapel organ, only to make a speedy exit when austere students arrived and then put in a formal complaint. The Apostolics claimed to be the most scriptural of all the Pentecostalist bodies in Britain as they retained apostles! Their headquarters was in Pen -Y - Groes, North Wales.

Bragging about the various sects I had visited resulted in being brought before the two senior students. They remonstrated that such visits on my part could not only bring a bad name on the Institute itself, but could also do my soul much irretrievable harm. Whereas there were one or two students who leaned towards Pentecostalism (the precursor of today's charismatic movement), I was clearly warned of its excesses: people occasionally rolling on the floor, foaming at the mouth, or falling backwards, supposedly by the Spirit; and then jabbering in incoherent tongues. Most of the student body was of Calvinist persuasion and many of them had, through allegiance to a 'Schofield' Bible, discarded much of the New Testament as being of no relevance for them. Their way of approaching Scripture was dispensational, but it would take more than a term in a later College to see the deceptiveness of it all.

For a second time the Principal asked to see me in his study; and unlike one or two of the female students who giggled whenever called for - implying he'd been 'a little too fatherly' - I had no such apprehension. Was it that more funds were available to meet my daily expenses? Regrettably, this time he wished to inform me that my efforts at college weren't as good as they could be. What was more, he'd heard from the warden that I was homesick and depressed, so suggested my finishing altogether at the end of term. "I think you should care for your mother and I, personally, don't feel there is any future for you in the Ministry," he said. As he spoke he led me to the door and uttered, "God bless you!" And before I could reason with him to the contrary there I was alone in the corridor; the door shut behind me.

Around about that time, while still smarting over this interview, the most pious and academic of visiting lecturers, a Rev. Dr Fitch, uttered strange words at the commencement of a lecture. 'He stated that he had been burdened for some time past, and was now led to affirm openly, that something, or someone, was openly grieving the Holy Spirit: the college wasn't as sanctified as it should be!' He left it at that; and the outcome was equivalent to the inauguration of a witch-hunt. Two students who possibly had homosexual tendencies were watched closely while a young couple, who were soon engaged, were watched like hawks. I well remember the couple coming out of his room together. They were exceedingly timid and, when they almost bumped into a group of us passing down the corridor, their faces flushed scarlet. We all nodded to ourselves. It is regrettable that I was one of that group who began a special prayer meeting, demanding that they became penitent or be punished. The sin that was in 'the camp' had to be rooted out as we were being robbed of blessing.

Perhaps my having to leave such an oppressive institution had its compensations. With increasing winter weather I could no longer study due to the cold and was occasionally being reeled over due to dizzy spells. Victor, who was married with four children, was training at an optical college. (This was through the sole generosity of a Christian 'Brother'.) As previously mentioned he bought me many a substantial meal without which, I sense, I would have succumbed to consumption. But to the oppressive atmosphere of this one term was to be added yet another occurrence. Within this weird, rambling edifice the old water lift, in the females' side, was making its way upwards, past the first floor on its way towards the top. Suddenly the pressure pipe burst open and the cage hurtled down to the basement, followed by torrents of water. The girls were fortunate. They were treated for severe shock and soon recovered. Consequently, the Principal, in his broad Scottish accent, thanked the Lord on the following morning at assembly for 'in wrath remembering mercy.' God had not allowed the cage to rise any higher before the disaster had occurred! "What hypocritical claptrap!" I said to myself: "The whole place is bewitched!" Yet it stood as a memorial to the Victorian evangelist Dwight L. Moody: a supposed powerhouse of prayer as well as a centre for intense Bible study.

On one of the last Saturdays of the term I joined a group of students in sharing an evening rally at the town mission in Ayr. There, for one other student and myself, tea would be provided at the home of the Town Missionary. Having previously been warned about the eccentricities of this particular individual I wondered what to expect. I can only say that no one reminded me more of the actor Alastair Sim, when he took an eerie role, than did our host. Old buildings, with pinnacled turrets, and old stone stairs ascending in spiral formation, are prevalent in Scotland. We ascended such a flight to arrive at the missioner's flat. With a broad Scottish accent he warmly welcomed us. His rather wild-looking eyes kept weighing us up, as indeed, they had every right to. His mannerism of taking out a penknife and habitually running his thumb over the end of it did seem rather odd. Unfortunately, his wife, a timid little soul, appreciated it less than ourselves. When she had a sudden outburst and rushed out of the room my fellow student felt like following suit. I must admit I quite liked the odd fellow. I think this was because he'd shown a marked preference to me, and had dubbed my fellow student a 'holy Joe'. After his wife's quick exit and, on her return, I fully acquiesced when he muttered, "Och woman, I meant nothing by it!" I admit it was a strange remark to make but he possibly got a perverted kick out of frightening others. Several students felt that he should be reported for mental cruelty to his wife, but more than likely, as was so prevalent, talk never leads to any action.

As you will have gathered the three months in Glasgow were intensely full of activity, oppression and excitement. I can only recall one other interesting event as that solitary term drew near to its close. The students were invited to a valedictory service at a Glasgow Kirk for one of the college girls. She was leaving to travel to some distant land as a missionary. Such an opportunity had been eagerly anticipated by many of the students of the college. To them, going out as a missionary sounded most exciting. At this particular meeting an elderly gentleman, a veteran missionary on furlough, brought any misapprehensions this young lady might have held of the mission field down with a thud. His sober statement of what would be expected of her followed the joy and chorus singing of the meeting. Though I looked upon him at the time as a dour old Scot of the United Free Kirk, I have since understood the wisdom of his words. So many of those Hallelujah Christians, bubbling over with religious clichés, needed to be brought down to sombre reality. Some, who set out to the foreign field with great gusto, would soon return with their ardour diminished, but thankfully their experience of life enhanced.

Each day, the humiliation of returning home to Wales, through having failed to make the required grade, troubled me deeply; and secular employment would need to be obtained. There was, of course, the dim possibility of securing the pastorate of Tabernacle Baptist church at Flint, but finances were low there and the deacons were not unanimous. During the time I waited in anticipation for their decision, a student on the completion of his full two years, whom I'd informed of this possibility, approached me: "May I suggest brother that you step down and suggest myself instead? You will appreciate, surely, that I as a senior student would be more suitable!" Well, although I furnished him with all the necessary particulars, this fellow from near Bradford had no need to fear. The chapel at Flint, of which I was a member, decided that due to finances they were regrettably not in a position to accept either of us.

I eventually turned my back on that Institute, founded by Moody, for the last time. I made my lonely trail to the railway station. Even the return journey to Holywell was to teach one a sobering lesson. Having purchased that clerical collar, and being still in my nineteenth year, I determined to overcome any sense of inferiority by wearing it. Yes, even if it were for possibly the last time. So I boosted up my ego feeling distinguished, indeed, in a compartment all by one's self. Eventually several folk were about to enter the compartment but, on noticing the revered collar, changed their minds! As the train rattled through the countryside and the darkness drew in, the reflections in the window of the bespectacled young man, with broad collar round his neck and an open Bible in his hand compensated for recent deflation. But then, all of a sudden an officer of the RAF, with a curled moustache and an accentuated flow of language, eagerly asked if the seat opposite was vacant. I could hardly lie. Indeed, they all were, as he jolly well knew.

On his eagerly wishing to make conversation I chose to make out that my stay at a 'Divinity Hall' was nearing completion. Scottish students, in their last year, were not averse to wearing a collar and all Methodist students were actually expected to whenever they preached, so why shouldn't I? I rationalized that it was all above board, yet eagerly sought to get out of the predicament of having questions put to me about the various Faiths of the world by someone constantly calling me 'padre'. As a station approached I seized the opportunity. "Well, it's been delightful meeting you. It's a pity mine is the next stop. God bless you!" Soon, through the convenience of a WC lower down the train, I replaced the collar with a tie, and slipped into another compartment. It so happened that the ticket inspector came round the second time. He looked bemused. Of more relevance, I had a sneaking suspicion that my companion in the previous compartment had decided to stretch his legs a little down the train. I just closed up my lapels and stared very hard out of the window, only wishing that I had a copy of The Times or Manchester Guardian in order to conceal one's face.

It was a sure relief when the train steamed into Holywell Junction. Soon I was boarding the quaint 'push and pull' train, which would build up steam for the steepest ascent of any normal line in Britain. The lone coach, with engine behind, pushed its way up the single track via Basingwerk Abbey, through the picturesque Strand Woods, past St Winefride's Halt, and then steamed into the terminus of Holywell town station.

I now walked home past the old Prince of Wales cinema where I'd worked previously on two occasions. The window of the projection box was slightly open as usual and the clickety-click of the film going through the projectors was audible above the crackly speakers. The light from the back of those arc lamps would have been discernible while the chief operator, Wild by name and nature, would no doubt have given me a friendly 'catcall' on passing.

Yes, I was back in sombre reality, back to where I'd begun and my dream for the ministry had come to its close. But even now there were compensations! Everything around was so beautifully serene. I was breathing the soft, relaxing air of my hometown - even though it occasionally reeked with the fumes of Courtaulds' artificial silk factory below! A marked contrast, nevertheless, to the harsh, bitter cold and grime of Glasgow. No longer were street trams rattling in one's ears till the early hours of the morning! I passed a few people, and all knew me enough to say, 'Hello!' 'Sut Mae!' or just, 'All right!' It was so homely and quiet now I felt I could have gone to sleep for a month.

Thrown Out After One Term!

The days of inactivity at home passed, and the quest for work terminated on my reinstatement as junior postman. It was about this time, while preparing myself to deliver a sermon for the following Sunday, that I sought solitude and opportunity to meditate, through a walk via Fron Park. I then made my journey along the top road, past the traffic lights in the Chester direction. I sat on the next bench in sight, in all sincerity praying for spiritual help and guidance. I then opened the Bible and began to read. Somehow, I had the arrogance to feel superior to the other lay preachers in the vicinity; for three months I'd been to a Bible College and they hadn't!

Much to my annoyance, who passed by but old Mr. Norbury, one of the inmates from the local workhouse. I became intensely irritated when he began to retrace his steps and plonked himself down on the same bench. He was not the cleanest of sights, salivating and conspicuous with his hairy workhouse suit - the cut and pattern shared by all the other poor vagrants now resident in Lluesty, opposite. Although I'd been very glad on previous occasions to lead a service or two within the chapel of this institution, I was not in the mood to discuss religion with one of its residents. Yet the old man forcefully pushed his presence upon me. With slaver running from his mouth through stubs of black teeth, he spoke to me: "I see you are reading the Bible." I hardly replied. It was obvious! Then with piercing, kindly eyes, which seemed to convey much past sorrow, he turned to me and said, "God is love, you know!" He repeated the phrase and it seemed as if he became intensely excited. Somehow, joy seemed to flow through that sad face as he told me to look around at the trees. "God is love and He is everywhere," he affirmed. "In the grass, the sky, the fields, there is God; and then pointing to himself he said: "and God is in me!" Yes, and such truth was being expressed through the radiance of his face. Then, without wasting any more time, he got up and continued his journey, and it seemed as if he were in personal conversation with Him.

What a lesson I had just learned! This inhabitant of the workhouse – not quite compos mentis - was intensely in tune with God. He was undoubtedly, to use religious jargon, 'baptised in the Spirit'. He may not have known the jargon, but he knew the experience behind it. Through this encounter, spiritual help and guidance had come in answer to my prayer, and in a way I was at first unprepared to acknowledge. Three months in a Bible institute and I was fast becoming a spiritual snob, convinced that I knew the ABC of salvation. It took a poor, despised vagrant to show how empty and puffed up I really was. 'Love edifieth,' said St Paul, 'but knowledge puffeth up.' What was hardly to be seen in any of those students, radiated from the countenance of a social reject: the Shekinah glory! Yet he was shut away, more often than not by the pious, out of sight and out of mind!

The Welsh Methodist minister, the Rev. William Price was saddened to learn of my return from college. He'd been generous in having sent me money but appreciated the fact that I had a real duty to do in caring for a widowed mother who would have spent her last coin on her sons. Before long, however, the principal of Cliff College, near Sheffield, was approached. It so happened that he and Mr. Price had formerly been students together. The principal was pleased to be informed of me and appeared keen to help. Cliff served as a preparatory college for those who wished to follow their studies for the Methodist ministry. It was called the college of the underprivileged as no one was turned away because of inability to pay. A letter received from Principal Broadbelt stated that a place would be reserved there on the proviso that I first affiliate myself to an English Methodist church, for it was through the generosity of individual Methodists, as well as their circuits, that the college was financially upheld.

Hardly a day would go by without passing the Reverend Price's home. His hand would be stretched out as if in blessing and he would ask, "How are you?" When most folk passed 'Llys Pennant' he would address them in Welsh, but, knowing that I was not conversant with the vernacular, would speak in English, except when he ocassionaly forgot! Along with the rest of those chapel ministers he was highly revered. If most vicars were respected for their position in the community, chapel ministers were deeply loved for their spirituality and care. This dear man had a cheery or comforting word for everyone. This was all the more remarkable in that he was, so the rumours went, in very poor health himself. He was a unique soul and an avid gardener. With a rake or shears in hand, a brown cap over his head and a broad collar round his neck, he proved a joyful inspiration on even the dullest day. His furrowed brow often expressed the marks of hidden pain. Nevertheless, he concealed it well.

This 'ray of sunshine' recommended me to look up the nearest English Methodist minister, and to get affiliated to one of his chapels. The nearest chapel was in Flint and the minister lived at Connahs Quay. He was most courteous but I'd visited him the day before he was due to remove elsewhere. "I'm awfully sorry!" he said, "but I suggest you contact my superintendent straightaway. He lives at Hawarden. Come back afterwards. I'd like to know how you get along." Arriving in due course at Hawarden I rang the bell of the manse with trepidation. The term superintendent reminded me, since my childhood days at Coldstream, of a strict police officer, but no doubt a kind cleric, with white hair and a tubby appearance, would shake my hand, ask my business and, with holy joy emanating from him, inform me what steps to take to prove my calling. Well, it so happened that the man's name was Diamond and he couldn't have been any harder or sharper than that stone itself. His dear old wife shouted up the stairs (it was about 11:30 a.m.), "There's a young man to see you down here" I waited a while. "Tell him to go away, woman!" came his reply. "He's waited a while, you'd better come down." "Oh, all right woman" he answered. Eventually a man, who looked past retiring age, descended the stairs with pyjama tops under his trouser braces. He peered me up and down. "What do you want, boy?" "Well," I replied. "Yes, yes, speak up boy."

"The Reverend Price told me to come and see you and ...". "Never heard of him!" he interrupted. "Well, he told me to see the English minister; and he told me to see you." "What about, boy? What about?" "I want to become a parson. I was confirmed in the church in Wales, but have spent most of my time preaching round chapels of all denominations. I can't get into the 'Church' ministry because, although I'm truly well up on Scripture and church history as well , all they're concerned about is that I have matriculation, and I'm hopeless at maths." He gleamed back at me as his dear wife looked on: "Tell me, boy, before you tell me anything else, is your mother a Methodist?" "No I replied!" "Is your father a Methodist?' he asked. "Well, no!" was again the reply, "Then, boy, you're wasting your time. You will NEVER make a Methodist." His little wife looked shocked. He grunted his annoyance to her, and speedily ushered me out of the door. I think I stood there on the step for a few moments, absolutely dumbfounded. Thankfully, I've never received such insulting treatment from a cleric since; though two came well close to it! On returning to convey the information to the other minister, he was hardly surprised to learn of the reception received. Regrettably I had not been the only one to be so insulted. His superintendent would learn some home truths within the next couple of days, which this kindly cleric was now in a safe position to impart. As for myself, it was merely another door shut in one's face. A future in the Methodist ministry was out!

If ever there was a time in those early years when one felt tempted to throw out Christianity, it was now. Christ had not failed me however. His presence was always near. Then, as if to counteract the slight I'd experienced, a strange incident occurred the very next day, when a knock came to our door. Two middle-aged ladies introduced themselves to Mother and myself as missionaries and Bible students of the Good News of the Kingdom. They didn't wish to inconvenience us in any way so they didn't stay for long. It was a welcome surprise when, a couple of days later, they returned with a young man only two years older than myself. He had a wonderfully radiant face as well as a cheerful brimming personality. His name was Leon Petit and, like myself, he was anxious to devote his life to the furtherance of Christianity. None was more understanding or sympathetic when I told him of my experience with the Methodist superintendent. "Yes, typical of most," he affirmed. "You'll find there's little to choose between them. They are religionists, the rulers of spiritual wickedness in high places. In

Scripture they are called Jonadabs," Leon affirmed, "and at the top of the whole system is the beast of Rome!"

I counted it a privilege, not only to discuss with Leon the Bible, but also to walk through the streets with him as he pushed his bicycle and its carrier bag that contained an assortment of delightfully bound Bible aids. The first book I received from him, at a very low price, was entitled 'Let God Be True'. We went through it chapter by chapter, in weekly sessions, while we sat on a bench in the Fron Park. Somehow I associated Leon and his companions with sunny, crisp weather. The books he circulated seemed to express the beauty of outdoor life, beautiful sunsets, Adam and Eve in all their innocence, and children playing in the streets of a New Jerusalem. Such publications, with their attractive bindings and pleasant illustrations, were a marked contrast to the drab, dry theological works I'd acquired at Glasgow. Even the very smell of the paper and the bindings of his books seemed to attract. Then to open up the title pages and find that the glory was not given to the writer displaying a whole host of his qualifications, but solely to 'Jehovah' was surely a mark of true humility on the author's part.

Leon told me there was no need to go to college to become a minister. I myself could be ordained, just as he was. Indeed, to undergo theological training would simply make me ten times more a child of the Devil than my instructors would be. Leon was proud to show me his own certificate of ordination proving that he was an 'Authorised Minister of Jehovah'. However, such proof of ordination had not exempted him from forced conscription in the services, as had been the case with many ministers of recognised denominations. This new friend had undergone persecution and a short jail sentence because of his stand as a conscientious objector! His reasons for being vindictive towards the clergy were the result of unpleasant associations with them plus the literature in which he was well and truly steeped.

If ever a man wanted to believe everything that Leon's literature taught, none ever did more than myself, for he and his followers were so intensely sincere. But it was gradually coming to mind that doctrines, which he and his Jehovah Witness associates upheld for themselves or denounced in others, were biblically far from flawless. It was, for example, their practice to refute the doctrine of the Blessed Trinity and to refer to its roots in paganism.

However, it so happened that my brother at this period was engrossed in religion too. He held little respect for Nonconformity and was at the time wavering between High Anglicanism and Rome. As I used to the full the Watchtower literature to denounce much traditional doctrine, he would use advanced Catholic publications to hit back, such as Apologetics and Catholic Doctrine, by Gill. Through weekly encounters with my Jehovah's Witness friend, corresponding sessions reading up my brother's works, plus studying the works I'd acquired on my own, I soon gained a first class knowledge of the major doctrines of Christendom, which throughout history had been repeatedly under attack. Not only was it possible to use Scripture to prove doctrine, but now the scholastic arguments for the existence of God were becoming intensely useful in argumentation. It seemed as if one's knowledge of Christian doctrine and denominations was superior to that of the local clerics whose education had been appallingly sectionalised, myopic and blinkered. Perhaps the Romanist priests and the Jehovah's Witnesses were the only ones, since my fundamentalist Glasgow days, who had any dogmatic lines of conviction.

My brother had seen how anxious I was to enter the ministry of the church and he also knew how often I'd been turned down. A friend of his had recently terminated a period of training for the Catholic priesthood. "No candidate in their church is ever turned down due to inability to pay for his training or through failure to acquire matric," he affirmed. Yes, their church's newspapers were full of adverts, asking young men if they had a vocation from God to the priesthood. "You've been to other churches; don't you think you ought at least to try the Catholic one?" 'Why not!' I thought, 'they must be public. Times of services are displayed on their notice board for all to see!'. I would just slip in at the back where someone would hand me a hymnbook, shake hands and probably say, 'So pleased to meet you!'

Arriving at the church, having read the words: 'Thursdays: Rosary and Benediction 7:30 p.m.' I walked up the steps, passed through the door and entered. Unfortunately, there was no one to give out a book, shake hands or give a welcome. So I slipped into a pew half way down. and felt quite inconspicuous. However, before long furtive glances were made. It was obvious that others were not unaware of a stranger and the looks were hardly a smile or a nod. The fact that I hadn't genuflected, because I didn't know how, might have singled me out. I felt somewhat nervous and hoped they didn't consider me as an intruder. God forbid! A dull service began, and after tedious and most repetitive prayers to Mary had come to an end, the whole atmosphere began to lift. The front of this church became a mass of glittering lights. A heart-moving hymn was sung as wafts of incense arose to form clouds above a raised vessel that glittered like rays from the sun. Soon the aroma reached the pew I occupied, and the atmosphere was so moving one had to fight back the tears. To me, it had become a foretaste of Heaven! Then later, a casket - which I was to learn, contained part of a saint's finger - was brought out for veneration. Worshippers started to leave their pews to form a line preceded by nuns and girls from the local convent school.

'What was I to do?' One could hardly join that queue as one wouldn't have known how to behave on reaching the front, and no one was likely to come to my aid. On nearing the Altar front they appeared to be bopping up and down and crossing their hands in front of their body! Yes, it was the concluding act of worship and the parish priest – with a large red sash round his waist – having now entered the church, was to acknowledge worshippers further down the opposite isle. Nervously and timidly I moved along to the far end of the pew to join them there. Each one received a nod and a warm smile on reaching him. I anticipated the same and wanted him to know what a wonderful blessing such a service had been to me. But when I reached him, he just stopped and horrifyingly stared as if he could have literally wrung my neck. I slipped past, turned around and his eyes had followed me. His hands might have been on his hips. I only know that if looks could have killed, I'd have been dead on the spot.

Returning home utterly deflated, I related the ordeal to the family. They felt that I might well have taken undue liberties. Had not Dad once said that the Roman Church was more akin to the temples he'd visited abroad? Only the initiated were expected to take part or even enter unless they had received special permission. 'Could they really be superstitious enough to believe that I'd contaminated the atmosphere?' I asked. Perhaps the proper procedure would be that of seeking information from a priest privately. If I put my cards on the table, surely he would be only too pleased to oblige.

Several days later and I was knocking on the presbytery door. After a few minutes it opened and a tall young priest, dark and with a long nose, looked towards me. I recognised him immediately. He was none other than the one whose attentions I'd repeatedly sought to attract, but without avail, in the Catholic church of Flint. That was many months previous when 'slipping in' from the Plaza cinema to pray, I'd noticed him performing his Daily Office. Well, he now gave a haughty nod of recognition and waited for me to speak. "Excuse me, but you are a priest?" I said - almost stammering as I smiled. He looked towards each of his cassock cuffs and back again towards me as if to say: 'What do I look like?'

Ushering me into a room, this young priest touched on Henry the Eighth seeking 'a divorce'; being turned down by the Pope, and as an outcome, creating the Church of England. Indeed, he also gave me a booklet entitled 'Why the Catholic Church is the one and only true church.' Well, I was anxious to interrupt him here. Unknown to this cleric, I'd now been to a Bible college and was certainly no ignoramus concerning Scripture. "Any questions can be asked at a later date!" he replied. "You are not the first Protestant to come here. I have several more enquirers!" Then, he coolly suggested a return weekly visit to which I acquiesced. "There will, of course, be no commitment on either side!" he added. Needless to say, lacking in character to tell him to his face how I felt about his cool and aloof manner, I proved more at fault than he for not keeping the future appointment thereupon made.

Strangely, I began to associate Roman Catholicism with something mysterious and alluring! Even the priest at the presbytery that night had appeared in a long, black cassock, folded cuffs, a multitude of buttons and, on his head, a kind of three-ridged hat topped with a large pom-pom. Indeed, such attire could even be a trifle ghostly! With the various Protestant churches everything had appeared open and transparent to behold, but now this Roman Church appeared in marked contrast. One began, again, to feel that it had an affinity with those temples St Paul had encountered on his missionary journeys recorded in the New Testament. Yet I would not be put off for long! In faithfulness to passages of Scripture the believer was exhorted to 'Search the spirit of the various churches to see which amongst them is truly of God'.

A month or two passed, and still occasional weekends were being spent in Chester. To call at Grosvenor Park Baptist Church, where I'd been through the waters of adult baptism was a means of renewing acquaintance with the Pastor who had the broad collar and Scottish accent. Though a little anxious to know why I'd been absent from fellowship for such a long time, he was still willing to shake my hand and extend, 'A hearty welcome in the name of the Lord!' His congregation was intensely warm, open-faced and kind; but now I was hankering after something on a deeper and more mystical plane. I'd had a taste of the aroma of incense, the flicker of votive lights and the sound of sanctuary bells; and now I was anxious to experience more!

Across from the Baptist place of worship near to a lovely Chester park, there stood the beautiful Catholic church of St Werburgh. Curiosity drew me to view its gorgeous interior. Then, while passing through the vestibule, I noticed a visiting priest. He had a ginger beard and piercing eyes and was about to don a soft, black trilby hat. "Excuse me! I'm not a Catholic and would like to know more about the Faith'" I said. He replied softly with a gracious accent as he viewed me with intensity. "May I ask where you are from?" "Holywell", I replied. "Why, what a coincidence", he said, "I'm one of the monks at Pantasaph." It was the very monastery, near Holywell, the boundaries of which had been traversed by us as a family enjoying an occasional afternoon walk. "But tell me," he said, looking with piercing, dazzling eyes, "you're not afraid of priests are you?" "Why, no!" I replied, rather taken aback at such a comment! "Well, you must never ever be afraid of a priest," he said "Some non-Catholic's have strange ideas." On being asked why I hadn't made enquiries about the Faith in Holywell, he was soon put fully in the picture. The parish priest, he affirmed, would be delighted to make my acquaintance. and it would be wiser to see him rather than one of his curates! "But first of all, allow me to clear the ground, informing him of our chance meeting here today. I think this would be most preferable!"

Father James, for this was the monk's name, added words to this effect: "You have been in a spiritual haze and God is steering you, in His great goodness, out of the mists of uncertainty and into His haven." In accordance with his wishes a few days passed before making a second visit to the presbytery adjoining the Catholic Church of St Winefride; and one of those intervening days was nostalgic indeed!

A Nostalgic Trip In To The Past

There was for me, however, more to life than religion but without the latter, life would be shallow, empty and, what was more, extremely lonely. Intense shyness had kept one from dating members of the opposite sex. Yet, deep down, there was a longing for a girl with whom life could be shared. The only girl who had ever truly occupied my thoughts was the one I'd known as a youngster in Shropshire, although at the time I'd been no more than nine years of age.. Absurd as it might appear to some, I had kept a little brooch, which had been given to me at that parting hour. It was from the Coronation a few years previous. Indeed, I often thought of the lass who'd lived in a square at the foot of that hill in Dawley and, as I listened to Gene Autry singing 'Blueberry Hill', I associated it with a rather scraggy hill, which became equally as romantic as Blueberry. A far-off childhood romance, which had involved no more than linking arms in the Saturday matinee and sharing some walks or errands together, still evoked strong romantic feelings.

Time and time again I'd reminisced over those childhood days. Indeed, since then, only two girls might have become sweethearts. One was anxious to accept a date from me when a chum approached her for me but when she agreed my nerves got the better of me and I ran away. The poor little lass burst into tears because she, also, was no doubt lonely too. She was truly lovely yet some less desirable youth had called her 'Spindle shanks' because, seemingly, they weren't as good as Betty Grable's! Another delightful creature had her friend approaching me on no less than three occasions. The request was that she liked me and wanted us to go out together. She also was of a sweet disposition but, as she had taken the initiative I considered her to be common. I spurned her offer, in no uncertain terms, only to learn a year later that her Dad was an under manager of Courtaulds where half the folk of Holywell worked. She was by no means common, simply open and honest!

My favourite novel was The Adventures of Tom Sawyer. Mother had bought me, from a local shop, an abridged version on which the film was based. Yes, the film was the one I'd watched as a youngster in distant Shropshire. Kathleen and Cathy had sat, linked to me on either side, when we were no more than ten. The place had been the Royal cinema at Dawley. Such far-off days seemed to haunt my memory; our little dog, Pat, perched on the wall, within the little lass's arm, as the furniture van was being loaded for Wales; the memory of playing among the newly made sewer pipes in the nearby quarry; the little church we'd attended and the girls with their Easter bonnets. Yes, their parents (or was it Kathleen's guardian?) were no doubt very poor and old fashioned, but their children were spotless and beautifully arrayed for Easter and Whitsuntide. How the memory of it all flooded back to one's mind!

Yes I was undoubtedly a dreamer. The world of reality was too hard and cruel to enjoy. Its mean, sadistic and pushy characters would tread down others to have their own way. No one ever dreamed so much about the past in Dawley or about a future in the ministry. Such dreaming was often indulged in while walking for miles over the hills. Occasionally falling on one's knees I would cry, 'O God, whoever you are, thank you for revealing yourself to me, and thank you for the gift of this glorious life'. Music also had its glorious contribution. One record, first heard on a Rex label at Lewis's department store in Liverpool, was speedily purchased and its very tune seemed to apply itself to a past childhood romance. Though that record had cost only 3/11d. I cherished it with all my heart. It was 'Stanchen Serenade', played by Trois and his Mandoliers. The heavy pickup arm carrying the stylus must have almost worn the record through to the other side. No other record in a large collection would ever take its pride of place, though 'Blueberry Hill' or 'Let me call you Sweetheart' were good runners up.

It began to dawn on me as never before that, having travelled as far away as Glasgow and back, there was really nothing to stop me from making a day trip to Dawley, provided I caught an early enough train. I would make the pretext of catching the 6.15 a.m. workmen's train to spend the day in Liverpool! The thought of telling others of a plan to renew a childhood acquaintance would have been far too embarrassing to consider. I had no wish to be teased or ridiculed. In fact, such an adventure seemed quite sacred.

Well, little can be remembered concerning the journey back, except that I breathed sighs of nostalgia on approaching Wellington station, where I was to witness again the beautiful livery and glittering green and gold of the Great Western Railway. One delightful loco, that day, had attached on the front of it a large brass bell. It was the 'King George Fifth', which had just returned from service in Canada. From Wellington to Dawley, as the local line might then have been annexed, I travelled by bus. The old Midland Red buses hadn't altered one iota. In fact they possibly looked more antiquated as I was now used to the superb Crosville 'Red' which would soon become the Crosville 'Green'! Those Midland Red single deckers had an extra-narrow driver's cab. It was confined to the very side of the engine cover rather than halfway across it, and a door, which only half shielded him from the elements, shut the driver in. The bus, once boarded, chugged on its way with a light purring sound, along the once familiar roads, way past Horsehay level crossing, up an incline and on towards the town of Dawley.

To alight from the bus, and walk once again past the old Cosy cinema, and then down Doseley Road to the outside of No. 211, where we'd once lived, filled me with nostalgia. Yes, the environment and district were just the same as when we left. Well, it was no use wasting time at anyone's house. Time was short, for the journey had taken longer than anticipated. So, past the old builders shed, where we'd played as young children, I travelled the road under the railway bridge and was soon in the vicinity of the parish church of St Luke. If the doors were found to be unlocked then I'd already made up my mind to offer a prayer thanking God for happy memories of childhood. It so happened that, not only was it open, but the Vicar was within and so was an elderly lady engaged in arranging the flowers. "If only I could be in that cleric's shoes!", I sighed to myself. "How I would love to be arrayed in that cassock while radiating love and kindness to others!" And then I wondered would young Kathleen of my childhood days be a real 'born again' believer? Would she love Jesus as I did?

Before long, my full intention in returning to the parish had been expressed to this young cleric. He told me that the elderly lady doing the flowers would be able to help. She was a retired mistress from the Pool Hill school. Why, yes! It was coming back into view. I now recognised her as the sweetest teacher in that drab, dismal establishment. She bore the same name as the wretched headmaster: it was Pickering! Mrs. Pickering seemed so pleased to meet an old pupil. Then asked me the name of the young lass I sought and where she had lived. "Her name was something like Kathleen Oitchinson," I said.""Why, yes!" she replied, "Hodgkinson is the name; but they always omit their H's in an odd fashion. The local dialect, you know! What a sweet, dear, dear child she was!" she replied, "I think she was brought up by an aunt or grandmother - well, some relation who agreed to have her... Very sad! Yes, she had such a sweet disposition; they now call her Mrs... ... "Is she married?" I asked, as if I really didn't care- when almost too choked for words. "Oh yes, she has one child. She now lives on a new estate. The old property that formed Pool Hill Square was condemned you know. Would you like her address?"

For a few moments I hesitated. Part of me wanted to say yes, but she was a married woman now and belonged to someone else. 'If she loved me now then her marriage could be ruined!' "No, it would be wrong, wouldn't it?" I said. They both smiled. "Well, it's up to you." "No, I won't," I replied with a lump in my throat. The young Vicar and the retired schoolmistress smiled again. I sensed I'd won a moral battle. On leaving the Church, it seemed the birds were chirping louder; the sun was shining brighter, and I was not walking alone: God was with me! "There are plenty more fish in the sea," were the closing words of the Vicar. I thought of the printer's words at Holywell - "Yes, but who wants a fish!"

Rome, Jehovah, Or Simply 'Chapel'

My second visit to the presbytery in Holywell proved quite a contrast to the previous one. The Parish priest, who'd stared at me as if my presence had contaminated that weeknight service, shook my hand, smiled and wondered if I'd mind being put into the very capable hands of another priest. "He'll keep me informed about your progress because I'm engaged throughout the whole diocese", he said. I learned that he was a vicar general! Naturally I agreed but wanted to be sure that it would be above board for me as a Non-catholic to attend services in his church. He said, "It will be alright for you to do so!" and appeared to give a smile that I interpreted as forced. Then he went out of the room and brought in a quizzical, yet jovial priest, and told me he was putting me into very good and capable hands. This Dutch priest was quite a boy with a wonderful sense of humour. He'd spent much time abroad and was proud to be quite a linguist. This middle-aged priest was obviously happy to conduct my weekly sessions of instruction and I was privileged to receive them. For several weeks, the more questions I fired at him from the Non-catholic viewpoint, the more delighted he was in demolishing them one by one. This endearing cleric was eager to assert from the start that, although I would never be cajoled into embracing Catholicism, it would actually be just a matter of time. "The pull of Holy Church", he said, "will envelop you more and more. Take my word for it: you'll not be able to resist all that she stands for." Such were the kind of words he would occasionally repeat.

At the first few sessions I was assured that all nervousness, as well as my occasional dizzy spells, would leave me as one learned to stop wrestling with doctrine and began to rest in the arms of the 'one true Church' which was established on Peter and had displayed itself down the centuries as a city set on a hill. "To help you to acquire such faith I want you to utter a prayer I'm about to give you, as many times in a day as possible" he said. "You can't say it too many times." It was this:

'My God I believe in you,
and in all that Your Church teaches;
because you have said it and your word is true'.

Before long my questioning of Catholic doctrine, through comparing it with passages of the Bible, led this dear priest to gently rebuke me for not repeating such a formula of a prayer often enough. It so happened that I was, even then, intensely interested in psychological works and knew the power of repetitive suggestion. I sensed the priest was playing a game with me, but lacked the heart and the guts to tell him so. He affirmed that, having found the true boat to Heaven - all others being counterfeit, I must no longer do the work of navigation. "Stop arguing over doctrine, bask in the sun on the deck and leave all the worry to the theologians, When a baby needs medical help the doctors and nurses rush round to do the work" said the priest "but the little child just lays back kicking up its legs and saying 'Coo-ee' unaware of what is going on." Again he reasoned: 'Leave the issues of Christian doctrine to Holy Mother Church!' One verse of Scripture stressed by this most genial priest, more than any other, was: 'Except you become as a little child you will in no way enter the Kingdom of God'. Only when I became humble and obedient - obeying and not questioning - would I be ready for reception into: 'the one true church which can neither deceive nor be deceived'.

By coincidence, during this period Holywell received a visit from the Wycliffe Preachers, known as Kensitites. They were Ultra Protestants who held a series of lantern lectures in the town hall, and they distributed literature, which exposed the teachings and practices of the Church of Rome.. I began to wonder whether or not the Roman Church could, indeed, be the scarlet whore of the Apocalypse as had been taught by Martin Luther, Archbishop Cranmer, John Knox, John Wesley and a host of others. Indeed, I reasoned that childlike questioning was good while childish obedience was bad. Nevertheless, I avidly looked forward to weekly instruction classes from that most endearing priest who was comparable to G.K Chesterton's own 'Father Brown'.

When, about this time, I asked about future possibilities as a priest, reference was made to Cardinal Newman's Apologia pro vita sua. He also had come through the hazes of Protestant heresy into the clear light of Rome, later to don a cardinal's hat!

Soon I was invited up to the monastery, at Pantasaph, to see Father Alfred there. "You'll remember the name? The one who burnt the cakes!" said the priest as jovial as ever. "He is expecting you and I'd like to know how you get on." Actually, I remember little about that visit except his bitterness expressed over some Protestants who, sometime in the year dot, had seemingly taken down an altar-stone upon which the holy sacrifice was offered, and had transformed it into a stepping stone for getting over a wall. There was obviously strong resentment held against the Protestants for things done generations ago; and what was more, recent Protestant gossip hardly improved relations. One was an utter fabrication that a secret passage existed below the complex of the convent opposite, which led into the monastery itself. Another involved monks seen with young women amongst the woods behind. There was little love lost between Catholic and Protestant, yet I wanted to be involved with both! I dare say I appeared as a young upstart, eager to ask too many pertinent questions and seriously lacking the virtue of a Catholic, who would not have asked but obeyed. Consequently Father Alfred appeared to have only the spiritual equivalent of burnt cakes to offer me on that first ever visit to inside his monastery

Indeed, in those days, there was not only a convent directly opposite the monastery, but also a large house to the side of it occupied by nuns. I remember the house quite vividly as, on a previous occasion, Leon and I had the audacity to visit it with our sample Watchtower and Awake publications. We'd only got as far as the gate when a nun of rather heavy features, with thick dark specs, peered at us. Though rather eerie in looks she was, nevertheless, a perfect lady. "These brainwashed nuns have slitty eyes because of the devotion they offer to their idols," stated Leon in a subdued voice, which I alone could hear. He was certainly no lover of Catholicism and our display of Jehovah's Witness publications brought forth no sale and no response. Not even when we later offered them free! Leon had, of course, anticipated this because all religious literature, which did not have the imprimatur of one of their bishops, was anathema. For a Catholic to read it would have been mortal sin. And to die in mortal sin was to be banished to hell forever. The nun had spoken softly in an Irish accent and, beneath an outer charm, would no doubt have viewed us as two more misguided heretics, fruits of the diabolic Reformation!

As a young man I was hopelessly mixed up: I received instruction at St. Winefride's one day, was out with Leon on another day and still preached in several Nonconformist chapels on most Sunday afternoons or evenings. Indeed, the religious literature assimilated was equally mixed. It could be said that, whereas so much of the literature I'd acquired from Catholicism was illustrated in the abstract and often with distorted or weird engravings, everything connected with the Watchtower was bright, colourful, simple and open to behold. Evangelical Protestant literature was likewise a contrast to the Catholic ethos. The latter had its 'Bambino of Prague', its Lady of Perpetual Succour; its crucifixes where the head was sometimes out of proportion to the body, and a skull and crossbones appeared near the base. All was clear to grasp amongst Leon's literature and, indeed, the pleading for money was absent as well. Yet, to any who would decipher it sufficiently, much of what the Watchtower publishers did teach could no more be reconciled with the Bible than could many of the doctrines of the denominations they preferred to denounce the most. However, be that as it may, Nathan Knorr, the humble Watchtower figurehead, was a marked contrast to the thin, weird Pius XII whose portrait, with finger raised, was revered in the corner of many a Catholic home. With round glasses and hooked nose, he was surely enough to create a shiver down the spine of any who were not of his fold. Yes, the portrait in those days of a 'Vicar of Christ', who'd signed a concordat with the Third Reich brought a very mixed response indeed.

If, as the Bible teaches, 'the Devil transforms himself into an angel of light' then one branch of Christianity, denouncing another, may well be no more than the frying pan calling the kettle black. So clever were the teachings adamantly expressed by Leon that many local folk were converted to his sect, including a village schoolteacher whose daughter fascinated me more than her mother because of her feminine charm. Leon thought that before long I would be a faithful witness of Jehovah, and preparations were to be made for my baptism by immersion at a local swimming baths. "You'll appreciate that your baptism as a Baptist was not enough" he said. "The early believers were baptized for the world to see, and not within four walls of a chapel!" Well, he had a point there, but it was not to be. I ceased commending their publications though I'd acquired a whole volume, which I went through with a fine toothcomb. One book, which had been presented to me, proved a mine of superb information and any high-pressure salesman might have treasured it. This was Theocratic Aid to Kingdom Publishers. Such subjects as how to answer a Roman Catholic, an agnostic, an infidel or Jew were all covered. The perception of body language, the need for right posture and a cheerful smile, were but a few of the factors included and it was a mine of information on how to organise activities.

At the side of the Prince of Wales cinema stood, in those days, a building which looked as if it could have collapsed at any moment. On passing it, on a Thursday morning and afternoon, one would hear the swishing sound of a vintage double-feed, flatbed printing press. Here it was that a local newspaper, the County Herald, was printed as well as published. Some folk would call it 'The County Liar'! For me it was a first class weekly even though, on occasions, one might get a copy in which they'd either forgotten to print the inside or else had printed it upside down. Thanks to the editor of this 'local rag' I was able to get my first articles on religion into print. This was due to the scathing remarks directed at traditional Christianity, which were now being sent to the 'readers' views' page by Leon. The local Vicar, himself, had been so misguided as to have written a letter commending these enthusiastic Bible students who were canvassing his parish from door to door! Leon had thought it worthy of a quite sarcastic reply: "If the Vicar knew his Bible why didn't he leave the heresy he was in and join them?" Although still remaining Leon's friend I now felt morally obliged to challenge him in the press over this. My ammunition was chiefly taken from an ever-growing library of books. Consequently, one week Leon's letter would appear and the next week my reply. Yes, then his, and then mine! Until the editor - an extremely patient and likeable soul - terminated the correspondence. The vicar, in all fairness to him, had congratulated me on defending Christian doctrine but, when I later argued as a Fundamentalist, he appeared on a different wavelength

These Jehovah's Witnesses of the late 1940s were a marked contrast to the Protestant denominations of the whole district who seemed to have been lulled into apathy and were completely void of any evangelistic zeal. Such denominations weren't all of Calvinist persuasion, but the term summarised their lack of zeal. If you were one of God's elect you would find your way to a place of worship, but it was a waste of time seeking those whom the Almighty had already destined for hell. The days of the Welsh revivals, during which most of the chapels had been built, were well and truly past. Calvinism and Modernism had combined to put out the flame. All one could do, as a local preacher, was to try and fan them back in to life.

It was about this time that elderly Mr. Phillips, from one of these smouldering embers, Ebenezer Chapel, Milwr, heard of my preaching abilities. One Sunday afternoon he called at our home to introduce himself as its secretary. He asked if he'd arrived at the right place and repeated: "Is this really the home of the young man who has excelled himself as a preacher? I receive such wonderful reports about him!" Mother modestly replied that it possibly was so. "Then you must be very proud of him." he went on. "Yes, well, it's gratifying to know! But I suppose you'd better speak to him, yourself about it". The request was that I conduct worship there about once a month; to which I agreed. Venerable Mr. Philips was an unusual personality. Though without education and, indeed, recently an eye as a result of a quarry accident, he could nevertheless be very much moved by the Spirit. When he was not moved by one spirit I dare say he could be moved by another! Well, at least, he certainly wasn't averse to alcohol. Of that I never had any doubt, not after the day he'd profusely apologised, to the extent of literally shedding a few tears. The afternoon worship had just finished "I'm unable to run you home this afternoon; I'm so very sorry." He said. "I feel so awful about it, but the car is incapacitated at the moment." Well, I failed to understand why he was so bothered. Walking meant nothing to me as a junior postman and, what is more, the weather was fine. I need only say that, as I was making my way out of the chapel gate, I had a strange urge to cross over and take a close look at his car which was on the far side. When I chose to peer through the back window, to my amazement, there covering the back seat, were crates of beer. Indeed, I wouldn't have minded a bottle myself at the start of the walk home. I've no doubt that Mr. Philips would have expected something better from a preacher! But perhaps I could have expected something better from one who was both a chapel secretary and senior deacon.. Beneath the surface we probably had similar if not identical vices. Yet we covered them with a veneer of 'nonconformist morality' on the surface. It is easy to denounce in others what we are guilty of in ourselves. The psychologists call it projection. Consequently, one needs reminding that in pointing a finger to another we usually find that three on the same hand are pointing back at us!

More often than not, however, on engagements at Ebenezer Chapel, the dear secretary would provide transport in his Ford Eight. As we travelled along the delightful lanes we would discuss passages from the good book, though I often wished he would talk less and drive with more care. The outcome of being deprived of the sight of his right eye was that he constantly veered to the wrong side and, on reaching sharp and narrow corners; one could be truly tense lest a car should suddenly confront us. Indeed, the fear of a head-on accident was accelerated by the knowledge that sticks of gelignite, for use in his quarry, were occasionally carried in the boot. On more than one occasion, as he rattled along, one would hear the sticks knocking against each other. When he actually became aware of them he would slow down considerably, apologising to his horrified passengers. More often than not, though, his mind would get so engrossed in the things of God that he became temporarily oblivious to all else. We'd sometimes burst forth into praise and, as we lustily sang either in a solemn key or a major one, the accelerator would go further down and the car simply rattled along until we gave him a nudge and a reminder.

This simple, saintly man, with normal human weaknesses, lived with his wife, an equally unique soul, in the small house that adjoined the tiny chapel. If the house was rather antiquated so, indeed, was the chapel.

To attend a service at Ebenezer was to go back a century and a half. You entered the building at its side and there, in the middle, was an old coke stove that the secretary, during the winter months, would often stoke up in the midst of worship or, if he didn't, a delightful young fellow called Tommy would. Sometimes it happened in the middle of a sermon. I once considered it most appropriate, when touching upon Hell, to hear more coke being cast into the stove and to see the glow that emanated from it through the door being opened. This, indeed, was a splendid visual aid to which each worshipper warmed. Mr. Philips would often sit at its side while close to him was a delightful Liverpudlian who played the old harmonium in the shadows. And, of course, to the left of the stove, and raised up above the harmonium, there was a boxed pulpit against the wall. Upon it was placed a copy of the Welsh Bible and, on having entered that revered spot, one was aware of oil lamps jutting out from the wall, one at either side. Once worship commenced you became aware of the close proximity of the congregation. Indeed, the chapel was so small one could be forgiven for feeling you could shake the hands of the worshippers across. The pulpit was raised high. Yes, but so were the pews in step formation, each with its own door!

The chapel door would keep opening and closing while, in utter solemnity as preacher, one sat in meditation as the time to start worship drew close. Worship was taken very seriously by these folk. At least, except for the time when Deacon Pritchard, from the mother chapel, came up one afternoon and introduced me to a strange, yet lovable lady whose attire was as from a previous century. She was dressed for worship in shiny black taffeta and lace while, under her very big hat, there dangled from her earlobes ebony earrings nearing the size of curtain rings. This particular deacon, who loved to amuse me as well as flatter her, beckoned me to her in the final minutes before worship was due to commence. "The preacher tells me, dear, that he is completely entranced by the beauty of your earrings: he has never seen any as lovely." She looked most pleased and elated. As she turned to sit down he told me, in an undertone, "they'd look better hung down from her nose!" Such comments, especially when worship was to be in such close proximity to the solemn worshippers, were to embarrass me to such a degree that the deacon's smiling, nodding towards her and winking towards me, were sufficient to make one burst uncontrollably in to laughter. Yet to do so would have been sacrilege indeed. These gesticulations from this rascal of a Deacon went on throughout the whole of that service. The only relief I was to experience was when offering a long extempore prayer with my eyes closed. Sadly, my preaching suffered very much that day. Indeed, because a chuckle or two escaped that I couldn't contain, I preached on how worship should be a happy occasion; that solemnity amongst God's people was wrong, and that smiling was a tonic to cultivate.

Unfortunately laughing is hardly the same as smiling. Yet laughter can be contagious and, as a consequence, not a few chuckles seemed to be evident on several faces. I sensed, by this time, that they were having as much difficulty in not laughing, when staring straight into my eyes, as I had whilst looking directly across into theirs. When that particular service drew to its end, I sensed it was a tremendous relief for a lot of us to get outside. Yes, to see the funny side in the most solemn of atmospheres has been my weakness. I have experienced it, while I have occupied several pulpits, but never as much as when I preached that afternoon at Milwr chapel up the Dolphin, near Holywell. Emotionalism was always manifest there. If it was not due to the lighter side then, far more often, it would be due to the wonderful fervour of Welsh hymn singing. The last verse of many a hymn would often be struck up and repeated once, or even twice, through the lead of that wonderful little chapel secretary. He really possessed a heart of gold and may well have a far greater place in glory than I might ever receive.

One experience at Ebenezer Chapel, which made an impression of mixed feelings upon the regulars there, was due to Mr. Phillips making the acquaintance of a GI chaplain at the nearby Sealand Aerodrome. Being an American Baptist, this padre was eager and anxious to conduct our Harvest Thanksgiving service. When the day arrived he was accompanied by several of his American friends. Dressed in American Air Force uniform, they made quite a change to the atmosphere of the chapel and they certainly stepped up the collection! However, the padre, in typical American style, started to auction off the produce before the service had actually finished. He began to ask, "What am I bid?" and then shouted, "Going, going, gone!" Some of the solemn regulars looked intensely horrified. Old Mr. Phillips was quietly 'motioned to', to intervene and stop such sacrilege in chapel. Nevertheless, he chose to ignore it and began to warm to the procedure. A couple, in apparent disgust, got up and walked out; and another soon followed them. One wondered who would be next. Fortunately, the Padre appeared oblivious to the disapproving gestures and kept asking: "What am I bid?". I can only say that I enjoyed every single moment of it; and the more shocked others became, the more I lapped it up.

As was to be expected, neither the American padre nor his friends were asked back again; even though the collection that night had been the largest in years! And what was more; the auctioning of the produce had been a common American Baptist practice. Indeed, whereas they believed that worship should be joyful and light the Welsh counterpart was one of solemnity and depth. And concerning the latter, I well remember the spiritual depth and emotion expressed when a young lady called Megan came forward to sing from the depth of her heart:

> *Into my heart, into my heart,*
> *Come into my heart, Lord Jesus.*
> *Come in today, come in to stay,*
> *Come into my heart, Lord Jesus!*

Yes, and on a later occasion this same gifted young lady sang 'The Old Rugged Cross' and it was the first time I'd heard it. The organist wept as he played for her. Mr. Phillips – obviously, spiritually choked by the words of the song - followed suit. We all joined in singing it over again and, perhaps, we all wept as well.

I began to compare, at that time, the ordered ceremonial of the Roman Mass at St Winefride's and the dedication of its priests with conducting, or even attending, a simple service at this cute little Chapel. As one pictured the utter simplicity of the latter, and remembered how the birds would be frequently chirping outside, I think I knew which of the two Christ would have preferred to worship in. But then, I may well have been utterly wrong!

Round about this time, when it was common practice to go to Milwr to attend Ebenezer Baptist Chapel on Sunday afternoons, I came across a visiting preacher, a mature Baptist minister, who was from the southern part of the principality. On learning of my desire to train for the ministry, he was pleased to offer sound advice. He declined the offer of a lift back to Holywell in order that we might talk together as we made the journey on foot. The recollection is vague and misty, but one remembers the weather as being sunny and beautiful. Before long the old Inn on the left would be passed, the crossroads would be traversed, and a short ascent would be followed by a decline which brought one to the main road that by-passed the top of the town.

Frequently from such a spot one had viewed the region of Pen-Y-Maes – prominent by its towering old mill – and had been conscious of how God was looking down on its many inhabitants; and this had been followed by silent prayer for those who seldom appeared to think of Him, except in times of trouble! Well, as we travelled this way, the Minister's request was that I first speak of myself. Then, on learning all he required and with a sad and yet searching look, he uttered words to this effect: "I'm not going to recommend you for the ministry! The ministry is more than preaching and these kind of people would destroy you. You've only seen one side of them. Don't think I don't appreciate what you want to do. Carry on with your preaching by all means. It seems as if you have a real gift from God there. Use it to the full".

Then turning towards me, as we came to almost a standstill, he reiterated: "But the ministry? No! You have far too gentle a disposition. Mind you, I'm not criticising you for that. 'Far from it!' I simply want you to know that once some of these worshippers are in business meetings they vie contentiously in a most ungodly manner. There is a ruthless side to their nature you haven't as yet seen. I've seen young men with stronger stamina than you whose lives have been hopelessly shattered by the church. If I were to recommend you as a candidate for the Baptist ministry then I wouldn't be able to live with my conscience. It would be too cruel to consider. 'Why, some of these diaconates would crucify you'! You'd be led as a lamb to the slaughter!"

This kind and courteous cleric was a realist, and I a young idealist. Down the years those words imparted were to be confirmed over and over again. But who is likely to influence a young idealist determined, at all costs, to fulfil a vocation, which he also feels, has divine backing?

Attached, as the mother chapel to Ebenezer, there stood at the bottom of Pen-y-Ball Street, in the centre of Holywell, Bethel. This Baptist place of worship looked smallish on the outside but much bigger within. It was a Welsh chapel, which held an English service in the evening and it was here that I was eventually asked to preach. This was undoubtedly a great honour, and before long the honoured evening arrived. The pulpit was high and ornate, almost level with the round gallery.

The chapel was also fully occupied by worshippers and one of them in the gallery was a fellow postman. I then traced my eyes downwards and directly below me, a trifle forward from the rest of the congregation, were the deacons in their exalted position known colloquially as the 'set fawr'. Two of them stood out in my mind from the others. One was saintly Mr. Roberts. Some called him Roberts the Post, while others called him Roberts of Bodgele, because he was a retired postmaster who lived in a house of that name. The other person present could have completely unnerved me, except that I never entered a pulpit without believing that I entered and shared it with Jesus. His name was Gomer Williams, my last teacher at school, fear of whom had contributed towards playing truant.

When the sermon was finished, and before I could announce the closing hymn and give the benediction, one of the deacons got up to express his deep appreciation as well as add his personal comments. And then my heart momentarily speeded up as Gomer Williams rising from his seat followed suit. He told the congregation about one of the thickest and densest boys he had ever had the misfortune to teach. He then turned round to me and said, in the hearing of all, that if anyone four or five years ago had said that someday I would deliver a logical sermon from this pulpit he would have told them to get their heads examined. "Well," he said, "this is the scholar to whom I refer. Well done, Thompson. Well done, lad, a thousand apologies. I take back all I once said about you!." The final hymn followed, the blessing was given and the congregation departed. During the following week several folk stopped me in the streets to thank me for having taken such an inspiring service. Some women who passed gave a kind nod of approval, while one or two men even raised their hats. Although still only a teenager, and merely a junior postman, I was now given respect due to being a preacher.

An, Idyllically Welsh, Post Round

As one looks back on one's past life one often becomes aware of a pattern in the process of being formed. At least, it certainly was so with my own life, and each brand of secular employment seemed to have contributed towards an evolving future vocation. I see it as more than a mere coincidence that experiences in a printing establishment were followed by those, which took me further into the cinema world. Even working in a factory had its purpose to fulfil. The printing company was the means of introducing me, to a marked degree, to contrasting members of the cloth. It was also the place where local church publications were taken through the successive stages of compositing, printing, folding, stapling and distribution. I was often involved in each. The projection booths gave me ample opportunity to repeatedly absorb films such as Joan of Arc, and the Ten Commandments, or the more sophisticated Bells of St Mary's, with its lovable priest, or the inspiring Lost Horizon with its Shangri-la. Even the less edifying productions, if nothing more, often showed the deceptiveness, the vanity and fickleness of human nature. The tool-room of the factory revealed to me the depth of depravity that can exist where men congregate. Much of the evil that I'd seen portrayed on the screen I found practiced in the tool room. Fiction was certainly followed by fact.

My calling into the postman's world was to be the means of discovering the many country chapels. It provided one with the opportunity to worship the God of the beautiful countryside; the glory of which reflected His love. Tramping the lanes, the hills, the valleys and the fields was not only a means of acquiring robust health, which the future would demand; it was equally a means by which, travelling along, I could be repeatedly singing my great Redeemer's praise. Such was the kind of spiritual education God was leading me through, before He ordained me into a greater vocation than any self-appointed academy, institution or sect could confer. Although I failed to realise it then, and bitterly kicked against it, such training would equip me far better for the Christian ministry than any coveted degree. The young mind fails to see it this way. It is only with the wisdom of much later years that some learn that those academic appendages, once so eagerly sought, are a very poor substitute indeed for the hard knocks at the bench which we share at the side of The Carpenter.

Work as a junior postman proved most congenial, even though it resulted in such an early start during all kinds of weather. The early morning atmosphere within the sorting room is something I still dream about sometimes. Yet once out of that office one was left entirely alone, and, while traversing the fields and country lanes, could converse with God. If one or two folk encountered were a little disgruntled over a bill received, the vast majority always had a warm welcome, for the Welsh folk are a happy, homely race with much compassion for others. Down the Well Hill one would go, with minimum pressure on the bicycle brake, and then I would peacefully pass through Greenfield, noticing Holy Trinity Church on the left and Alpha Congregational Chapel opposite. 'Ah, if only I were the minister of Alpha! I would sigh to myself.'

Soon I would be round the sharp bend at Greenfield, making my first call at the Congregational manse occupied by a layman. Then I would cycle towards Llanerchymor, making another call at the home of a Welsh nationalist. He insisted on addressing me in Welsh and only on learning of my Scottish roots did he become civil. Provided I addressed him in a little Welsh he would welcome me. Then, along the lane the little hamlet of Trefor would soon be approached: two rows of old Welsh cottages! The row nearest to the Chapel was nicknamed Nefoedd (Heaven) while the first row encountered - once nearest to a colliery –

'the first row --- referred to as Uffern (Hell)'

was referred to as Uffern (Hell). These cottages mostly had stable doors and one remembers stone cobbled floors. Standpipes were just off the roadside, as was a Victorian style post-office that also served as a general store. The chapel, in a homely austerity, stood beyond. As for the people: they were the very salt of the earth and to deliver their mail was an honour and a privilege. I sometimes prayed to God for His blessing on each house as the letters were pushed through each respective letterbox

All was very beautiful with the aroma of wild flowers, though not so beautiful on either a Monday or Tuesday morning when the open sewerage lorry came round for the toilet buckets to be poured over into it. The sloshing of the contents, as the lorry slowly passed, was rather frightening because it was followed by a permeation of the atmosphere, which remained on the road a good while afterwards and in one's nostrils longer still. For some unknown reason I nicknamed the lorry 'the dragon'. If I could possibly deliver my mail in advance of it then I would do so, but more often than not it would eventually overtake me. I'm sad to say that Trefor no longer exists. Yet the post office, with shop combined, was as quaint as the two rows of houses. It also seemed to be a hangover from a bygone age with its old fashioned counter, scales, gas lamps and, what I remember most of all, massive round tubs of butter and cheese. Flies were not unaccustomed to descend upon such dairy produce, especially in warm weather. It seemed many weeks before the tubs or vats were replaced by new ones. No doubt on Monday or Tuesday mornings the flies would descend fresh from playing about round the sewerage lorry. Such was the way of life and no one ever seemed the worse for it. Many lived to a ripe old age

To make one's way along the old coast road was a real pleasure as the birds sang in one's ear. And to ascend such hills as Stockyn Drive was equally a pleasure. It was here that several wooden houses had been erected. It was not uncommon to enter them, and one in particular is not easily forgotten because of the smell of smoke through improper ventilation in the chimney. All I can remember about it was a humble young woman, with several children who ran around the house with jerseys, but no pants. It always seemed to shock me that the children's private parts weren't covered; but then surely it wasn't all that necessary in one's own home at such an early hour. It would be no more than 10.30 at the latest. 'Nevertheless, money spent on kiddies' clothes,' I said to myself, 'should come before money spent on Woodbines or Players Weights.'

Well, up Stockyn Drive one would go until level with a spot on the left. There one could cut across a large field with a hollow, and climb up the far side to deliver letters at Old Stockyn farm. I was always relieved to arrive there as bullocks occupied the field. These would nosily weigh you up, and sensing your trepidation decide to walk across towards you. On such occasions I would usually engage in singing a hymn while thanking God for His love and constant protection. The bullocks would quite sportingly come close up. I sense they might have been curious to know what was in the post sack. I liked them, but it was certainly a relief to arrive at the farm on the other side. The occupants there were an elderly, rather dour couple. They'd previously had little to say; but now, having learned via the grapevine that I was a lay preacher, opened up and spoke eagerly about spiritual matters.

'Old Stockyn Farm. I was always relieved to arrive there'

Before long the opportunity to preach at Trefor chapel was extended to me by them and this I gladly accepted. The chapel was of Welsh Calvinistic Methodist persuasion. And, though I took the service once, it was not to be offered a second time. That a service given in the English language had taken place was a fresh innovation. A forceful minority - during the week that followed - voted for no service at all rather than have another one, when all but the hymns would be in English.

In all fairness it needs to be mentioned that they had borne no malice towards me. Indeed, several on the post round commended my humble efforts profusely. During that Service one couldn't have been made more welcome, and yet one was merely a teenager! How the memory of it comes to mind. I see it all as if it were yesterday. That Sunday evening service was held in an atmosphere all of its own. Indeed, the building was idyllically Welsh as from a previous era. The pulpit was more like a straight platform with an open banister rail running along its length. Half way along there was a ledge; jutting out on which was laid a large, revered volume from which I was to preach. Regrettably I couldn't because it was in the vernacular, but I would use it as a base upon which to place my notes, if not my copy of the King James Bible.

If one's memory is correct, oil lamps were used for illumination but, being a warm summer night, were not lit. Two such lamps jutted out from the wall, one on each side of where the revered preacher took his place behind the hallowed book. The windows were long, narrow and all of plain glass. There was also, above the rostrum itself, a text in scroll pattern high up on the wall. It was appropriately in the country's vernacular. I know that the noise from the harmonium was solemn, mellow, reverent and in a minor key. It conveyed such tremendous adoration when accompanied by the Welsh voices of those worshippers. One such hymn, the numbers alone of which I could announce, started up as if it was almost a wail. I could have wept with gratitude to God because He had given me, of all people, the privilege to lead such worship directed towards Him.

Disconcertingly, however, and irrelevant as it might seem, the very commencement of such an engagement had a strange effect upon me of which it was difficult to rid my mind. I made a practice of entering the toilet before entering a pulpit, and this occasion was no exception. One was directed to an outside closet and, on entering it, was confronted with a bench of double width with two holes in it. One was smaller than the other. Well, if the thought of a male and female being busily engaged side-by-side could tickle one's imagination, the foul stench that arose from two half full buckets beneath more than tickled the nose. My nostrils became permeated for the whole length of the service that followed. And, somehow, the thought of those genteel ladies, who gave off a beautiful aroma of lavender, being engaged over these buckets, was something too disturbing to contemplate. During the hallowed hour of worship I was frequently being put off by the thought of not only flies in the hot air circling round those buckets but, what was possibly more disturbing still: sweet and genteel ladies arrayed in best Sunday refinery, busy using portions of a well inked Flintshire Observer while squatted in the Ty Bach. 'Can't the chapel afford a roll of respectable Izal Germicide?' I asked myself.

As a postman I was used to seeing the farmer and his hefty wife in their rough, ungainly, gear and failed to recognise them at first. They made themselves known to me. How smart and immaculate they now were! For them the chapel and the Sabbath were events they looked forward to throughout the whole week. As for scrubbing potatoes for a grand Sunday dinner, most of it would have been prepared on the Saturday. Yes, such folk truly hallowed their hard earned Sabbath and, though the age gap between them and myself was so vast, we were on the same wavelength: their God was my God and we knew Him personally. I sensed our lives revolved round Him. Nevertheless, half way down Stockyn Lane, from that delightful farmhouse, there stood a quaint old wooden bungalow. This was, amazingly, the residence of a Baptist minister, the Reverend J.B. James. He was a most unique personality. The lady at the farm above owned the bungalow and expressed concern over the way it was occupied. She was horrified because its occupant chose to hang out dilapidated washing on Sundays. A man of the cloth, she said, should set a better example.

Well, 'J.B. Jesus' (as some called him!) never actually wore the cloth! "I wouldn't be seen in it dead or alive man" he said to me. "Take it from me, the preacher's collar covers a multitude of sins man. Yes, indeed: a multitude of sins man!". And then he would say straight afterwards, his eyes repetitively blinking: "Have you any winners for me today man? Any winners? Any winners?" The farm lady would have been more shocked still if she'd known that this reverend gentleman received more football coupons through his post than anyone else on the whole postal round, and such is no exaggeration. Until it actually dawned upon me that he was a minister I had viewed him as a scruffy lay-about who was too lazy to work. He was, in my opinion, dirty because he kept hens inside his house each night. On opening the door each morning the hens would start to chuckle out from between his feet. More often than not, my hammering at the door would act as his alarm. At last he would respond by knocking at the bedroom window: "Just a minute. Coming!" When there was no post for the farm I would sometimes refuse to make the frightening journey across the valley merely to deliver his Vernons or Littlewoods coupons. I often dishonestly kept them for a couple of days at the bottom of the postbag.

J.B. James was truly eccentric. Many felt sorry for him as his wife had found him unbearable, and subsequently left him. Being a man he was not so gifted as some in looking after a home, and that's putting it very mildly. Occasionally, he would utter odd remarks, Yet this unpretentious man was known to have tremendous preaching ability. He could work himself up into ecstatic fervour and, what was more; he would have gone out of his way to help anyone. The advice he gave me to train for the Baptist ministry was the best but, at the time, I foolishly failed to put any importance on what he advised as I actually thought him to be truly 'three masts to the wind'. He was, however, an accredited Welsh minister who trained, I was told, at the united Bala Bangor College, and his joint pastorates were those of Greenfield and Ffynnongroew. Going to, or returning from the former he would often pass me on his bicycle (the old 'sit up and beg' style). Raising his hat in a semi-circle he would ask, smilingly, "How are you, man?" Yes, one couldn't help but truly warm towards him.

On my way back, nearing the end of the usual daily round, I had to again pass the cottage occupied by the roadman who was a nationalist. Slogans, such as 'Down with the English', were whitewashed on walls near his home. The Welsh flag would often blow in the breeze and, as he spoke to me in Welsh, woe betide me if I didn't try to reply in the same. That I had lived in the principality so long without acquiring the language would have been unforgivable.

Soon a large rambling building, known as Greenfield Hall, would usually be visited. One of the occupants of this now semi-derelict, loose set of flats was an evangelical Christian. Consequently, it was always a spiritual uplift to climb the many stairs so as to deliver her mail and then discuss 'the things of God'. She had a sister who worked in the Liverpool City Mission. This resulted later in having dinner at the mission's headquarters; but at the time, much to my regret, there were no vacancies going. The trip to Liverpool, however, had become an opportunity to have fellowship with evangelical believers who were overjoyed on hearing one's personal testimony of faith. Nevertheless, they warned about the 'sinister' allurements of

Catholicism and discouraged my pursuing further instruction from "this harlot church of the Apocalypse!"

Further up than this old rambling hall, now almost crumbling into a ruin was another house with a differing fascination. It was a wooden bungalow in a wood. The occupant here was young, with children, and I was quite turned on by her charm. I sensed rightly or wrongly that it was mutual. She possessed a pretty figure and usually wore Wellingtons. Yes, sometimes my thoughts fluctuated between divine aspirations and human appetite.

During the last lap of the daily postal round one was brought into the vicinity of another farm. It necessitated crossing a field occupied by a bull. Here it was that an unforgettable experience occurred one day, which was factual through and through. It was living proof to me of divine intervention. In order to save half an hour's walking time it was necessary to climb up a steep hill to reach the farm above. The hillside was a field, and on this particular occasion, unknown to me, a bull was grazing.

To my horror, on getting into the centre of the field, I perceived this lonely beast coming speedily towards me. I felt petrified. I knew that to run might merely antagonise the creature and, what was more, I would never be able to get out of the field in time. A passage of Scripture came rushing to the mind: 'Prove me now in the day of trouble that I am God!' The opportunity to put such Scripture to the test confronted me then, as never before. I closed my eyes and stood perfectly still. I cried, 'Lord, I trust you! You will never fail me.' I waited a few seconds, opened my eyes, and the creature was actually trotting away. On reaching the farm, where the farmer stood, he looked both astonished and relieved. He collected the mail and walked away deep in thought. On narrating the experience to others, it proved the subject of much humour. 'The bull mustn't have liked you and changed its mind!' they said. Others stated that it was purely coincidence. But for myself, I felt sure that God had saved me from a bull that was ready to charge. 'The prayer of a righteous man availeth much,' states the Scripture: and, though I had many faults, I guess I was pretty righteous in those days. The next day, word was sent to the post office that the proper approach to the farm must be used. The short cut involved not only real danger, but to take it was to be guilty of trespass.

Amongst Dear Ulster's Proddy Dogs & Papists

Many months had indeed passed since returning from the Bible College at Glasgow, and I'd only made one lasting friend, Victor Gilmore. Having returned to his home and children in Belfast, he was now qualified as an optician. Only one or two letters had passed between us but, in reply to the last one, Victor had shown deep concern about me receiving instruction to become a Roman Catholic. As a means of getting me out of their, supposed, clutches he was now offering me work in a Christian soldiers' home. The letter suggested that I leave for Ulster as soon as possible to avail myself of such an opening. A fellow Christian, of the Brethren persuasion, had liased between him and the proprietors on my behalf. 'Praise the Lord', I thought, full-time Christian work has come at last. With minimum delay plans were made to leave Holywell, to embark on the steamer at Liverpool and sail out for the Emerald Isle. Poor Mother would never stand in the way, even though she was a widow and doing some cleaning for a little extra money.

Victor had embarked for his home in Belfast from Glasgow several months previous via Stranraer, on the Princess Victoria. A short time later, this very steamer, making the same journey, sank through the hold doors not being properly bolted. Most, if not all, lives were lost! I had no wish to go via Stranraer, and made my way to Liverpool which was much closer.

The night was getting on when boarding the Ulster Monarch. After the ship had left the docks we were soon slipping past the night-lights of New Brighton, which was then a seaside pleasure beach of some considerable size. An elderly gentleman, with a soft, refined Irish accent, spoke to me of his joy to be returning home. On the other side, viewing the romantic setting stood a youngish looking fellow of a seemingly ordinary background. I turned towards him, smiled and said, "Isn't it a lovely evening?" Whereupon he turned to me and bluntly blurted "Are you saved?" The question was put to me as forcefully as a thunderbolt. I was shocked! Out of the whole crowd of passengers, here I was next to a believer, a hallelujah Christian. We exchanged accounts of our conversions and I was told that the hand of the Lord was in our coming together. It was made equally clear that time mustn't be wasted in exchanging further experiences for there were souls to save during this crossing. We must get on with it immediately. He then put his hand in his coat pocket and withdrew a large bundle of cheaply printed American gospel tracts, plus several more dignified ones published in Northern Ireland by a Mr. Gilpin, an affluent businessman and member of the Brethren. A gentleman I would one day meet and the one who'd paid for all of Victor's training! Well, going down into the saloon, it was crammed with scruffy and inebriated folk, the penalty for travelling third class or 'steerage' as they termed it. We singled out a young Air-force man at the foot of the steps. 'Excuse me, but do you know the Lord?' asked my new travelling companion. 'What do you mean?' came the reply. 'Are you saved? Are you under the blood?' asked my companion. (His words, if not identical, were similar to these.) The fellow in RAF uniform looked exceedingly embarrassed to the point that I felt intensely uneasy for him. Somehow, I just couldn't imagine our Lord using such a blunt, rude approach, which seemed to be without any tact or courtesy. But then, perhaps, I lacked such courage and needed my new companion's boldness. After all, if you're rescuing folk from imminent fire, you don't waste time with niceties; you've often to be very blunt. Perhaps we're rescuing him from hellfire I thought.

After having spent an hour or two evangelising ruthlessly with this 'Brother in the Lord' I eagerly sought an opportunity to slip out of his way, getting lost in the crowd. The hours passed and the ship began not only to shake and shudder but to roll from side to side and we sensed that this could lead to real danger should any of the cargo break loose. I still felt very seasick even after having vomited many times. My stomach was wrenched and I felt ready to die. Unable to procure a seat I lay flat on the floor of a saloon, which reeked of the mixed smell of salt water and alcohol. Peering through the misty windows as the vessel raised and dropped. I saw waves like mountains and turned to read the warning notice. Even if the siren had gone I wouldn't have had the strength to do anything. One felt too weak and tired. Yet I was afraid of taking my eyes from my 'attaché' case least it should be pinched. It came as a relief in the morning to awaken and find the boat in a great calm. The case with all its belongings was still at my side.

I was just beginning to appreciate the calmness of the early morning when suddenly the sound of a pipe band struck up to the full. The tune was so lively that it made one feel like dancing and it was repeated many times. Some of these pipers made their way past, and though their eyes still looked exceedingly glassy through the amount of alcohol consumed the previous night, it was obviously no deterrent to their playing. Another tune was struck up and similarly repeated. I recognised it as 'Three Cheers for the Red, White and Blue', while another was to the tune 'God Bless the Prince of Wales', but they had been well and truly speeded up. Eventually an hour or two's silence followed. Then the band struck up once more when land was sighted and the words sung to one tune concerned the wearing of a sash. This was my first encounter with a group of Orangemen, and this was to be one of their great days in Belfast. Though they claimed to be Christians and loyal Protestants I felt they were nothing more than a motley crowd of alcoholics. I questioned even if they knew the first thing about the Bible, but I wouldn't have dared ask them. Several of them were reminiscent of the razor gang I almost encountered in Glasgow.

Eventually my evangelical colleague again made contact with me and apologised that, somehow, he'd lost me in the crowd. He then went on to tell of two or three who'd shown a deep interest in the things of God. He remarked on the appalling roughness of the crossing and told of how gracious and long suffering the Lord was to have spared us all from a watery grave.

Walking up the cobbled street from the docks, I passed horses and traps. I truly felt as if I'd slipped back in time. Soon, however, I was in the midst of a very modern, clean and beautiful city, which was swarming with colourful trolley buses. The air was crisp and cool from the nearby river and there was something romantic, fresh and welcoming about the people. When I arrived at Victor's home in Orby Drive, I was introduced to his family and made exceptionally welcome. There is no hospitality I've yet experienced which is comparable to the homeliness of many Ulster folk, be they Catholic or Protestant. For me the Gilmore family were exceptionally delightful because they were Christians, not just in name, but also in deed.

The next day soon came round and I was off on the most expensive coach journey yet paid for such a distance. A green single-decker took me past lakes and scenery unsurpassed for beauty while the grass and foliage were a most delightful green. Cottages were soon quite sparse. Their occupants appeared so fair with eyes that were so open as to almost look through you. Then, on alighting at the 'Sande's Soldiers' Home', one was faced by barrack-like buildings which were near a long stretch of idyllic beach. While opposite, across the water, were the mountains of Mourne sloping down to the sea. However, it appeared that a mix-up had occurred for, whereas I'd come to evangelise to the troops during their leisure moments in this Christian establishment - complete with its canteen and cinema - a Mr. Snow, many years my senior, had beaten me to it. Consequently, my task ended up being just one more of the voluntary workers. In return for services, as a general mug, I was given free food and accommodation. The hours worked were to be long and tedious and, if money were needed for personal expenses, a special request had to be submitted to the two elderly spinsters who were in charge, the Miss Maguires.

I must confess I was hardly suited to convert hardened soldiers who were mostly older than myself. I felt that Christianity could be expressed through kindness and often turned a blind eye to accepting the stipulated price for a mug of tea or a bacon and egg sandwich. Because of this, when it came to meal times and I joined the other staff behind the long counter, a queue would form in front of me while the other assistants felt humiliated as hardly any of the soldiers would queue up in front of them. A dear old sergeant, with a lovable, friendly nature, in order that he might avail himself of a free mug of tea from me, would rattle the mug with his spoon. Detecting a slight Welsh accent he would keep repeating iechyd da (good health) while giving me a few winks and tapping his empty mug on the counter. There were, of course, those who were always ready to tell and, before long, I was brought before the two spinsters and gently reprimanded.

On one occasion Mr. Snow couldn't fulfil a pre-arranged 'Christian Fireside Meeting' in the large lounge, so I was asked to step in for him. I think Mr. Snow had caught a cold that night, so now was an opportunity to wear my dark preaching suit, with white shirt, starched collar and black tie. Yes, I walked in to the packed lounge with a big Bible, out to do business for God; and as I looked round I saw several attractive members of the Auxiliary Territorial Service included. One of them offered to play the hymns on the grand piano.

I told those present how God had saved me 'from the guttermost to the uttermost', and what he could do for me, he could do for them also. They were not a little amused! As I forcefully preached on avoiding sin, two or three members of the ATS began to cross their legs and hitch up their skirts. When I went on to relate the evils of lust and drink, one actually revealed her suspender belt and gave me a wink and a 'come and get me' gesture. The men folk were joining in with shouts of 'woe!' and 'shame!' Indeed, they were an extremely happy crowd. No doubt Mr. Snow would have swiftly brought them to order and frowned on the whole affair. Unfortunately I ended up as if I were one of them and my prestige was lost. Yes, as far as the two spinsters were concerned, their choice of Mr. Snow had no doubt been the right one.

Sande's home also possessed its own cinema. I'd never come across such antiquated projector equipment and one could hardly make out the picture on the screen, while the muffled sound gave the effect of coming through a sack. Then, as soon as the national anthem was finished, a visiting member of the Open Brethren jumped onto the stage and pleaded with the members of the audience to give their lives to Jesus Christ. He spoke most eloquently, and with sincerity, which I considered immeasurably superior to that of the two army chaplains who frequented the place. They spent most of their time sipping tea and chain-smoking. The Anglican one couldn't preach for toffee and, indeed, when he spoke, it seemed as if his mouth was full of marbles.

Within weeks I was back in Belfast; those spinsters having got me to Ballykinler under false pretences. I would soon see how the broad-minded worldling lived in marked contrast to the narrow-minded Christian. Yet the pleasures of the world held little lasting appeal and the fellowship of practicing Christians soon attracted. It seemed as if, in such a city, you were either one extreme or the other. Little respect seemed to be shown to 'middle of the road' respectability. While Clonard Monastery proselytised for the Roman Faith, the Baptists, Brethren, and Evangelical Presbyterians went all the way with the old time gospel. The former flirted with the world the latter frowned upon it.

On several journeys in a trolley bus, I became envious of a fellow no more than four years my senior who had the initiative I lacked. He would be in bondage to no man and solely responsible to God. This forceful preacher, though proudly attired in a garb similar to a Roman priest was, however, no lover of Rome and strangely enough, in later years, Ian Paisley would cross my path more than once. After training in Wales he'd acquired his own following within the Ravenhill area of that memorable city. He sought decisions for Christ while he also exposed the glaring superstitions of Rome. Knowing, for instance, of a multitude of RC chapels, which claimed to have parts of Our Lord's cross, a relic of the Virgin, or some other saint, he would allude to the multiplicity of these. Yes, he stood for the truth but his sarcasm and scorn stirred up the baser elements in those of the opposite camp.

Ian, largely self-appointed, was not, of course, on his own. Minnus Mills, a Baptist and a builder, had erected his own little centre. He was a self-styled pastor and was to inaugurate a thriving work at Orangefield. Minnus never wore the Roman collar. It was not the Irish Baptist's practice to do so, but he became conspicuous as the pastor with the bow tie, who had a big congregation in a tiny church. What was more, I sensed he also had a large heart and was out to help me. However, I soon ruined any chances at Orangefield because, at the closing of the afternoon Sunday school, a hymnbook, which had been scribbled on was shown to Norman, the secretary and Minnus, the pastor. Looking grave and extremely shocked towards each other, it was then handed for me to view as they looked for a reaction. It was the scribble of a little man with a very well endowed weapon! Well, being the kind of fellow I was, I just about burst my sides with a spontaneous laugh I couldn't suppress. So while they looked at each other, completely aghast, I speedily made a quick exit, never to return.

On several Sundays I attended another Baptist church, which I thought resembled a mission hall because of its school like forms rather than pews. Pastor Wilson had welcomed me warmly and told me of several churches which would soon be on the lookout for a young pastor. "But meanwhile, dear brother, you'll need a temporary job; and we'll make that a special priority at our prayer meeting." he said. Well, I thought: 'the Lord helps those who help themselves.' Anything would be better than joining the dole queues so I accepted the post of third projectionist in the luxurious Strand cinema. Indeed, to have secured a job at all was quite an achievement in those days. The only antagonism was towards folk who came from the south. "They're prepared" it was said, "to work for a pittance while they breed like rabbits!" The Protestant majority with their small families felt threatened and young men like Ian Paisley were warning of what could occur in Ulster, just as people - such as Enoch Powell, a decade later - would similarly warn of what could occur in Britain.

Well, a couple of weeks later I eagerly returned to Sabbath worship at Pastor Wilson's church. "The Lord has answered our prayers and I now have a job" I said. "Hallelujah, dear brother! What are you doing?" "Well, It's just temporary, but it's in a cinema," I said. He looked utterly aghast, literally turned his back on me and began conversing with other believers. 'Was his response really intentional?' I asked myself. 'Surely not!' Sadly, information was soon circulating which came back from a trusted source.: "It's the funniest joke I've heard in years" said a deacon, "A young man who claims to be saved, and is seeking a pastorate, works in a cinema!" The deacon's job was that of a butcher.

It had to be admitted, that the first night employed in the cinema industry had hardly been advantageous to spiritual growth. Indeed, my first impression of my cinema 'digs' was that they were little better than a brothel. As a lark, the landlady's rum daughter had shoved a nude statue under my bedclothes. Well, I can't say I objected to that. I could have put up with four letter words too, but I couldn't stomach the blasphemous remarks any more than the breakfast. The frying pan was black, gritty and full of fat from previous use. I felt more like vomiting than eating, and I could never swallow enough tea to stop the smoky fat from prolonging its taste on my palate, while to burp was to re-taste it all. Nevertheless, the conversation at the table was full of fun. When they constantly used the Saviour's name in blasphemy I was tempted to be a 'wet blanket' by saying, "Don't you realise you're speaking about my greatest friend?" I hadn't the guts to say this. If I had I wouldn't have been appreciated, so I did the easiest thing and got out the next day.

Within three months, due to a restless conscience heightened by the 'born again', I terminated my post at the cinema. I had no doubt the post would soon be taken. But all those men of God surely couldn't be wrong in denouncing the cinema world! 'Those who honour me, them will I honour,' said the good book and by the grace of God I would obey it. I then set out to visit a member of the Brethren who was a millionaire and ran a thriving furniture store in Sandy Row. Mr. Gilpin was delighted to learn of my step of faith. Though he couldn't make a job for me, he there and then gave me what must have been a highly substantial amount of money. "Come back whenever you require more!" he said. I sensed that he would have helped me to acquire a post if I'd identified myself with the Brethren. However, parts of their theology, such as that which taught 'Once Saved, Always Saved', one couldn't accept. I simply had to be true to God. Yet the gentleman at the local labour exchange had advised me personally to well consider them. "There's a saying in Belfast it may well be worthwhile for a young man like you to consider. It is this: 'If you can't join the Masons then join the Brethren!" Well, while dining one day with a Brethren family, a marital row occurred and I undiplomatically took sides with the wife and, as a consequence, was told to get out by the husband. Later, things were soon patched up and apologies exchanged. But it had been enough to convince me that so many hot gospellers are frequently spiritual schizophrenics. Indeed, I myself was a young man of extremes; so on being informed of a mission to be held that night in the Church of the Most Holy Redeemer, attached to Clonard Monastery, I was soon amongst the crowds outside this large edifice off the Falls Road. Several stalls selling novelties were erected in the precincts and coloured lights were displayed around the entrance. From the loudspeakers hymns such as 'Soul of my Saviour', 'I'll sing a hymn to Mary' and 'Hail, Holy Queen' were being sung. Was it any wonder that the next day I was ringing the bell of the monastery door to continue instruction in Ireland from where I'd left off in Wales?

The door opened and I was escorted down a beautifully scrubbed and polished corridor, and then ushered into a small side room. Father Arthur was undoubtedly a wonderful priest, quietly spoken, taking everything in through eyes, which were not unlike those of a Chinaman. "Before we discuss religion, I think you could do with a nice meal," he remarked, whereupon I was taken to the refectory where a lay brother kindly and graciously waited upon me. Later, the priest pushed a couple of pounds into my hand and advised me to return to the Strand cinema and ask to be reinstated. "There is no harm at all in working in a cinema," he said. "I enjoy the films myself." Well, who's right? I asked myself. "Oh my!" said Victor, "you've got mixed up again with Rome. They'll never rest until they make you ten times more a child of the Devil than they are themselves. God forbid that you should ever become a Mickey. You could now contaminate my house and family. Oh, it's all very sinister!"

Father Arthur was exceptionally generous and suggested in return, that rather than be idle, work could be done no doubt for a little remuneration, helping out at the Old Black Hen pub. "Don't be astonished, but offer your services to the odd character who runs it. He may be able to help you."

Eventually I arrived at a quaint, dilapidated pub on the very corner of two streets, an area that was near enough in parts to slum property. One felt the pub was really no more than an old-fashioned off-licence corner shop. The stable door was opened at the top, and one could see behind the dark counter a row of beer barrels with taps added to them. From out of the shadows came a burly Irishman complete with a black patch over one eye. As he approached he seemed to be muttering curses under his breath. "What do you want?" he asked. "Father Arthur wondered if you could offer me a job, possibly helping in the cellar," I replied. "Has the priest gone mad?" he asked, "Is this some kind of a joke he is playing? Tell the priest I've no job for you here," he added. "He must be stupid - typical of a bloody priest. He's getting at me because I haven't been to Mass. Can't he see me himself instead of sending a young lad?" Father Arthur was keen to know the kind of response I received. "Yes, I thought he'd be like that," he said, "I hope you didn't mind going."

On another occasion, an attempt was made to secure work at a cinema owned by a couple of devout Roman Catholics. The Clonard was an eerie old building, even more so than the Diamond nearby. One ascended a high staircase to get into the tiny projection booth, but no work was forthcoming, though the couple were truly delightful.

An interesting place in which to pass the time philanthropically was in the Star of the Sea hostel down the Falls Road. Here it was that a rather eccentric Frenchman cared for the down-and-outs. His name was Mr. Deeong, Well, if that was how you spell it! Amongst the dust and between the old beds, on ledges or tables, several statues had little blue or red lights flickering in front of them. The French gentleman was most mannerly, and very helpful though not a little erratic and nervy. It was here that loaves, large ones, were cut into no more than five slices. They fed the hungry, poor souls who lived there, as well as others who walked in for warmth and shelter from the streets.

Yes, there was a romantic atmosphere about the Catholic district and the old St Mary's church was regularly frequented so that I might kneel before the Blessed Sacrament to offer devotions. The more such devotion was practised, the more spiritual blessing was derived and, at times, I actually began to believe in Christ's presence within the tabernacle. The precincts of that particular church, however, were a haven for beggars and scroungers. These would glance away from the statue of the Virgin and offer to say a special prayer for you if you would give them some money, supposedly for a bite of something and a cup of tea.

In marked contrast, the Protestant areas of the city seemed to breed a different type. Though sometimes poor they would have been reluctant to beg, yes, and as reluctant to gamble or possibly booze. Their places of worship were contrastingly only opened for services and gospel meetings. They were often drab buildings with mere benches, and a raised rostrum to the front. The only exception to size I saw was St Anne's cathedral. Though it provided a place for devotion I sensed it lacked atmosphere and ornamentation; an architectural shell but, for me, void of the numinous.

To return one day to my new lodgings, that were truly superb, and casually inform my landlady, Mrs. Scott, that I was taking a course of instruction for the Roman Catholic faith was equivalent to dropping a bomb on her. The normally placid soul flew into a hysterical rage. She became livid, and was actually undecided as to whether or not I would immediately have to get out. This dear, lovable soul knew very little about either Faith, but to switch one's Faith was to her mind the mark of a traitor and that's what she called me in no uncertain terms. Thankfully, within a few hours she was as placid and caring as ever.

Father Arthur was truly sympathetic when he learned of my ordeal. He advised me never again to mention my leanings towards Catholicism while in Belfast. However, there was undoubtedly a Catholic link and bond, which went on beneath the surface of everyday living. This priest truly went out of his way to help me, even though my unemployment was due to acting on the advice of evangelical Protestant ministers. Whereas they would now merely keep me at the door and promise to remember me at the prayer meeting, this dear man of God furnished me with a confidential letter addressed to a prominent person in the employment exchange. The outcome was that I was welcomed privately by a top man and had refreshments thrown in. However, the only immediate offer of employment to follow was in an establishment where almost every sentence spoken by the interviewer included a blasphemy, and this I just couldn't have tolerated. Remarkably, this prospective employer was a loyal son of the Holy Church! Was it hardly surprising that a Belfast priest had recently spoken from his pulpit of the appalling lack of respect shown for the Saviour's name amongst the whole Catholic community?

My inability to acquire work compatible with my desire to share it with Jesus, and the recent hostility from my wonderful landlady, resulted in a decision to return home to my neglected mother. The dear priest appeared sad to learn of it. He knew, however, that my mind had been made up and he sadly said goodbye. I would never again see that strange, yet most gracious monk. His last words to me were, "Don't be too eager to resume instruction when you return home. There is plenty of time." For several months I would wear around my neck the little medal he had given me. It was called a miraculous medal, and it contained these words: 'Oh, Mary conceived without sin pray for us who have recourse to Thee!'

That beautiful church building briefly was visited for the last time. After my period of instruction with that caring priest in the monastery itself I would enter the adjacent church and offer a prayer. Yes, within the large, impressive twin-spired edifice of that Redemptorist community, there were contained two priceless treasures well worth witnessing: part of the true cross of the Saviour (a strange coincidence, I thought, that St Winefride's in Holywell should have another part), and also a relic of St Gerard Majella. The latter was displayed openly for veneration and, wonder of wonder it was still seen to be bleeding. Ah, if only I could have believed it all.

Which Is It To Be? You Can't Be Both!

Returning to Holywell was truly pleasant. Whereas the voyage out from Liverpool had been exceptionally boisterous, the return was as calm as a pond and, what was more, I'd acquired a berth. Mother had very much missed her unusual son and, as employment was so difficult to procure in Belfast, returning home had obviously been the wisest thing to do.

Soon I was pestering Mr. Williams to reinstate me as a printer, but all to no avail. Night after night, I would help him, temporarily, whenever urgent jobs came in hand. Work was usually accompanied by singing delightful songs of those far off years, many of them made famous by that singing cowboy, Gene Autry. The boss would start off the singing and we would join in. They often spoke volumes to one's heart. Our favourite was undoubtedly, 'Jeannine, I Dream of Lilac Time'. The other two favourites were 'Let Me Call You Sweetheart' and Ivor Novello's 'Shine Through My Dreams'. Such songs were expressive of a pure, clean romanticism, which was more akin to the spiritual rather than the sensual. It is a quality, which is now so much lacking. Women, in that delightful 'Well town', were held in very high respect and in that small establishment they received a great deal. They were often the focal point of love, but hardly ever of lust!

Reinstatement as a postman was not difficult and, though twenty years of age, I was also the 'telegram lad'. I had more than once cause to regret this. I had been known to put urgent telegrams into my pocket for several days, as the mind was more concerned with heavenly matters than down to earth ones. The resulting ordeals of being reprimanded on two occasions by the chief postmaster were something horribly deflating for many weeks to follow. Indeed, whereas urgent telegrams failed to be delivered because of absent-mindedness, the casting down a mineshaft of dozens of Vernons and Littlewoods pools coupons was deliberate. It was reminiscent of the Belfast Protestant temperament, which associated gambling with the Devil. Such rationalisation saved one from having to make a tedious journey on several 'howling wet' days merely to deliver to outlandish farms football coupons, for which, in fact, most people hadn't even applied. Consequently, part of the morning's round was associated with prayer and a glimpse or two at the pocket Bible; an occasional furtive glance round might occur when passing a disused mine shaft. This would then be followed by a bunch of coupons being speedily dispatched down old workings. These workings were quite numerous. They were fenced round on all sides; all that remained on the surface of these lead mines.

News that the young lay preacher had just returned home resulted in a trickle of preaching invitations arriving. Several scattered Bethels of the Welsh countryside opened their pulpits to me and, oh, how delightful and truly idyllic so many of them were. Hardly a fortnight had elapsed, however, when I came face to face with the dear Dutch priest walking up the High Street. He was most anxious to know why I had ceased the course of instruction so many months earlier. On being told of my staying in Belfast he expressed surprise; though a slip of the tongue later made it obvious that he had been informed of my presence there!

I couldn't help but like this priest and within a week, I had resumed instruction. But now, it was not so much from him as from a new curate under him who was a convert from the Protestant world. The Dutch priest considered this more appropriate. This new instructor had none of the finesse of the older man. He was cockney and proud of it. The dear man murdered the King's English in the pulpit and obviously had been taught nothing whatever about sermon construction or biblical exegesis. However, he was a qualified priest with seven years training behind him, and I truly coveted his position. So once again - possibly snatching at straws - I threw my lot in with the Roman church. I was delighted when the older priest repeated what he'd said to the vicar-general on seeing me that first time: "I feel we have a future Cardinal Newman in our midst!" It may have been no more than flattery, but no Protestant cleric had commended me in such a fashion.

The curate, being a convert, seemed extra zealous and, on learning of my library of around eighty religious works, suggested they be handed over as heretical and dangerous literature. Indeed, to read or leave around any religious work, which did not have the Roman stamp of approval on it -the Imprimatur -, was to be guilty of mortal sin. Consequently, although It was a great sacrifice to part with these books, the zealous priest felt I'd scored quite a victory when, with mixed feelings, I handed them over to him. He said they might well end up for selected scrutiny at the local monastery!

However, this was not the only sacrifice I would have to make: a more difficult one swiftly followed. Having turned down several preaching requests I was now approached for yet another. It was to be guest preacher at a special anniversary service in the Ffynnongroew Congregational Church: a nonconformist chapel dedicated to St Andrew. Nevertheless, as a prospective convert to Catholicism - whose date of reception had been fixed for over a month ahead - I very much sensed that I would be forbidden to accept the engagement. It came, therefore, as some surprise to learn the possibility of a worthy alternative. Did I not know my apologetics and Catholic doctrine? Could I not point from appropriate Scriptures to the existence of but One Holy Church, visible, infallible, and founded on Peter?

"Could not such an occasion be used as the final time to enter a Protestant place of worship? ... As its preacher, could you not affirm from the pulpit that you are now leaving to enter the one and only true church, outside of which there can be no salvation?" The priest was keen! ... "Yes, the result might create one big hullabaloo; but think of the publicity it would create and the soul-searching that could follow!" Such were the kind of words this eager cleric uttered. "I'm not asking you to do it, It's just a possibility you might like to consider. You certainly wouldn't be the first". And once more reference was given to the life of Newman!

Well, this zealous 'reverend father' could have mentioned nothing better to the ears of a young man who though sincere, was far from averse to the sin of pride. As the date for the preaching appointment drew nearer, a spiritual battle began raging within: I could be hailed by the curious Catholic community should I go ahead with this scheme; but I would have betrayed simple chapel folk void of guile. 'Is this the way Jesus would have worked to get converts?' I asked myself. It turned out to be more than a relief, indeed an inward blessing, when the young priest rode up to our home on the Friday evening, before the Sunday appointed, to say that the vicar-general very much commended my willingness, but could see snags that might ensue if it took place.

Well, there was not sufficient time to notify the chapel of my cancellation by letter. The memory is vague. I certainly can't remember visiting them. Perhaps I wouldn't have had the guts to. The posters would have been distributed. Poor souls, on turning up for the anniversary service, they may have waited and waited. Maybe some deacon would have taken it upon himself to step in and just do his best on the inspiration of the moment. Remarkably, the memory haunts me still! At that time, perhaps, letting down those I was starting to associate with heresy could have been sufficient justification in itself. Or could it?

Within a week or two things were to come to a head, which very much affected my course: this was in 1950. It was the year when the Catholics commemorated the centenary of the restoration of the Roman hierarchy within England and Wales, and made the assumption of Mary a dogma binding on the faithful. Big events had been planned especially in Holywell, because it was the Lourdes of Wales. Indeed, not only did this Catholic centre have its miraculous well and its relic of Winefride -part of her finger for daily veneration - but I dare say of even more importance, they had part of the actual cross of Jesus Himself. You'll remember I'd witnessed another part of it back at Clonard where young Ian Paisley had once said outside that, if all these bits were put together, one would have enough wood to remake Noah's Ark!

The great day came to Holywell when pontifical High Mass was to be celebrated in the presence of His Eminence, the Apostolic Delegate. I'd wisely acquired a pew at least one and a half hours before the worship actually began. However, once it did commence I felt oppressively claustrophobic, hemmed in by numerous poor, semi-illiterate devotees from Merseyside. They were jingling their rosary beads and grovelling almost on all fours after the asperges (sprinkling of holy water preceding the Mass) had passed round the aisles. Then a corpulent cleric, a delegate to the Holy See (Rome), appeared to be venerated as if almost divine. Whereas I'd expected to find a man radiant with the glory of God, I considered this prelate to be less handsome than the late Mussolini though not unlike him. I imagined oneself to be surrounded by lurking spirits. Once the service was over, and I was outside, I truly felt as if I'd left an abode of Dracula. The incense, which I normally loved, had been extremely overpowering as if to make the atmosphere deliberately sinister, and the organist had chosen to play the heaviest and harshest of church music which was more in keeping with Dracula's castle than with a meeting of Christ's children.

About this time, and possibly to coincide with this Catholic celebration, a Protestant lecture within the local town hall was once again given. It was under the auspices of what was termed the Protestant Truth Society. John, a dear printer friend, a Liverpudlian and an Orangeman, had informed me of it. Well, having spent a considerable amount of time reading booklets from the back of Catholic churches called 'Catholic Truth', I was only too eager to acquire further information from the other side, particularly as I no longer had any books of my own. Well, such books proved most enlightening and confirmed many of my suspicions. Some certainly sounded extreme. If 'The Awful Disclosures Of Maria Monk' appeared questionable, Pastor Chiniquy's '50 Years In The Church Of Rome' did not; while a more recent book: 'The Popes And Their Church' by Joseph McCabe appeared to confirm the worst.

I'd gradually come to the conclusion that Rome was one of two things: the one true church outside of which there is no salvation, all others being heretics; or else she must be a counterfeit, sufficient, if possible, to deceive God's elect; yet with intensely sincere worshippers within her. For had not God said: "Come out of her my people!" Had not the priest himself used words akin to Newman's in order to convey that there could be no half way? "The claims the Holy Church makes for herself, if not true, must be nothing short of utter blasphemy". Yes, I was convinced of such logic. As a young man I'd recently wrestled for hours in prayer over this. I longed for God to show me the next step to take.

Well, the atmosphere during that Pontifical Mass, plus the supposed indulgence of a whole period less in Purgatory conferred by the corpulent cleric, had brought me to a speedy decision: Roman Catholicism, though as alluring as an Elysian siren, regardless of her trinketry and mysterious rites, was far removed from what she, at that 'pre. Vatican two' era, so haughtily claimed for herself. She was not supreme, and neither were the worshipping Protestant communities heretical! To enter other places of Christian worship was not a major sin but frequently a means of untold blessing. Consequently, I avidly purchased publications from this newly introduced Protestant Truth Society, decided to build up a new library, and relinquished going for Catholic instruction.

A myth was then prevalent that Rome would never 'push' for any convert and, indeed, her attitude was at times contemptuously arrogant. Nevertheless, the moment my instructor knew that his prospective convert had lost interest; he became as persistent on the knocker as a Jehovah's Witness. The sound of his auto-cycle approaching resulted in even Mother - who was renowned for her straightness – agreeing with me not to answer the door. But then, what followed from such unsuccessful visits resulted in both of us wanting to leave the district. Hurtful attitudes and occasional remarks were being muttered from isolated Catholic quarters, not only against myself, which I most probably well deserved to receive, but against Mother.

Looking back with hindsight, it was obvious that the young priest had been sorely humiliated and, via the grapevine, several members of the Catholic community were not unaware of this. Amongst these were two young Irish spinsters of an exclusive inward beauty. Yes, regular worshippers at weeknight Rosary and Benediction, where I'd been cajoled in to 'taking up' the collection and had almost slipped back, with the full plate, on the highly polished floor. Mother was equally snubbed in a Newsagent's, though she had wanted no say at all in the matter.

That my grandparents, at Newcastle-upon-Tyne, should have felt no longer fit to look after themselves, and had sent a letter asking if Mother and I would care to move there to live with them, seemed an absolute blessing in disguise. "I'm not religious like you are Jim; but the hand of God surely seems to be in this; and at a most appropriate time!" affirmed Mother. So now, after eleven years in glorious Wales we would move to the city of my birth. There, Mother would care for my aged grandparents and I, in my religious searching, would bring yet more headaches into her sad life. Yet it seemed she would radiate a smiling face down to the very end of her life. What a wonderful mother!

A Newcastle Protest & Then Off To London

Selfishness and irresponsibility in a man of twenty had proven most apparent. For when my widowed mother needed me most, I availed myself of the opportunity to go to yet another Bible College. Mother would not be a burden to me! This time it would be down in London. Mercifully all the training would be free, but the condition, which I would later fail to keep, was that, on the termination of the two year course, one would normally be expected to travel round exposing the schemes and errors not only of Rome, but more so of Anglo-catholicism. Indeed, the offer of such a course with this Protestant society was basically due to their becoming aware of a Lutheran-like protest against idolatry, which I'd recently staged on having arrived on Tyneside. It took place within a high spired Anglican church less than two miles from my grandparent's house.

At the far end of Westmorland Road, nearest to the town, there stood this spiky church dedicated to St Mary the Virgin. In the past year the vicar had been defrocked and was now serving a two year prison sentence for homosexual misconduct towards young choir boys. A more mature priest had taken his place. This man also was of spiky and ritualistic persuasion, and I was more than horrified to find that the doctrine of transubstantiation was professed. This was, at that time, in strict contradiction to the doctrines of the Church of England as set out in its confession of faith, the 39 articles of the Book of Common Prayer.

Upon these articles each priest had to swear strict allegiance at his ordination. Well, when a sacristy bell was rung thrice, the bread and wine being elevated in Romish style for actual worship and adoration. I simply had to protest! If there were any truth in transubstantiation at all, I'd reasoned, then only a priest in valid orders could perform it!. Anglican orders were unanimously considered by Rome as invalid because of a broken line of Episcopal succession at the Reformation.

To worship what Ian in Belfast had previously called a miniature pancake - as God! – must surely be brazen idolatry? Consequently, I got to my feet and roared at the top of my voice: "This is idolatry within the Church of England; this is contrary to the Book of Common Prayer. It is an illegal act and is breaking the second commandment!"

Indeed, hardly had I finished these words than did two gentlemen gently ask me if I'd kindly mind leaving the church. I agreed and was very courteously escorted to the door; outside of which I felt as if I could have danced or cried with joy. The blessing that came was indescribable. I sensed I'd honoured God in line with Wycliffe, Luther Cranmer, Latimer, and so many more. Indeed, I felt so proud of the honour I'd shown to God that – on reaching ones new home - I foolishly informed my mother and grandparents. Indeed, it would appear as if one had dropped a bomb! They appeared fearful and horror struck. Throughout the Sunday dinner they even anticipated the heavy knock of a policeman on the font door; but, of course, it never came.

Such a protest had been 'chewed over' for some time, following a visit to a High Anglican church in the city centre. For here it was that one had discussed with the Vicar a possibility of entering the Anglican ministry via Mirfield or Kelham college courses. "My dear I can certainly help you. You've come to the right one! Let us sit down together dear!"

He hutched up close on the pew; and though I hardly minded the affectionate term of dear, he went on to say. "Your first step, dearie, is to come to Confession, for a young man like you, dearie, must have much to confess!" Well, when he then squeezed my thigh, breathed heavily and asked me to call him Ian my suspicions were aroused.

Fortunately, at that point, a lady in deep distress approached him with heavy sobs, so I used the opportunity to get up and distance myself. He appeared to want me to wait at one side. Well, as I walked away, this short corpulent cleric now glared through his round rimmed specs at me. His hand was fumbling in his cassock pocket as he whispered: "What you need is a good whipping!" Yes, my suspicions had well and truly been confirmed; and one was hardly surprised to learn later that the defrocked past vicar of the church where I made my protest had been his previous curate!

One fact was now clear: the Anglo-catholic priesthood - quite unlike the Roman priesthood it largely aped – possessed an over abundance of flaunting homosexuals. Consequently, awaiting the commencement of the college term at the Protestant Truth Society in Finchley, London, I considered sampling the far healthier, and morally superior, world of Tyneside Nonconformity. Indeed, I couldn't have chosen a better temporary spiritual home than the first one visited: the Wycliff Baptist church along Elswick Road. It was truly a beautiful place with a cheery, round-faced young minister whose one concern was to do business for God. As with others of his persuasion there was nothing furtive, scheming or effeminate about him. Frank Applin was as open as his face, and his Faith was just as bright and cheerful. I remember well the first morning I attended his church.

Though past memories of the three months undergone at the Glasgow Bible Training Institute were certainly mixed, I was still not averse to wearing their blazer badge for it served as an evangelical witness. Well, it so happened that even from the far off elevated pulpit, the cheery pastor had noticed the same, and on entering the vestibule at the close of worship he gave me the kind of welcome that only a cheerful saint of his persuasion could confer. It was the beginning of a comparatively short yet happy friendship. Short because the church itself was not as evangelical as its pastor, and though Frank's gifts were enormous his preaching was not at all his most redeeming point. Be that as it may, he immediately remarked on the BTI as a place of profound learning which he as a past chartered accountant and now a bona fide non-collegiate minister would love to have sampled. Through him I would later be inundated with requests to take Sunday services in North Shields, South Shields and Alnwick Baptist churches as well as in Newcastle.

As for our new home surroundings, Mother soon felt that she and I were now little better than lodgers in my grandparents' home in Elswick. This was in marked contrast to Wales. Yes, I remember Brunel Terrace as if it were merely yesterday: sloping steeply upwards from Scotswood Road, which was now truly notorious for its slums. At the top of this terrace stood the gracious Catholic church of St Michael and a little below it I can still visualise infants who were often terrified of the nuns at that school, should they happen to arrive within the yard once the bell had already rung and the rest of the children had been ushered into the building. It was interpreted by some that, whereas most of the teaching sisters were kind and gracious, others were utterly sadistic. Grandmother had shed many a tear for those helpless, sometimes-barefoot 'bairns' quaking outside in the play yard.

At the foot of this once distinguished terrace, another large church was situated, for if the top of the slope typified Catholicism then the bottom of it was the epitome of Protestantism: St Stephen's was renowned for its high spire which was constantly under constructional repair. The gracious building had a cold interior, wide and spacious. It was 'North End' Protestant in worship! No fear of any Popish innovation here! Yet it might well have benefited by the warmth and homeliness a few lighted candles would have conveyed. The church was attended twice but not frequented a third time. The formal acknowledgement received on leaving, from an incumbent with a traditional Anglican voice, was not likely to draw one into its fellowship. I sensed his manner was reminiscent of a headmaster, and such characters had left an unpleasant taste.

Mother, bereft of her husband, and her elder son living away, was soon left to tend her ailing parents. The commencement of my session at Wycliffe Bible College drew near. Word had been circulated concerning my church protest, and the college body - particularly old Mr. Kensit himself - were most eager to welcome me into their midst.

'a ramshakle van'.

Alas, for quite a different reason this time, the course would again last no more than one solitary term. It was to be my own decision and very much against the wishes of the principal! There was not only my own incompatibility with the college warden, who was a fiery, ardent Pentecostalist and an ex-miner, but I was so much of a dreamer that in the midst of group conversations, I would occasionally be brought to reality by the uncouth bawling of his voice directed at me to pay attention. I was not prepared to tolerate this for two years (well, certainly not on meeting a female!), and lacked the strength of character to tell him where to get off. Yet, paradoxically, I could never thank this 'rough diamond' enough for broadening out the Scriptures to me. The warden gave me my first driving lessons in a ramshackle van Yes, with much patience and humour Mr Gautry taught me the art of double-declutch: a real necessity in those far off days.

Accepted As A Kensitite, And Then Engaged

Three months can seem an eternity when one has barely reached twenty-one, and those days are still vivid with many glorious experiences. The college and its grounds were a marked contrast to that grimy, grotesque Bible training establishment attended previously in the centre of busy, smoky Glasgow. Here, the Finchley air along Hendon Lane was pure and clean. One could listen again to the song of birds, and, walking round the spacious grounds or along the lanes, one could make time to converse with one's Maker and one's God. The students in this spacious, bright building numbered, for this term, no more than six. This afforded one plenty of personal tuition from a Mr Ashdown. He taught Church History in a far more interesting and vivid manner than the writer would ever subsequently experience. These lectures were not factual lists of occurrences, as Mr Ashdown made many of those martyrs live again. Love emanated from his eyes as well as from his voice! He had a pleasant wife, and an attractive daughter one could not fail to notice even though she was still a schoolgirl.

As an added source of remuneration, part of the downstairs of the college was used as a kindergarten school. Amongst the mothers who brought along their little girls was none other than the renowned Forces sweetheart, Vera Lynn. Some of the students would have occasion to speak to her. One could hardly come across a more unassuming, sweet and friendly soul.

Sunday tea was a prominent occasion. It was there that Mr Kensit and his wife invited others into their flat. We all shared in the family meal together. Not only were none in the establishment excluded, but any who wished to be excused had to offer a very good reason. Stout Mr Kensit always proved a jovial old fellow who relished telling such stories as that of his father being martyred by 'Romanists' in Liverpool, or of his own travels around Rome and within the Vatican itself The numerous nails of the cross, the chains of Peter, the bumps in rock caused by the apostle's head; or the aerial journeys of the holy house of Nazareth, the various phials containing the blood of Jesus or the milk from Mary. These were the kind of subjects he delighted to enlarge upon. Humour was always high. Though the dear man was Calvinistic in doctrine one could never have called him a killjoy. One simply warmed to this aged yet most likeable fellow of wit, dignity and eccentricity.

There were occasions when jokes uttered and practised by the students became morally questionable. Some students in a particular prayer meeting asked God for forgiveness for having nicknamed the principal 'Old Double Belly'! The situation certainly wasn't improved when the most sensitive of them 'felt led of God' to inform the principal of the nickname they'd previously given him. "Well, dear Blackburn, I suppose young men will make fun out of an old man!" he replied.

Needless to say this most open student hardly appeared in a favourable light amongst the rest. Walter, for that was his name, had come from a very humble yet caring background in Lancashire, and his great love of Jesus was clear for all to see. This Pentecostal brother believed in thanking God for everything. Nothing had to be excluded. When relief came after several weeks of persistent constipation he just couldn't keep it to himself. At the prayer meeting – "Praise the Lord, I've done it. I've passed a stool. Glory to Jesus!" he cried. The distinct possibility of entering hospital had been averted. Yes, even in a Christian establishment a weaker brother can become the focal point for fun. One evening the waxwork effigy of a martyr's head was placed under the same student's pillow. Walter was of a nervous disposition and consequently let out such a loud, shrill shriek on retiring to bed, it reverberated along the corridors.

The short period spent at Kensit's College became a marvellous eye-opener to the forms of Catholic propaganda used, much of which other Christians were totally ignorant. To see with one's very eyes booklets of a religious nature identical in layout and style, apart from title and cover, was to become aware of the liaison that sometimes existed between the High Anglicans and the Romans. "The harlot of the apocalypse has an active daughter," they said, "within the English establishment!" As for any who might have viewed such ultra-Protestantism as bigotry, books such as Walsh's Secret History of the Oxford Movement were readily available. So was Blakeney's Manual of Romish

Controversy. Having two years previous studied a reputable Roman publication of two volumes, Gill's Apologetics and Catholic Doctrine, I was now able to study in equal depth writings from the opposite extreme. Indeed, Foxe's Book of Martyrs now superseded Butler's Lives of the Saints. As for some of the contents in a manual for father confessors, what they sought to illicit from children, as well as married women, were enough to make one blush, and I was no angel! .Future prospects looked great, I knew, should I complete the course, and, after a period of practical work on the caravans, every opportunity would be given to do a brief course as a mature student in an Anglican theological college such as Oakhill, Tyndale or Clifton. But whereas students had used Kensit's course as a stepping-stone into the Church of England ministry, several others were immediately accepted and ordained into one of two Episcopal English churches recently merged into one. It now formed 'the Free Church of England.

The college course, was most intensive and weekends were eagerly anticipated as the Saturday afternoon and early evening were free. This had enabled me to walk quite a few miles round the vicinity and this included Hendon. It had provided an opportunity to visit some churches as well as frequent a peculiar American religious community, which possessed the strange name 'The Pillar of Fire'. Indeed, this delightful American monastic-like structure was as much opposed to the dogmas of Rome, as was the Kensit's Protestant Truth Society. The only difference was that the former was Armenian in theology while the latter was predominantly Calvinist. Little did I then realise that I would again visit this religious community at Hendon, in quite a different role, three years later.

While Saturdays were occasions for free time from study and work (and we all had chores to do such as gardening) Sunday evenings were equally and eagerly anticipated. Thanks to the warden and his lovely wife we were able to accompany them to several places of worship. One Sunday we visited the local Baptist church when the renowned Alan Redpath took the service. He was a non-collegiate minister who, having filled the small Baptist chapel at Richmond, was now using the local Odeon cinema for the evening services. How I longed to follow in his footsteps! Could not such a wonderful future one day await me? Some other Sunday evening services were far from inspiring: those who preached in the 'tin tab' within the very grounds of the college left much to be desired. One wondered why on earth they had ever taken to entering a pulpit at all! This dark building, which smelled, of wood was furnished with a wheezy harmonium, rostrum and forms. The preacher would often be sombre, attired in a pinstripe suit, stiff white collar and black tie. A large Bible would be carried, and it all seemed geared towards generating depression, morbidity and solemnity. A truly delightful contrast to such an utterly depressing hour and a half would be the singing of lively Pentecostal choruses, accompanied by the warden's concertina while we were sitting around the supper table afterwards!

Ah, but then there was one Sunday that had far-flung repercussions for the rest of my life; and should the warden have known about it, he would never have allowed the event to occur. The dear man, along with his wife, had been in the habit of attending the Wittington Hospital not all that very far away. On one of these particular Sundays we had all been given permission from the principal to visit the place. We were to take part in either distributing tracts or else in a short service that the warden and his wife were to hold in several of the wards. We were all equally convinced that these patients would endure a lost eternity unless they repented of their sins and got right with God by 'being saved'! That others needed the same experience around which our own lives were governed was something none of us could ever doubt. Nevertheless, though we were highly conversant with the threats and encroachments of Romanism – and mostly via Anglo Catholicism! - we usually felt that our first priority was to get 'the lost' converted to Christ before picking fault with any rival branch of Christendom.

While visiting the old Wittington Hospital it so happened that the warden had made the acquaintance of a young Pentecostal lady from Islington. He and his wife made the point of inviting her back for tea the following Saturday. Indeed, throughout the days that subsequently intervened, we were more than once warned about the oncoming visit of an extra guest for Saturday's tea table, and how we would need to be on our best behaviour. As for myself, I was eager to have a closer look at the privileged lady. It need hardly be said that when the day arrived she proved attractive and utterly charming. Indeed, so charming did she appear, that somehow -and without too much effort on my part -we found ourselves first of all having a stroll around the grounds and somehow this widened out to walking almost to Hendon and back! The warden was rightly annoyed that I'd monopolised their guest. Yet he was not without a great deal of humour when he told me that if I didn't watch my step she would be getting me to put a ring on her finger. I kept to myself for some time the fact that I'd already asked her for a date and that she'd gladly accepted. It was for the next Saturday.

Well, the week in front seemed to drag. When the eagerly anticipated afternoon arrived I've no doubt we had a wonderful time. One thing I can remember was that one or two 'ring shop' windows were momentarily stopped at, as the young lady was without doubt a lover of jewellery. But what seemed to occupy her interest far more was the desire to start up in business with her own dressmaking establishment. For the moment she was working for someone else. "Why shouldn't I start up, accumulating the profits for myself? Buy my own warehouse!" she said.

I remember the atmosphere on perhaps the most primitive of those tube lines, the Islington one. It took both of us to a station called Angel. There was a homely mustiness about the journey and, through the mist of bygone years; I faintly recollect the cage lift in contrast to the all too common escalators. On alighting, we grappled with the smog of the district and eventually came across a pub in the centre of Islington. Along the side of it, having climbed some stairs, I was pleased to make the acquaintance of a delightful working-class cockney couple the type who are the salt of the earth. They were the parents of my newfound girlfriend. Yes, I had a sweetheart at last! I was not alone. Someone else, as well as my dear mother, really loved me. It seemed so mutual! When I told her I liked her company she told me she liked mine. Later that evening it would seem as if spring was in the air even though I was returning to college via the smoggy streets of Islington.

Now the weekdays were to linger and drag as never before. Saturday lunchtime would eventually arrive, but then Saturday afternoon and evening would pass only too quickly. The few hours of ecstasy on those afternoons spent in the sunny streets of London suburbs are quite vague now and, try as I have done to remember young Hilda, she is now little more than a name, and even that was forgotten for many years! Such a temporary repression was no doubt a means of buffering me against a heartache almost too hard for a sensitive mind to consciously carry. It was not, however, to occur before she'd taken the initiative to choose her ring and pay for it. I, a penniless student, would then place it with an appropriate prayer upon the relevant finger of her left hand. Yes, it was an engagement ring, even though the romance was to last less than five months!

Those months were traumatic and far-reaching. During the romance we were not only to anticipate the formation of our own dressmaking establishment, in which I would be the representative and conveyor of the goods made, but these were also months in which, due to my nomadic walking of London streets on an occasional Saturday when Hilda wasn't free, I chanced to find the headquarters of a rival Protestant establishment to the Protestant Truth Society. The title was the National Union of Protestants. It was situated along Gloucester Road in Kensington. The secretary, Mr Perkins, was truly delighted to make my acquaintance. I would have to fulfil the two-year course to qualify as a Wycliffe preacher at Mr Kensit's establishment. Mr. Perkins would be prepared to offer me immediate free accommodation in his headquarters, providing I would assist in a voluntary capacity as an iconoclast. Papal objects and practices had been illegally and deviously introduced into several Anglican churches; they had to be removed or stopped. There would also be ample opportunity to spout regularly at speaker's corner as well as give lectures in sympathetic churches, chapels and city missions. However, there was one drawback; the Union were not in a position to offer me full-time remuneration, as they just hadn't the funds available. The secretary lived with his wife, Ruth, on a mere pittance within a pleasant suburban flat. What was I to do?

A visiting Baptist minister - a convert from the Anglican ministry, over baptism! – lectured weekly at the college on the art of speaking. He spoke of my emotional way of preaching to the extent that it could lead one to cry! "You must get rid of it" he said "and become strictly factual! Be your true self and do not ape some emotional Welsh preacher you may well have encountered in your past travels!" Well, the gracious man meant well, but I was not prepared to have anyone alter a style that congregations had so often commended me for. Consequently, after further clashes with the college warden - and even protesting about them to the principal with no lasting effect – Hilda and I talked about a united future together As the college term drew to its close for the short Christmas recess, I thereupon resolved not to return in the New Year.

The National Union of Protestants, based directly across from that epitome of High Anglicanism St Stephen's, Gloucester Road, had surely more to offer a man who couldn't wait to follow in the steps of Cromwell and couldn't see enough of his fiancée. I can still visualise a crisp winter evening at the close of that solitary term, and a visit made to the headquarters in Gloucester Road. I can still see before me that half-Spanish stalwart of Protestantism in the company of his delightful wife, dark and in every respect a real lady. I was, indeed, very privileged to spend one evening in their flat in the suburbs. Dear Ruth seemed at times to be in intense pain, which eventually passed. It was hardly a surprise to learn five years later of her tragic death through dreaded cancer. Though she was a married woman, and I saw her only twice, I felt that I could have loved her. She appeared so virtuous. My carrying a Bible, and daily wrestling in prayer, was not enough to ward off covetousness.

Christmas was spent with my beloved mother and grandfather at home in Newcastle. It was a sad Christmas. Grandma, whom I dearly loved, and who'd understood my spiritual inclinations more than the rest, had passed to her reward quite suddenly. Mother had found her as if knelt on the side of the bed praying, but she'd entered glory at last. She'd believed, through the revelation of a previous dream, that I would be instrumental in awful chains which had bound her being broken Grandma never forgot that dream. whereas, Granddad was not a believer and he opposed most of what I stood for. Yet he was normally a humorous and equally a cantankerous soul. I sensed he was, in every sense, an Alf Garnett of his day and Mother was left to care for him.

Though away from London for no more than three weeks, letters between Hilda and me were being sent and received every other day. Mother was so pleased and was eager to meet her, but fate – or rather divine providence! -   had decreed otherwise.

A Fickle Fiancée & A Fanatical Friend

The January weather arrived and a long distance journey in a cold unheated bus terminated at Victoria bus station. Soon I was ascending the steps of 54 Gloucester Road. It was a sturdy building, which housed those champions of British Protestantism. Indeed, their emblem of a Union Jack plus the words of Scripture, 'The righteous are as bold as a lion' summed up the fidelity and boldness of the cause. The staunch and fearless secretary warmly welcomed me into his office, and, during the conversation that followed, made me aware of a fellow who was a little older than myself. He was doing a truly courageous work for their cause over in Belfast. "I'd like you to meet Ian," he said. "I already have," I replied. "Then I'll take you upstairs and show you your room. Up to last week a converted nun, Miss Monica Farrel, occupied it. You must meet her before she goes to Australia on a tour" "I already have," I replied. "She filled a large hall when I was in Belfast!" Monica's story had been quite breathtaking. Though, when she had spoken of how several Romanists had tried to poison her because she'd not only become a Protestant but was now exposing the corruptions of their church, I had my doubts. The more outlandish her accounts, the more they had flocked to hear her. Ultra Protestants called her a godly lady – she might have been. Only eternity will tell! – But I was not impressed.

When we approached the top landing, the secretary looked a little disturbed and said, "Would you mind all that much, brother, if you shared a room with a fellow Christian? You don't have to, it's just a thought and it would save using an extra room." For myself I was only too pleased to acquiesce. Arnold seemed pleased but then he went on to tell me that this roommate was a Pentecostalist of a very fervent nature. 'You don't have to remain with him unless you wish to do so," he said.

I knocked at the door on the top landing where the roof sloped inwards, and, on receiving a request to enter, found myself staring across towards a bed. There sat on it, with rather piercing eyes protruding from a tall and bony frame, a sad looking undernourished soul. When I'd told him my mission he looked rather startled and then asked if I had sought secular employment. When I told him I had not, but would no doubt be getting work in one of the Lyon's coffee houses, his whole face lit up: "Don't work, brother, the Lord has sent you here! I have enough money for six months on me and we will share it together, provided you are prepared to fast and live meagrely like myself. "My stomach is empty, brother, through much fasting and abstinence; listen" said William. Then looking down to his abdomen he began to shake his stomach. I heard liquid swishing inside; "I think there must be something wrong there, brother! - besides, the old devil has really been afflicting me lately. However, we will overcome him by prayer and fasting!"

William Butterworth and I held several things in common: particularly an Armenian outlook on the gospel and a willingness to follow the example of a John Wesley or a William Booth should the Lord be leading us that way. Believing that we were living in the last days, the task of evangelism was considered so very urgent that Brother Butterworth considered that all 'born again' Christians should leave their jobs and take to converting the masses. If God had met the financial needs of a George Muller in Victorian England - one who had never begged for a penny, yet had established and run several orphanages - he would surely provide for us provided we were faithful.

I still remember how very tired I became that night due to the long journey on the coach from Newcastle to London. My eyes kept wanting to close and it was a relief when praying together came to its close. It was followed by a deep sleep. Suddenly I was being shaken awake. My eyes opened and the brightness of the early morning was now shining into the plainly furnished attic room. "It's time to get up, Brother James, and give glory to the Lord. Hallelujah! Praise God for a new day! 'This is the day which the Lord has made; we will rejoice and be glad in it'. Amen, brother!" Then, looking down at me and seeing that I was drifting off to sleep again, this dear Pentecostal room-mate cried out, "Don't let the Devil get in, brother: let's get down to what William Booth called 'Knee Drill' On your knees, brother, in prayer!"

"What time is it?" I asked. "Four o'clock, brother. We can pray, as did Wesley, until eight! Get up and discipline the flesh, brother. Keep the flesh well and truly under control," he continued. I was either too hypocritical to do so or perhaps I just didn't wish to hurt his feelings or dampen his ardour, but I could have gladly thrown something at him as well as sworn. But then, true enough, I felt all he said was biblical and because Christians were not as keen as he was the churches were only half full. Strangely enough, eight o'clock soon arrived, when Brother Butterworth each morning would go to a cupboard and bring out a packet of pressed dates. "These are very nourishing, brother, and in line with our task. I've no doubt they are Palestinian. They were certainly the fruit of which many of the prophets must have partaken'," he said. It was purely a matter of just eating enough to live. Pleasure derived from it savoured too much of pandering to the flesh and was not to be encouraged at any cost.

William later went to a drawer and from between some clothes brought out some silvery white material. It was old barrage balloon material of which there was then quite a surplus. This had been made into the form of a waistcoat by a dear sister in the Lord. On it was inscribed, upon both back and front, a biblical text. The words might well have been 'The wrath of God is at Hand' and 'Believe in the Lord Jesus Christ, and thou shalt be saved'. William was to fasten this strange affair round himself thereby displaying to others from back and front, through dazzling red letters, two important texts from the infallible book. "What do you think of it, brother?" he asked. On learning that I was quite impressed, he thereupon promised to get one made for me. I no doubt diverted his mind from such a kind offer, as I would have lacked the guts to wear it. To have told him so to his face would have resulted in being denounced as ashamed to confess Christ to the world.

One morning we divided a large bundle of gospel tracts between us and walked along Gloucester Road towards the shops of the fashionable West End. As we walked along I was highly embarrassed because William repeatedly shouted out biblical quotations. "Don't be ashamed, brother, do the same," he would say. On the rare occasions I did open my mouth, I would be much encouraged by him. "We must spur each other on in the Faith." he said.

That such a mission as ours should be viewed as eccentric, he stressed, was merely to imply that we were in line with the early Methodists and Quakers. If George Fox could have shouted out around Leicester: 'Woe to the bloody city!' why shouldn't we around London? Indeed, the corruptions of the fashionable West End were open for all to see. If the world was not ashamed to advertise through sandwich board types of publicity, as did many of the theatres, then why not the Christian? As we walked along, a youth, hardly left school, looked intently at the biblical text on my colleague's chest: 'Believe in the Lord Jesus Christ, and thou shalt be saved!' William's eyes lit up. Pointing towards the text he eagerly asked, "Are you interested in the message?" The young teenager affirmed he was. "Have you accepted Jesus?" The reply was in the negative. "Then, 'Behold, now is the accepted time; behold, now is the day of salvation'," said William. The young lad was truly cornered. "We'll pray together now, the three of us. We may never see each other again!"

Although it's very many years ago, I still remember that scene. We faced each other while Brother Butterworth and I commended the young lad's soul to God. "Now in your own words thank God you are saved," said William. The young man said something. "Hallelujah! The Lord bless you!" replied William. We then left the young convert, believing that the Spirit was leading us elsewhere.

The hours of that day were passing and we were both feeling the pangs of hunger. It was an embarrassment when my colleague referred to a high-class vegetarian restaurant to which we could go. "They may not appreciate our dining there because of the way I'm attired," he said, "but our money is as good as anyone else's and it will be an opportunity to witness." If I remember correctly the entrance was slightly off Kensington High Street and, as we pushed through the swing doors, palm trees seemed to surround the place while tail-coated waiters were hustling about. A gentleman, busily enjoying his soup, raised his head but, when he saw William, he spluttered and spilt some of it. As I turned towards William he was pointing to the print across his chest and saying to the man: "Are you interested?" 'Oh that the ground might swallow me up,' I thought. The manager appeared, as if from nowhere, and refused to serve us. He rocketed us out in a couple of minutes. "Have you ever come across such conviction before?" asked my colleague. "Obscene adverts, and suggestive underwear is openly displayed down the escalator tubes as well as on theatre hoardings. And these cause no offence whatever! 'But the word of the Lord is sharper than any two edged sword', brother" said William. Yes, the word of God convicts to the core! I reasoned. Though one part of me could have burst out in laughter the other part was much impressed by William's tremendous courage - a courage, which previously he'd expressed single-handed.

On another occasion the call of nature necessitated William asking the commissionaire of the Odeon if he could use their toilet. The commisionaire agreed, but on his way out William asked the man whether he was 'right with God'. Well, if this wasn't embarrassment enough, greater was yet to follow.

The venue in view for one afternoon was a pedestrian island halfway across a busy thoroughfare situated near Victoria station. A miniature, resembling Big Ben, was placed there in those days. To arrive at our destination it was necessary to travel on the underground and, whatever hour it happened to be, this was obviously a London rush hour. The tube train we boarded was full, and William and I had difficulty squeezing ourselves into the end of a compartment. Hardly had the train moved out from the station when Brother William felt the urge to preach the Word. "I feel led, brother, and I mustn't be ashamed." It was no use trying to restrain him: so I waited with hidden glee for the reaction. "Repent and turn to Jesus!" he cried. "Boo... Woe.... Shame...." came the response, reverberating down the length of the compartment. A beam and sparkle seemed to emanate from very many faces. Poor Brother Butterworth was instantly silenced. As for myself, I longed to get back to relate the incident to Arnold Perkins; but first of all the day's mission had to be completed.

Leaving Victoria station the little clock on the island soon became visible and, true enough, two shabbily dressed, middle-aged creatures were holding forth 'the word of salvation' to the hell-bent sinners passing by. I shook hands with the Pentecostal sister. She smelt strongly of BO. Through her unlovely teeth, or what remained of them, she told of her task in proclaiming the full gospel, four square, to the unconverted masses. She and her male colleague were also attired in barrage balloon waistcoats to which texts were appended. In fact, she'd made William's. Though her sincerity was as deep as his she was not as cultured or as clean as he. Hers was the voice and courage of a cockney, with the message of an evangelist. 'Good God, I've ended up with a couple of mucky loonies!' I said to myself. I could hardly get away quickly enough lest I be identified with them.

During one of the evenings that followed my return to London, having been across to Islington to spend time with my fiancée, a row ensued between us because of her consuming desire to be baptised in the Spirit and speak in tongues. Over the weeks I'd seen her becoming more excitable, nervier, and seriously neurotic through an urge to manifest this gift of gibberish. For this - according to the theology she followed! - would confirm that she had been immersed (baptised) into the Holy Spirit. After a row following such an excitable and frenzied meeting, the rift between us widened. Being 'puffed up' by biblical knowledge, my own pride worsened the situation; yet to sever our, relationship was the one thing I had no intention of doing. Had I not terminated college and returned to London so as to be with her?

That evening, following the row, which had even resulted in her taking off the ring, I sought to make amends. On leaving Marble Arch tube station as midnight was approaching, I made a phone call to her. This was before making the journey on foot to Kensington because I had missed the final connection. The call was of no avail. She was now adamant in her intention of never seeing me again and, of course, the more I grovelled the happier she was to refuse me. In a fiery temper I ultimately slammed down the receiver as hard as I possibly could, and the mouthpiece literally broke into fragments. I was heartbroken. I made my long and weary night stroll back to Gloucester Road. Creeping up the long spiral stairs, worn out, wet and weary, the door to the shared room was quietly opened. To my astonishment William Butterworth was still awake and pleased to see me. Indeed, I was even more pleased to see him. Evil forces, he said, had kept him awake that night. "Listen to the wind -it sounds evil!" He was looking up with glittering, piercing, and yet, as I remember them, very sad eyes. "My dear brother, it's over," I said. "My romance is finished." "Hallelujah! Praise the Lord," came the reply and his face lit up with new hope. That God had graciously delivered me from a dreadful snare was my roommate's interpretation, because in the last days it was wrong to get involved in marriage. 'Let him that is without a wife, not get involved with one,' were the teachings of Paul. If I were to keep faithful to those Pauline epistles then singleness, because of the imminence of Christ's return, was obligatory to the Christian.

The next day, with a single purpose in mind for the advancement of the gospel, we agreed to go out to the fashionable suburbs of Wimbledon in order to distribute tracts and proclaim the good news. Wesley had preached in open spaces within hearing distance of the crowds and we would do likewise. Some affluent flats were soon approached there. I think they encircled a lawn with the flats forming a circumference. So, with all the volume we could muster, we began to preach the message of repentance. Hardly had we begun when a uniformed commissionaire seemed to appear from nowhere. He told us, in no uncertain terms to move away before the police arrived on our tracks. We were upsetting the residents, he said. We no doubt retaliated by telling him that it was a free country; we might well have told him that he would burn in hell unless he repented of his sins and committed his life to the Lord Jesus. Indeed, I can't remember if William was of a gentler temperament than myself. Although he was filled with zeal he was never arrogant. This convert from Catholicism was as meek as a lamb though as bold as a lion. He tried to reason with people lovingly. Be that as it may, hot gospel preaching was often very wearying and exhausting. Before long I was limiting my share of it to a more respectable witness at Hyde Park Corner. The need for home and my mother in Newcastle was being experienced. Soon, with luggage packed, I was to make my way to the Victoria bus station for the long, weary coach journey northwards to Newcastle. I would be back at base again or, should we say, square one?

Poor William was also to experience mounting obstacles. I later learned that prayer was not supplying the answer to all his needs; and no one living had ever more Faith than he. The offer of working as a lift attendant had come his way and it would meet his financial needs. However, so sure was he that each day might be the last before Jesus returned, that, even when the interviewer said, "I think you've as much as got the job but I can't confirm it until the end of the week," William couldn't let the opportunity of witnessing for his Master pass. He got as far as the door then turned to his interviewer, saying: "May I ask you a personal question: are you ready to meet the Lord? You see, it's not your job I want so much as your soul for Christ!" Dear William ended up securing neither. Yes, if he'd lived in the first century he may have been later hailed as a heroic saint, but because he lived in the contemporary world he was ridiculed as a raving nutter.

Varied Experiences Upon Tyneside

Now that I was back in Newcastle, back to where I'd started, it seemed as if all thought of a future in the church really had to be discarded, as Mother longed for me to get my head down from the clouds and face reality. What should I do with my future? Employment was not easy to obtain. Several weeks passed, and eventually the post of an assistant in a radio shop on Northumberland Street presented itself. Everything went remarkably well at first. The work was the easiest I'd yet experienced and was like earning money under false pretences. I was assured, however, that the profits made on a Saturday more than compensated for the slackness of the rest of the week. Yes, excepting for Saturdays, most of the time was spent dusting the many radios and radiograms on display, creating the impression that we were busy when we weren't. One young lad, just fresh from school, was going through the mill due to the manager making him a constant point of attack. The poor lad would often appear on the point of bursting into tears, red-faced and trembling. "What would your parents think of you if they knew you were inefficient in your work?" asked the manager; while in all reality the lad wasn't inefficient in the least. While he was cursing the youngster for his supposed inadequacies the manager would often give a side-glance and a smile towards me. Indeed, I often felt a hypocrite smiling back and was very tempted on one occasion to intervene on behalf of the lad who was having a raw deal. An older assistant, very caring, warned me in no uncertain terms not to unless I myself was willing to bear the full brunt of all future hostility. "It's just something we have to turn a blind eye to. Otherwise they'd make working conditions completely unbearable for us. Unless you're prepared to get out, and can be sure of getting another job, you've to learn to hold your tongue in such situations, hard though it is!" Such were the gist of his comments.

After several weeks of plain sailing, during which time another fellow had become an object of attack and subsequently left, the focus of the manager then turned itself upon me. Indeed, I sensed I might have accelerated this by wearing on my lapel a 'Jesus Saves' badge. Hardly had I worn this than did a delightful elderly gent from the warehouse look disdainfully at my lapel and take me to one side. "Like yourself, I am a Christian" he said. "I do not want to dampen your dedication but do you think this is wise?" "Why?" I asked. "All the bosses upstairs are Jewish! They come in to the shop and say nothing. But they are taking everything in. There's nothing they don't miss. Be careful". "But two of their names are Welsh" I replied. "Yes, but they often take British names for business reasons! Just be on your guard" he added.

Rightly or wrongly it is my contention that anyone who tries to follow the teachings of Jesus, no matter how far he falls short, will sooner or later, because of this, find himself a target for unpleasantness. Either the pretext will be that his work is not up to scratch or else that he is a 'holier than thou' -a killjoy. I don't think anyone could ever have branded me as one of the latter. If my work was ever criticised, the only legitimate reason was due to my being quite a mystic. I was repeatedly telling God in secret I loved him, and would occasionally slip into the staff room to pick out a verse from my pocket Testament so as to meditate on it while doing the dusting. I suppose it was hardly likely to accelerate my sales drive. Nevertheless, my commission was never below average. However, the manager was having a domestic difficulty as his wife had become seriously ill. My mention of a God of love (which may well have been overheard) was hardly likely to foster a good relationship. 'All who live godly lives in Christ Jesus will suffer persecution!' said St Paul; and whatever my shortcomings I was endeavouring to live such a life.

Most evenings were absorbed in meetings at the Eldon Mission, Wycliffe Baptist Church, or Central Hall, Maple Terrace. If the former is remembered mostly because of the fervour, sincerity, loyalty and utter devotion of its many ex- miners who preached the word of God on the Quayside and in the Bigg market, then the latter was memorable due to the ministry of a Rev. W. Mills whose sermons were amongst the best I've ever heard. He was prominent as a Keswick Convention speaker.

Newcastle, in those days, had its 'Cowan's Monument' as well as Bigg Market and both were centres where one could stand in the city and preach from the Bible without any fear of the police moving you on. At the former, a sweet soul by the name of Margaret became a friend of mine. Although seven years older than myself, she actually looked younger. In a softly spoken voice, which she might have used to effect, she witnessed to the love of Jesus. She had that 'little girl lost' image and she certainly used it, while she remained utterly loyal to a mission hall of strong Calvinistic sympathies. I, young and not a little conceited, opposed her in her strongly held belief that, having committed her life to Jesus once, she could never ever be lost. I reaped the force of her wrath by telling her she most certainly could. The more I'd expressed my feelings towards that particular lady, who'd first shown interest in me, the more reticent she had become. "I don't think it's the Lord's will," she would say. "I don't feel the same towards you as you do towards me!" Yet whenever I'd ignored her, she did all she could to get my attention. I sensed that her outer expression of seeking God's will had been no more than a charade; beneath it she had been treating me as a cat plays with a mouse, and enjoying it. Indeed, a godly Mrs Cully, previously an alcoholic and once banned from every pub in Newcastle, got converted at the Westgate Citadel of the Salvation Army. Her life had – without a shadow of a doubt – been supernaturally transformed. Wherever there was unjustice dear Mrs Cully was there: and one night she got this Christian flirt of a girl to one side and dressed her down over her dealings with myself.

But of more relevance, the breaking of this brief relationship culminated in me entering the Church of St Thomas the Martyr; and in that hallowed place, pouring out one's soul to God. A feeling of desolation, as well as of contempt for human fickleness, had resulted in agonising in prayer before a God whom I'd given second place instead of first. Pulling out some scrap paper and a pen, I wrote a poem of six verses within twenty minutes. Later, a member of the Plymouth Brethren was so touched by it that he had it printed for free circulation. What happened to my copy I really don't know. I only know that I've never since been able to compose a poem in such a brief period of time. Well, at least, not until compiling hymns for God's animal kingdom three decades later!

Of all the open air meetings attended, and that includes Hyde Park, none was enjoyed as much as those witnessed in the Newcastle Bigg Market on a Sunday evening, and to a lesser extent on a Saturday night. There was the Catholic Evidence Guild, denouncing Protestantism and claiming to be the one and only true church; there were the Free Thinkers, denouncing religion altogether; there were the Communists; there was occasionally the Salvation Army; but almost without fail, and always in full fettle, stood the members of the Eldon Mission in a circle. They were complete with an accordionist and a host of bluntly sincere and fiery preachers who were zealous to proclaim the whole counsel of God. These people had a Faith to be proud of, and a knowledge of Scripture, which could tie the priests of the Catholic Evidence Guild into knots. The latter had a number of devout adherents whom the priests occasionally allowed to spout. Of these, none was more prominent than that lovable soul, a firebrand for Catholicism, whom we nicknamed 'Betty the bead worshipper'.

Dear Betty, was getting past middle age, yet she would have been truly glamorous if she had worn fashionable clothes. As it was, she was fast becoming a recluse when not engaged in theological warfare. Betty never minced her words, and her underlying hatred for heretical Protestants was never far beneath the surface. She idolised her priests who largely tolerated her. Often, proudly holding her rosary in her hand, she would start repeating its five decades in full view of all. Awkward questions such as 'How many heads of Peter has the Roman Church got?' or 'How many nails from Christ's cross does Rome have?' would be asked. The motive was to get Betty infuriated rather than expect an answer. This dear lady, the keenest exponent of the Roman church I've ever met, was later to become a close acquaintance when yet again, and for the final time, I underwent a brief course of instruction in order to try and do full justice to Catholicism. Strangely enough, on my inability to go through with it yet again, Betty, much to the utter embarrassment of the Roman priests, turned away from all the dogma of her church and became a 'born again' Christian, Protestant through and through. Somehow, I feel there'll be a large crown in heaven for Betty, the ex-bead worshipper, and it'll be heaven to meet her there. I still visualise her, tall, thin, and old fashioned in dress, and yet not unlike the Jesus people of a later decade. Betty wore a soft hat with a wide brim. She'd no doubt experienced all shades of what the world offered, and her features portrayed that she'd known much heartache and suffering in her life. A laughing- stock to the young, flippant, and spiritually smug, she equally conveyed a long story of conflict to those who'd mellowed in life. She, whom we'd viewed as being a pawn in the hands of the priests, was at last, I sensed, a jewel in the hand of the Master.

I suppose I switched jobs like forms of worship and, during that last course of instruction which barely lasted three months, secured work as a projectionist in a dump of a cinema, once a Nonconformist chapel. It was situated beside the big lamp at the top of Westgate Hill, and though it was called the Gem, the locals nicknamed it 'The Lop'. The projection room was directly under the old bell tower and from it one looked down directly on to the prefabs, which were visited, in many cases, by my hard but good instructor from St Mary's, Father Urquhart.

The sleaziness of this picture palace didn't of course; mean that those who worked in such a place were immoral, though I'm pretty sure that some of those delightful ladies were more liberated than most. The manager was a former army sergeant, getting on in years, and he taught me a great deal about human nature. He knew women better than most men, and he could see through outer scheming and fantasising to the real lady beneath. This was something I was totally incapable of doing, and I was most vulnerable. One usherette was referred to by him as no more than a butterfly and a dolly-bird. I willingly took her to an afternoon's performance in another cinema: a kind of busman's outing, and before long my heartstrings began to throb for her. Once again, I was infatuated by a member of the opposite sex! She stated that she felt deeply towards me, but she couldn't guarantee a lengthy future. "I'll let you in to a secret" she said: "I've lived beyond my time. I have a weak heart and should have been dead six months ago. I'm really little more than a freak." How my heart went out in sympathy towards her. "As long as I die happy and laughing I'll be satisfied!" she said. The young lass was far from irreligious and perhaps I would be able to help her to fulfil this wish! But then she added that though she very much liked me, she might never be able to love me. I would never be able to take the place of an ex-lover, called Bill, who had gone out of her life forever. How deeply sad it was!

At this delightful lady's suggestion, I accompanied her on a Sunday evening trip to Seaburn. Thankfully, the Gem never opened on Sundays, so we alighted from the coach, left the others and walked along the sands, in the direction of a fair. "How I love the sound of the sea!" she said. Then narrated how it took her back to the seafaring days when her Dad, the captain of one of the largest ocean liners. (the SS Normandy) had taken her, as a child, walks along the sea front. Alas, he'd been drowned at sea, she said, and nuns had brought her up in a convent. "But the sound of the sea!" she said: "It makes me want to walk out in to it". Ths way she might die happy! All she said was so moving and touching that I could have wept for her. Before long, we would touch on spiritual things as she was not averse to such a topic and I later bought her a Bible. However, what sticks in my mind most, from that night's trip, was our turn on the 'Chair-a-Planes'. They swung out to a great height, and not only was I on the outside, but with a sudden vigour and excitement she grasped and twirled my chair and was asking me to do the same to hers. "I want to die happy," she said. Well, I didn't want to die at all. The mechanism was creaking and groaning as we glided over the canvas tops. And, as one was swung further outwards by her capers, it looked as if the other end of the hook supporting the chains to which my chair was attached was about to come out of its ring at the top. A petrifying experience for myself; yet she'd enjoyed every moment of it.

Each weeknight on kissing this most attractive girl of twenty-one good night I would say, "I'll see you tomorrow," and she would reply, "Perhaps, or perhaps not!" She had already outlived her time. 'How could I make her happy during her last weeks or days upon earth? I asked myself. I must do all in my power. But, first of all, I needed to be really sure as to the seriousness of her condition. She referred to her doctor as being nothing less than a second father to her. So, as we'd agreed to the possibility of getting engaged, I sought him out for advice. I can only say that he rudely blasted me out of his premises. Well, I wouldn't be put off, so off I went to the convent to meet a Sister Patricia whom she idolised. The Convent was quite a weird place but not without its own delightful rose garden. However, to meet this dear nun I was escorted along a long corridor. Indeed, it was along this that a host of novices made their way towards my direction, led by one of the sisters. As these young lasses with their short veils came closer the ones at the front looked me up and down and began to give a gentle titter. But then, following a gentle whisper from the sister leading them, they swung their heads back and across to the left, just as I was starting to pass them on the right and had started to give them a smile.

But then, once escorted in to a side room I found myself confronted with Sister Patricia who was as lovely and as caring as the picture my recent girl friend had painted of her. She was most interested to know of the spiritual side of my life and then went on to enlighten me about the one with whom I was infatuated and had lost so much sleep. "Poor, dear soul!" she said, "She never knew who her father was. It now appears she is creating a world of make believe as her real background is possibly too unbearable to face. As for her heart being weak, I'd be inclined to very much doubt it. She was abandoned as a child, you know! Her mother ended up in a bad way; and that's how she came in to our life." Then looking towards me this compassionate Nun added: "She is not the kind of girl a person like you should be considering a future with." It appeared that a make-believe world, filled with romanticism, had been created by her to compensate for a harsh and exceedingly cruel reality, and her mind had probably been twisted into believing what she said. Well, it was the end of yet another brief encounter.

Such experiences with the gentler sex as I'd undergone were hardly likely to endear me towards them. Women could be the objects of lust as well as love. Indeed, although I'd indulged in many erotic fantasies with the pin-ups of the Picture Post and the Daily Mirror, I'd never as yet experienced sexual intercourse. Many friends told me that my sexual education was, consequently, deeply lacking. Well, why shouldn't I? Why continue to respect that species which dangles you in a cat-and-mouse relationship, or lies to you over and over again? Well, soon such an opportunity presented itself. It followed after attending the public service of Rosary and Benediction at the cathedral. Making my way in the Scotswood Road direction, past the bus station and the wholesale meat warehouses, I noticed a youngish lady in the shadows near the entrance of an old pub. She was conspicuous, with patent leather shoes, a fur coat, and a chain round her ankle which was an obvious cue. She smiled towards me and asked if I happened to have a quid handy; this was after she'd asked for a light. On affirming that I did, she then linked my arm in a public manner, which proved extremely embarrassing. We speedily crossed the busy thoroughfare towards waste ground behind a high wall where, looming above us, were large warehouses. "We're alright here, deary," she affirmed and then, making sure she'd got the pound first, asked that she might inspect me as I had to be clean. The embarrassment heightened as she then directed me to the correct spot. Then to my question: "Is it in?" she merely replied, "Yes, deary, you are a big man!" Well, she seemed as if she wanted to remain emotionless throughout the event. When it was over, as it very soon was, I can only say that I left the spot very much deflated.

This episode was immediately followed by taking the shortest cut to an all night chemist's. There I promptly bought a bottle of Dettol ointment! The ordeal was followed the next morning, by the cinema manager – an ex. Army sergeant - giving me a rollicking for having used a woman from the city's grottiest suburb. Well, that same female would spot me on subsequent occasions, but her offer was only to be taken up once. She looked such a frail and extremely vulnerable character, complete with a handbag crammed with so many notes. On a subsequent occasion a sinister feeling, associated with power, which was not unlike the kick experienced by Stevenson's Mr Hyde, came over me. Why not threaten her with a knife and snatch the bag from her side? My eyes began to glitter. It was as if some luring force was urging me on, and it was connected with a feeling of dominance. I would use women in the manner they had recently used me! Fortunately such a Satanic urge was soon overcome. The dagger, which I'd procured, was cast into the dark Tyne from the bridge. It was the eerie old Redheugh Bridge. Indeed, if I'd given vent to such a diabolic deed I dare say my body, rather than the dagger, would have ended up in that murky river late at night. The prostitute might well have had a pimp at hand. Yes, there are forces at work, demons as well as angels. We can so easily become their agents when we are young.

(Newcastle's Gem, before closure).

Following the most recent let-down by a girl I now no longer descended the Gem's spiral staircase in order to chat up an attractive usherette who was within the balcony. No, I would now descend the steps during performances until I reached the bottom of this well-like structure, not to push open the door, which led to the gallery, but to kneel in privacy within that dark and dusty chamber. There I would pray, worshipping my God in as deep and fervent a manner as I had done years previously amongst the fields and within the idyllic white quarry region of Holywell. Somehow, the blessing derived was just as real.

After such spasmodic periods of meditation and intercession, and on retracing my steps up the winding stairs to return to the projection platform via an iron door, I felt that my face literally shone with almost a divine brilliance. Indeed, the young fellow, who assisted me, seemed to sense it also and he would often see a pocket Testament in my hand which was much the worse for constantly being used. Such a dear lad was of poor and humble background. He was conspicuous for always wearing a trilby hat throughout his working hours. I always felt that he was impersonating those American gangsters and 'tough guys' of the movies, and yet he was a fellow for whom I somehow held the greatest respect. I knew, also, that a similar respect for this young fellow was held by my priestly instructor, as the lad was truly proud to be a Catholic. Certain weeknights, while on his parish rounds, Father Urquhart would look up towards the old bell tower with a searching smile. Before long, we would both be waving back with glee.

This authoritarian priest, one sensed, was the kind of cleric who felt most at home amongst the less privileged and least prosperous of this world. You couldn't help but warm towards him. Yes, indeed, this gracious priest had been kind towards me until a fellow priest, literally 'a Father Divine!' informed him that while I was receiving instruction I had also been throwing up the trickiest of questions at the open air meetings of the Catholic Evidence Guild. Well, so sarcastic and utterly contemptuous did he now become towards myself, and the whole Protestant world, that I terminated instruction for the final time. This had been accelerated by two prime factors. One was being made aware of official Catholic teaching, which I had no right whatever to question but must in humility submit to: 'Animals have no soul. When they are dead they cease to exist!' Well, I considered this most callous and in conflict with Jesus redemptive plan for all creation as revealed in the Bible! The other factor was witnessing within the walls of this hard yet most devout priest's cathedral, a horrifying spectacle in the middle of worship:

"Clear the isle!" bawled out an authoritarian priest from the front. And then - following a slight commotion from the very back - a hush of unexpected horror appeared to descend on the worshippers as a cripple, minus a leg, and with no supports, dragged himself forwards along the whole length of the floor where, on reaching the chancel steps he struggled to climb them; there to kiss a large crucifix held out by an austere priest. This done, the fellow turned round and with a marked agility made his way right to the back from where he'd started. Well, whether this was voluntarily done out of extreme devotion, or whether it was done – as appeared more likely - as an enforced penance for some horrific sin, I'll never know; but somehow, it quite turned me and sticks indelibly in the mind.

Indeed, if St. Mary's, on the inside – with its penitents queuing up outside confessional boxes and lighting candles in dark corners before lifelike statues - had an uncanny atmosphere, its exterior was uncannier still. For right outside its very gates was a notorious spot for the prostitutes! I well remember two 'ladies of easy virtue' walking back and forth along the length of their respective patches and meeting up at the gates that divided them. "How is business doing tonight, Veronica?" asked one. "Very slow Theresa. Very slow!" replied the other.

Newcastle certainly had its share of denominations as well as devotees. The Holiness meeting of the Salvation Army citadel in Westgate was a most inspiring service. One was always assured of a warm welcome and though Salvationists hadn't been baptized and for that reason, said my former priestly instructor, could never enter Heaven, I chose – with scriptural support - to think otherwise. Yet, a future in 'the Army of the Lord', void of Sacraments, hardly appealed; even though I had gone forward to the mercy seat and afterwards signed 'The Articles of War', which made me a bona fide Salvationist! Perhaps I was hypersensitive, but the coldness that followed the warmth of those meetings seemed most pronounced. The congregation would disintegrate in to cliques where one family knew another and a new convert was left in the cold - except for a brusque: "God bless you! Where are you from? Do come back!" at the door..

Mind you, going to the Army on most Sunday afternoons was not without its titillating fascinations! The platform at the front was highly raised: and upon it, often denouncing the sinful lusts of the flesh would be a firebrand of an officer. Sat at either side would be several other uniformed Salvationists: and the females were not at all averse to crossing their legs, thereby revealing a bit of bare thigh above a sexy black or navy blue stocking top above the garter. It could really turn one on. I noticed that quite a few elderly men, sometimes down-and-outs of the locality, were very keen to hobble to the front benches. I often felt it was hardly consistent for these female members of the corps to be shaking their tambourines to 'yield not to temptation' and 'dark passions subdue' while the elderly men near the front looked upwards boggle-eyed.

Brunswick Chapel was the centre of much activity. Here a Methodist clergyman, who publicised his qualifications, attracted yet more publicity to himself by having toured parts of Yorkshire in John Wesley style, on horseback. Recently he'd published a book on it. Indeed, he was also engrossed in running a psychology clinic. He knew how to draw folk in. I dragged dear Mother along to this Methodist metropolis, hoping that in response to some appeal from the front she might be 'saved'. It didn't work, as the man was a Modernist. Mother felt the man was much in love with himself, and I began to think I'd been listening to what the Bible calls a preacher 'with itching ears'.

Fundamentalism, I had decided, was the only legitimate way to approach the Bible. Either you believed the whole of the volume or you may as well discard it. Once you reject one part where do you draw the line regarding the rest? A dispensational approach to the Scriptures, as propagated by the Brethren, was something I despised, for in practice it discarded much of Scripture as irrelevant to our time. Curiosity, together with the desire to find fellowship where the whole of the New Testament was deemed relevant, led a pal, Tommy, and I to visit several peculiar missions. While others used weekend newspapers to find out what was on at 'the flicks', my kind and I would find out what was on at the churches, missions and gospel halls. One title attracted our attention immediately: 'The Church of God at Newcastle'. Well, off we went to sample it.

We arrived at a large Georgian house, facing Leezes' Park, made our way up the wide staircase to a moderately sized room and, on entering, were confronted by several young ladies clasping their gospel song books and singing lustily. A time of prayer followed and this was notable for its inarticulate groanings: the presumed promptings of the Spirit. The only words that appeared discernible were 'Jesus, Jesus, Jesus; bless Him; He's been through it -poor soul! He did it for me.'

Those sounds, which weren't expressed in words, were anything from a sobbing sound to a dog-like whimper, or occasionally a noise not unlike a steam train. Often on such visits the repeated interjection would be a simple 'Hallelujah'; but even then it was occasionally uttered at a most inappropriate time. The preacher might cry, "Lord, we are sinners ... we have grieved you, Lord," then someone might well respond with: "Amen, Lord! Thank you Jesus!" The worship was what people of a few decades later would be actually terming Charismatic renewal.

The traditional churches then knew nothing about such glossolalia! When the worship had worked up to a high pitch, then it would be that some hysterical woman, often trembling from head to toe, would burst into a flow of gibberish. Phrases, very often repetitive, would be uttered in a guttural tone. Then, after a pause for silence, a young, handsome pastor would interpret the meaning, "Thus saith the Lord, fear not my people. I know your burdens but I have come to liberate you. ..." etc, etc. As before, I often felt it strange that, though the gibberish was so repetitive, the interpretation was hardly ever so. Much of it bordered on the hysterical as well as the sensual and, if the young pastor had had a wife, we wondered how many of his female flock would have remained. Yet, though so critical of the Pastor myself, I'd love to have been in his shoes. His job was a contrast, indeed, to my projecting films at the Gem; known to some as 'The Lop' or more unkindly by others as 'The Knocking Off Shop'.

People today talk about the need to get back to New Testament Christianity. Well, none was more worthy of the title than 'The Church of God at Newcastle'. They not only had a ministry of pastors, prophets and evangelists, they also had a surplus of apostles as well. We were once introduced to a visiting preacher from Ulster. He was quite a humble man who frowned upon wearing a 'Roman' collar. He wouldn't wear a cross, as it was pagan. He refused to give himself the title of reverend as he felt it was contrary to the teachings and example of Jesus. He merely called himself 'Apostle' and placed it as a prefix before his name. Yet I couldn't help but like him. He gave a big smile and a big handshake. I sensed he had a heart as big as his head.

Talk about meetings going with a swing, one could gladly dance to the rhythm of the choruses and the shaking of the tambourines. There was no doubt about it; the worshippers enjoyed themselves and the tithes and love offerings kept flowing in. The Charismatics of today are forty years too late! Indeed, so excitable could things become that sometimes Tommy and I could no longer restrain ourselves from laughing. We took it that such manifestations would be interpreted by the rest as 'laughing in the spirit', of which they heartily approved. But for the fact that the Almighty must have a great sense of humour we would surely have been struck down for our profanity.

Dear Frank Applin, the round-faced, cheerful minister of the elite Wycliffe Baptist Church sought to straighten me out on several occasions during this period. He was grieved at my unwillingness to anchor down at his own church where there was plenty of help needed. He'd gladly secured preaching appointments for me elsewhere within the Baptist denomination, but eventually, he quite despaired. My 'going the rounds' of the various denominations revealed a lack of character and stability.

This baby-faced pastor, whose face equally revealed how he felt on less happy occasions, was not only feeling let down by myself; he felt let down by a. deacon who'd recently professed salvation. Brother Hopwood, previously quiet and a little withdrawn, was becoming more vociferous each week in evangelical zeal. Alas, his new found spiritual perception was leading him to cast doubts on the morality of a sedate senior deacon: Illicit liaisons were inferred between prim and pious members whose features, the pastor whispered, were 'not unlike the back of a tram'.

One day, returning homewards from work, awaiting an appropriate bus in Grainger Street, this newly converted deacon approached me. After mentioning the Good Book and the need to abide by it, he assured me that ones battle as a Christian was against spiritual wickedness in secret places. Well, he had one's full sympathy until he told me to modulate my voice. "There are concealed cameras directed to entrap the believer'", he affirmed. Then, beckoning me to come away from the wall of Kemsley House, he whispered, 'walls have ears!' It was an expression reminiscent of recent war years. When he mentioned further modulation because of manholes and pavements ones suspicions were confirmed. The Deacon was sadly undergoing delusions and, on several Sundays following, a compensating zeal to 'shout out' for Jesus became his practice. The round-faced pastor found now, not only sour faced deacons on the front pew but a disturbed singer repetitively shouting hallelujahs further back. I enjoyed assessing this situation from the side isle opposite.

On a later Sunday when the deranged deacon stamped his feet, as though marching, while singing in high volume, 'Onward Christian Soldiers, I found it exceedingly difficult to look as 'sour pusssed' as the rest who'd left him to sing solo after the first verse. Alas, soon that dear soul was taken off in a 'green maria! "My ministry is a failure" said the minister. "The congregation is dwindling; and Hopwood, whom I felt was an answer to my prayers is off to the loony bin. As for yourself Bro. my suspicions are confirmed: you are a Spiritual Tramp!"

A Pastor To Paupers Comes To My Aid

Not so far from the fashionable Wycliffe Baptist Church, yet in a much poorer area and amongst the back streets, there stood an old, derelict- looking building known as Mill Lane Mission. A tiled pub stood at the bottom right hand corner of the lane, which adjoined Mill Lane and Elswick Road. The houses on either side of the lane appeared hazy in a frequent smog. And as one walked up on the right hand side there would be a hissing sound from the gas lamps, plus an occasional whiff from the fish and chip shop; and then, looming up: the mission itself!

This building was more like a warehouse, except that a solitary bell was suspended from the side of it. Strangers to the district would no doubt have considered the building semi-derelict or condemned. Yet, as one pushed open its door, a number of benches and odd chairs came into view. Its congregation were a handful of poor, simple-hearted souls singing out their hearts to Jesus. An old man with curvature of the spine would look as far up as he could; that's if he wasn't already sitting at an old harmonium playing one of those plaintive yet beautiful Wesleyan hymns. One would occasionally detect a tear or two in his eyes as he worked away at the pedals, and sometimes a dear old soul would sing at his side. One such solo, frequently rendered, was 'Out of the Ivory Palaces'. The place was very drab and yet it was spiritually beautiful. As for its minister, he was away holding missions as often as he was present. Whoever led the service would remember the minister's work in the prayers that were offered. Indeed, their pastor was quite unique, living by faith from day to day, just as Muller and others of a past age had done. Yes, the Rev. Willie Hudson was one of the humblest of men; he was never ashamed to do a lowly task for anyone. Indeed, he was conspicuous at times through carrying his ladders to clean windows for some of the poor and infirm. That this man didn't discard his collar to do so, was seriously frowned upon by some sedate and snooty clergy of the district. A local Presbyterian preacher, whose church attracted a cultured, refined and genteel flock had actually told the pastor to his face that he had no time whatever for back street mission halls. Did this worry my friend? Not in the least,

Willie Hudson had broad enough shoulders for such abuse. He knew men for what they really were because he had mingled with some of the vilest.

Respectable ministers would occasionally question Willie's credentials, as their predecessors had those of our Lord and His cousin, John the Baptist. To the clerical snobs of 1951 the Roman collar and the title 'Reverend' were marks of scholastic attainment, much more than marks of a man's mission for God. The scholastic had taken first place over the spiritual and its disastrous fruits were expressed through ever-dwindling congregations. Mind you, in all fairness, Mill Lane Mission attendances were often sparse, but it was the quality that mattered. The attire of the folk and the drabness of the building were ugly. Yet, paradoxically, they were beautiful. They loved God and they loved their fellow worshippers too. A Methodist lay preacher, who regularly assisted the minister, so radiated the love of Jesus that his face shone and his eyes were as clear as crystal. But then saints are varied. If the pastor himself had the meekness of Jesus then a colleague, whose ordination he'd taken part in, had the sheer boldness of the Baptist.

Ian Paisley had come all the way from Ulster to hold a mission in the slums near where I lived. He held no fear at all of the roughest of characters and he equally refused to water down his words. Yes, I'd known him previously in Belfast, our paths had crossed in London, and now he'd come to Mill Lane. It seemed a small world. Willie and Ian were both men of tremendous stamina. Whatever their shortcomings, and I dare say they had quite a few, they were out to do business for God rather than sip cups of tea with old ladies. But even then, tea had its place at Mill Lane. There was more than enough available at the annual treat for the poor. Cakes, buns and trifles were included. This was followed by games for the tattered little children of those back streets who'd also come in from the possible cold. They idolised this minister who so cared for them. I remember how he would gather them into a circle to tell them a story of Jesus; indeed, he would willingly get down on all fours to entertain them and, as conjuring tricks made their hearts happy, he always had a few up his sleeve. The old folk, some who had been gentlemen of the road, would be prompted to sing 'What a friend we have in Jesus!'

On one such annual treat, this 'Firebrand for God' turned to me and said, "Not much of a building to the glory of God, is it? The rain is coming through in several parts up there. The place is drab and condemned; but you know," he said, "Jesus is here tonight. I tell you that I can feel him here!" Truer words were never spoken to me. Jesus was there. I felt His presence closer there than at any subsequent church gathering. (The only exception being animal blessing services; but they would be decades later!). Indeed, being in that Mission resulted in a spiritual rededication; for 'doing the denominational rounds' previous - though feeding one's pride and intellect - had resulted in a stinted, superficial spirituality. The words of a gospel hymn became most poignant:

In tenderness He sought me, weary and sick with sin
And on His shoulders brought me back to His fold again;
While angels in His presence sang until the courts of Heaven rang.

O' the love that sought me; O' the blood that bought me!
O' the grace that brought me to the Fold. Wondrous grace
That brought me to the fold!

He washed the bleeding sin wounds and poured in oil and wine.
He whispered to assure me: "I've found thee. Thou art mine!"
I never heard a sweeter voice. It made my aching heart rejoice.

Several weeks were to pass and this wonderful pastor to the poor offered me a full-time post as superintendent over a tiny mission hall. My employment in the cinema industry had created no barrier to him; he said it would have given me good insight into the world. As for my knowledge of the Roman church, it would prove most useful. 'At last my prayers have been answered,' I thought. I can now live every hour to win others to God.

Incidentally, one of the strangest experiences in my life occurred around this time. It was in connection with a Buddle Road Baptist Church. I'd passed this place of worship on several occasions while going along the back streets off

Scotswood Road; had also met the temporary pastor there and, indeed, must have so coveted his position as to dream of taking a service there. But what a strange interior it was with panelled walls and a set-in organ. Many months later, and quite out of the blue, the opportunity to take a service there occurred. As I entered, an uncanny feeling crept over me; the interior was identical in every detail to the way I'd seen it in the dream!

But now I return to Mill Lane and the post that was opened to me. It concerned a tiny mission down in the lovely Yorkshire town of Harrogate. The building was largely financed by a Mrs and Miss Rudd: two elderly ladies who lived together and were much respected by the community around Chatsworth Place. The mission occupied the top part of the building and underneath, except for the vestry in which I would sleep, was the undertaker and joiner's premises. One approached the mission from a door which took one directly across to the vestry, or else up a flight of stairs into a long mission room neatly furnished with individual seats, a raised platform at the front and a harmonium at its side. Though small, the mission was clean and neat and a warm spiritual atmosphere seemed to permeate the place. Most appropriate therefore that above the door of the mission, sometimes swinging in the breeze, was a sign bearing the words, 'Hallowed be Thy Name'.

The first night in Harrogate was quite exhausting due to what seemed a long journey down from Newcastle. But what a great honour to have travelled on the coach with such a reverend gentleman at one's side! Then, on reaching our destination, we were warmly welcomed by the sedate ladies who made us supper. To save unnecessary work for them we agreed to use the same bedroom, indeed, the same bed. My reverend roommate was an upright man of God, so I only hoped on retiring that I did not express flatus while asleep or subconsciously roll in the wrong direction. I always had a dread for sharing sleeping facilities with another, unless of the opposite sex! However, my fears were unfounded; that solitary night his snoring was so voluminous, it could have blown one out of the bed. This followed on from his very lengthy period of prayer and Bible meditation. His valued companionship, however, was short lived. This saintly new boss would return to

Newcastle late the next evening, which was a Saturday. I, then left on my own, would be expected to evangelise the district. Nevertheless, this was not to occur until I'd been officially inducted on the Saturday afternoon.

Walking out early next morning, my saintly mentor had made a new acquaintance. In fact, he'd felt constrained to stop a middle-aged cleric in the street to ask him if he would care to take part in a service of induction for a young man. Well, though the invitation was at such short notice the cleric seemed only too pleased to oblige. This strange, though cultured-looking parson, turned up at the appropriate time. I can't remember what was said at that service, but before leaving, while offering me future hospitality at his home, the lavishly attired cleric placed into my hand his visiting card. He was a Master of Arts and a Doctor of Divinity. 'Why, your qualifications are equivalent to that of a bishop,' I said. He beckoned to me to draw closer, and in a voice he didn't wish others to hear he said: "Between you and me, I am a bishop. But I want you to keep that to yourself." Then, before we all dispersed he came back to me and again as if he didn't wish to be overheard, said: "Call round and see me sometime, I'll tell you more about it. I could help a young man like you, but be sure to ring me first." Why, I thought, I've made it at last. Not only am I a full-time Christian worker, but I'm on close terms with a bishop. It seemed as if all my prayers were being answered at once. 'All things come to those who wait;' and now the sky was the limit!

Later that same week, an appointment having been made, my steps were directed towards a house in Deferrious Avenue. The bell was rung and my eyes looked down the passage past the open door. Then, completely attired in a long flowing robe of scarlet, plus pectoral cross and chain, my latest clerical acquaintance beckoned me along the corridor and ushered me into his front room. This I'd noticed was not without him first of all telling a young lady, seemingly many years his junior, to get into another. "You will see that I am in my Episcopal robes," was the comment he then made. It was certainly a remark, which seemed superfluous. Well, the dear man seemed kind, but his suggestion that I was ordained by him as a deacon for twenty-five pounds - a large sum in those days - gave me the impression that money would be a deciding factor in his willingness to help me. Suspicions were aroused further when he went on to state that the period lapsing between ordination to the diaconate and the priesthood could be negligible, provided I could provide another twenty-five pounds. Tea and cakes were kindly handed to me!. "What kind of church will I be offered once I am ordained?" I asked. "Well, most of those in our movement are part-time," came the reply. One of them was seemingly proud to frequently swap between the attire of an engine driver and a parson. Even the archbishop was a contrast to Church of England prelates as most of them, like the Bishop of Ripon, were utter snobs. "Once I've ordained you, you'll be able to wear a collar and append reverend to your name. That's what really counts," he said. "You'll find it opens up a new world of opportunities to you."

The more I listened to the cleric in front of me, the more suspicious and unimpressed one became. The whole offer just didn't ring true and I began to question whether his strange denomination even existed outside his own mind. The fact that such a slack-knit movement did exist with many strange characters from an Archbishop of Glastonbury downwards was not to be learnt until several years later. Homosexuality amongst ritualists was not uncommon in shady parts of the metropolis; yet the bishop before me was married with an attractive young spouse. He could hardly be branded in such a way. That he was polite and pleasing to wealthy, elderly ladies - possibly to further his own ends - was an undoubted fact. He later suggested a scheme to win over the Rudd sisters in to the ceremonial and ritual of his movement. It was their wealth that kept Chatsworth mission going, he said "Just imagine the front with an ornate high altar in place of a mere rostrum!"

As suspicions increased one later became eager to enlighten the dear Rudd sisters, as well as acquaint them with what had been confirmed by a local vicar. The cleric had been defrocked by an autocratic Bishop of Ripon who had shown no mercy towards him. Yet, this most convivial cleric now taught at a private school where he'd won the hearts of both pupils and staff. The two maiden ladies did not appreciate me enlightening them: "How dare you call that dear reverend gentleman a con man!" said one. "He calls so courteously to see us". "Yes, and he never leaves without asking if he may offer up a prayer," said the other. As a young man I had, apparently, been sorely lacking in Christian grace. My utterances, they said, were nothing short of gossip. .

These sedate maids ate and drank from beautiful bone china and cut off the crusts from around their sandwiches. The reverend in question - conspicuous by his ten-gallon hat, umbrella and sometimes gaiters - not only dined sometimes with them, but was now occasionally receiving donations as well. In marked contrast I was hardly genteel due to several nervous tics such as sniffing, blinking and an ocassional twist of the neck. Yes, these dear ladies were most particular and, as a consequence, I had a fear of putting my foot in it, and therefore sometimes did. In the words of Job: 'That which I dreaded most has come upon me!'.

One morning, conscious of one's sweaty socks and shirts with grease round the collar, I resolved to have a washday which was well overdue and never, as yet, tackled. There was, in the vestry, a new wash boiler, which had been used for heating water to make tea for the prayer guild and faith suppers, and I decided to use it. The fact is previous nights had had their problems in that vestry. I used to awaken with the sound of mice while endeavouring to sleep across several chairs over which I'd placed sheets of corrugated cardboard so as to lessen the hardness. Indeed, the mice became so bold that they eventually ignored my movements and even the beam of my flash lamp. They just carried on squeaking, and I learned to tolerate them until one night they began to run boldly over me. After that I chose to sleep on the floor of the rostrum upstairs. But, as there were no curtains I often awoke early in the morning, exhausted at the very commencement of the day. This particular morning was one of them!

Feeling extra-grimy, as well as whacked through lack of sleep, I decided to boil some water for a drink and to use the rest for boiling my cast-offs. So in they went under the lid of the boiler, complete with plenty of Oxydol, or was it Rinso? Then, as the morning was young, I went off to do some visiting. There was an aged seaman who was quite ill, and it was needful to spend time with him before setting off to Harrogate. Well, absentmindedness was always a personal weakness and somehow the hours seemed to pass very quickly.

On returning to the little mission around 2 p.m., one was not only confronted by the kind lady from the bakery opposite who'd given me free under-weight loaves which she dare not sell, but, to my horror, the two elderly Rudd sisters were waiting with severely censorious expressions as they witnessed steam belching up like smoke from under the mission door. I alone must have possessed a key on me. We rushed, groping our way through the denseness, to be faced by a reddish glow as the lid of the boiler was opened. Sharp comments were passed. Before long I was left on my own, picking out what appeared to be tar from the sides and bottom of the boiler. This was all that remained of one's socks, underpants and shirts. The rest of that day is remembered for emptying lumps of soda into the boiler with the unfulfilled anticipation of it becoming shiny and clean again.

The most pleasant part of those mission days was taking some of the local youngsters for a picnic to a little wood on the way to Knaresborough, which was near a stream. I had them sitting in a circle while I taught them choruses and told them stories of the Lord Jesus. One or two of those youngsters really loved me, particularly a young lass of about nine. I really loved them too as an aspiring young man of God. Sadly, soon I would leave them and they would wonder where I'd gone. I was always anxious to better my status wherever it might happen to lead me.

Those few months certainly seemed packed with activity. A couple who befriended me for a short time suggested moving in with them; but in no time atall asked for a rent which one could not afford to pay. They had been going through a sticky patch and mistakenly considered me a young fellow of private means. Another fellow, a regular worshipper was certainly a man of means, a wealthy widower who was fond of a lass twenty years younger than himself. I must admit I much preferred this air force officer with a curled moustache and debonair twinkle to the elderly, sedate ladies. It could have well been a matter of envy with them that, while this widower and the young lass sat hand in hand during the worship - him sometimes touching her knee! - that they gave such disapproving glances of shock and horror. I sensed the couple knew what they were doing; shocking the sedate, puritanical and pharisaic; and I quite liked them for it.

One old dear, a regular worshipper whom I visited frequently, would ask if I had enjoyed her homemade cake. She would have brought out a bought one, having removed the telltale crinkly paper first. Because of this practice others talked about her. Well, I used to boost up her supposed cooking ability and this seemed to gladden her heart. The same dear soul had a strong fascination for cats and, consequently, the atmosphere was sometimes strong. I ate her cakes and her deception didn't offend; in fact it proved enjoyable.

One delightful soul was much more open-minded and, indeed, humorous too. This middle-aged lady decided to 'step out in Faith for the Lord'. She'd received various visions, as she termed them, and one had to do with evangelising farmers. So, in obedience, she sent for bundles of free tracts, which were offered to believers for prayerful distribution. Having acquired a large assortment from various sources, she would then send them out with her own stamp added, to scattered farmers. A personal letter would be included with these and she was not averse to suggesting a donation from any who might wish to further her cause. Indeed, they would receive a regular newsletter from her. She was equally willing to address weeknight meetings providing a collection was taken for her cause. Consequently, her enterprise became well known as the 'Farmers' Christian Tract Society'. Her Harrogate base to the farming world flourished and as she once remarked, with a big smile, "It is scriptural teaching that the labourer is worthy of her hire."

Pride Before A Fall: Experienced And Witnessed

Now in full time Christian work, I was becoming a little shrewder. Though most of my shirts had been ruined in the boiler, I'd brought out my preacher's collar on the odd occasion or two. One's horizons were now on a higher level and I would use the present as no more than a stepping-stone. One such occasion comes very much to mind concerning what transpired during a break back home in Newcastle. Such were not to be idled away as I knew of one or two places of worship, which were without a resident minister. One of these was along Jesmond Road, a delightful looking Congregational Church in an upper class suburb. Well, I was soon knocking on the door of the Church Secretary's home where I offered my services to him while donned in a collar. "What a pity you hadn't called four months sooner!" he said. They had already secured a student fresh from college. However, there would be a pulpit vacancy in three weeks. It was the new minister's Sunday off! This was extremely short notice; could I possibly oblige? I gladly replied that I would and left a visiting card in his hand.. It contained the words 'Pastor Thompson, M.R.P.S.' Such letters appended went back to those Belfast days, as much like the Royal Geographical Society or the Royal Society of Arts, there were a whole host of other 'learned societies' to which one could seek affiliation, provided you were duly nominated and paid an annual subscription fee. Letters, I sensed, looked impressive so I appended these, rationalising that in so doing one was no more vain than a whole host of British clerics whose photos and particulars had appeared in an American Naturopathic Directory. They were now styled as Reverend Doctors outside their churches and the one, I'd known, had no more interest in alternative medicine in those days than I myself. Indeed, if stacking letters to one's name was vanity, then the vainest people in the whole world must have been amongst the professional followers of the lowly Galilean. Indeed, I sense they still are!

The Sunday evening of that Newcastle preaching appointment soon dawned and, what was more, it was an unexpected ego booster to find displayed, on the large notice board of that beautiful church, 'Special Guest Preacher this Sunday Evening: Pastor Thompson, M.R.P.S. from Harrogate!' I think I stood for quite some time, viewing it from the other side of the road where I alighted from the bus. I viewed it, not only with pride, but also with real inward humour. Then, raising myself straight while conscious of my collar and large Bible, I crossed the road, entered and introduced myself in the vestibule. Others were making their way in. I would no doubt be escorted personally down to the vestry, not unconscious of side-glances towards me to see what the visiting preacher looked like. It was, not a little funny, and made one feel great. I can remember very little about the actual service itself, except for a feeling of elation at finding my Mother and my dear Aunt looking quite radiant amongst the congregation. The service in which, in all humility, I seemed to excel as a preacher, I attributed to God who'd already ordained me in His way.

After the service I was invited to mingle for a short while with the young people of the youth club. Well, hardly had I begun to do this when, to one's embarrassment, I saw the secretary walking towards me with a young, studious, introverted kind of cleric. "I've come round specially to introduce myself to you," said the latter as the secretary moved away.. "This is actually the Sunday in the month when I am usually free. I hear very favourable reports about the service - they like you! Tell me about yourself." My temperature began to go up. My mind would have to think and act quickly. "'Well, I'm pastor of a town mission down in Harrogate. But tell me about yourself," I replied. "Are you a college man?" "Well, I've a degree from Cambridge for what it's worth!" he answered. "But tell me, you've a qualification I haven't. What exactly is it?" Good God! I thought how do I get out of this one? "Oh well, actually, nothing really." "Oh, go on, I'm quite intrigued. It must mean something," came his reply. "Er tell me," I said, "whatever are those young fellows doing over there? Let's join them." "No, go on, tell me," he said; "I must insist." You would, you awkward so and so, I thought to myself. "Oh, just a little bit of philosophy," I answered. "Oh, what a coincidence!" he replied. "I took up philosophy at Cambridge but nothing, I sense, to the degree you must have studied it! Tell me, what period of philosophy?" "Sorry - I just didn't quite catch what you said as I'm really interested in those teenagers over there. I'd like us to join them." "Please, what period of philosophy?" he again asked. "Oh, just a little of Hume, Kant, Socrates ... and 'Hegel" I said. "Y -e-s," came his curt reply, and then he turned with glaring eyes to stare contemptuously at me.

At that moment the church secretary joined us. "Would you excuse me a moment?" I interjected, "Is there a toilet near? I'll be back in a moment. I must pay a call." I scuttled off round a corner, looked for the nearest exit sign and, at an appropriate time, slipped out into the open where the air seemed cool and welcoming. 'Stupid bigot,' I muttered to myself. He probably can't preach for toffee. I doubt whether he believes the fundamentals of the Bible, and he's obviously never worked manually or witnessed human nature at factory level. I reasoned that the 'Union' of the Congregational Church gave credence and support to him merely because he was a Cambridge graduate. 'He'll eventually empty the church', I said to myself 'whereas with my personality and God, it would thrive!'

The next evening, who called round at my home but the church secretary himself. He'd come from the wealthiest part of the city to one of the poorest. He hadn't time to enter, he said, but wanted to know why I'd hurried away as he'd so much enjoyed my sermon. I, thereupon, told him that I was really no more than a pastor of a small mission hall and I was not an educated minister with university background. He looked at me so kindly and lovingly and the words that followed almost led me to tears, "I speak, not only for myself, when I say that we wish we could have had you instead of the fellow we've got. He isn't a patch on you and he's merely relying on a bit of parchment." Such words were to return to my mind down subsequent years. The proof of one's calling to preach is surely the ability God gives to the one He calls. There is a greater ordination given than can ever be granted by men or institutions.

On my returning to Harrogate, full time work at the mission hall was expected of me, but one pound per week, even in those days, was hardly enough to exist on. Thankfully a rota to furnish me with one good meal a day proved a blessing, without which I couldn't have continued. But sleeping without as much as a cushion, either with the mice in the vestry or without Curtains in the hall, was not conducive to stamina. So I decided to put out further feelers. Although I had attended two Bible colleges, and no theological college, I had obtained a sound knowledge of other denominations by attending their services and learning their respective interpretations of the Bible. I knew that this had given me an all-round knowledge well in excess of accepted clerics. Then why should I ever feel inferior!

One day, after much time spent in prayer, I visited the Harrogate library. Then, having taken from the shelf a copy of the Baptist handbook of churches, I prayerfully opened the book while my eyes were closed and placed my finger on a particular page and spot: On opening my eyes I found my index finger resting between two churches in the Bradford vicinity. One was Bethel Chapel, Shipley, and the other was Eccleshill Baptist Church, Bradford. Both these places were without a minister so I would seek God's guidance all the way.

Later that week the journey was made to that strange city down in a hollow, Bradford. I went to the suburb of Shipley. By this time I had just reached my twenty-third year and strongly felt that if Alan Redpath, from my native Newcastle, could cast aside his job as an accountant, don a dog collar, and become renowned by packing a small chapel at Richmond in Surrey, transferring evening meetings into a local cinema, then I could be similarly successful in Bradford! If I lacked a high secular education I was not alone. I was compensated by fearlessness, an ability to preach, and a drive, which was apparent in Lockyer, Redpath, Olford and the other leading evangelical Baptist ministers of the day.

So confident was my manner, on approaching both chapel boards that eventually an offer came from both churches. Would I be their minister? Well, admittedly my preference was for Shipley Bethel. It was a solitary, high building set on a small hill; and the interior was furnished with a high pulpit, which was level with the gallery. The deacons, however, took far too long in deciding, so meanwhile and much to their annoyance, when the offer came from Eccleshill I accepted it and would not go back on my word. Regrettably, the salary, although there were perks, would only be three pounds three shillings and sixpence per week. The promise was, however, that, as soon as congregations increased, the salary would rise correspondingly. I considered it a worthy challenge and agreed- to be inducted two months later. All formalities were signed, sealed and settled. And now, without wasting further time, I would spend the intervening couple of months with Mother at Newcastle - using the time to prepare a large series of sermons to see me well into the winter, and getting all the pastoral advice I could from quite a famous minister there.

Yes, it was during this period in Newcastle that I had deep fellowship with this prominent ex-Keswick preacher, who was semi-retired now, but was caring for the spiritual flock at Maple Terrace. This was a church built for the Norwegians but was now a meeting place for believers associated with the Fellowship of Independent Evangelical Churches. Indeed, it was across from the old St Mary's, where three years previously I'd made my one-man protest against idolatry.

The Rev. E. W. Mills, for such was his name, encouraged me no end. One memorable occasion was when he invited me along to a Saturday missionary rally, at which tea would be provided between meetings. As I'd received a call to a pastorate, and was about to be inducted, he felt it appropriate that I should wear my collar for the occasion. "You'll have the opportunity," he said, "of meeting evangelicals from different parts of Tyne side; brothers and sisters in Christ from varying denominations." He was a Baptist, an ex-student of Spurgeon and no mean scholar.

Things went remarkably well until we gathered round the tea table in the hall at the back. A young looking curate, with a gawky wife and two extremely pampered children, joined me after our respected host had introduced us. This Church of England fellow, tall, thin and rather nervy, had only recently 'professed salvation!' He asked in rather an affected tone: "Where did you train, dear brother?" "Me?" I smiled; "Oh I only did a very short spell. Two Bible colleges for only short periods; I'm mostly self taught!" In response to such a meek and humorous reply I was startled to see his face drop considerably: "But you're wearing the collar; and certainly no bishop has ordained you!" He still stared and moved his head back in horror. "I really don't know that it's right to be sitting next to you!" Well, I thought, I've got a real Anglican Charlie here; I'll bet he can't preach for toffee! He seemingly knows nothing about the Nonconformist world. I'll bet he knows only the practices of his own Church of England and then only of his own churchmanship within it. The fellow had played right into my hands and I was firmly determined to bring him down to rock bottom. As he was comparatively new to evangelicalism and was boasting about the need for credentials, I decided to question him on the differing schools of evangelical thought. However, it was then that our gracious host intervened to ask how we were faring together. The young priest was uneasier than ever, so I took the initiative and told our lovable host that my fellow partner thought I was some impostor. The affected creature then learned what he should have already known, that denominations vary considerably in customs as well as practices. To learn, for but two examples, that Methodist students wore clerical attire on Sundays, when they would probably not be ordained for another three to seven years, was a fact of which he was totally ignorant. Indeed, that the collar was of Roman origin appeared to flummox him more.

So as our host, on leaving, had hardly deflated him I thought 'I'll deflate him!' "As an evangelical, what brand do you follow? Are you a Calvinist, an Arminian or a Dispensationalist?" The man looked aghast. He obviously did not know the difference. When I asked him his views on the Schofield Bible, and also of the leading schools of prophetic interpretation down the ages, he just couldn't answer. "It seems your knowledge of the basic book of Christendom: the Bible, is at an all time low," I sarcastically commented, "Yet you have the nerve to question me. I can see that, although approved by some pompish bishop, you are quite ignorant of the foundation book of Christendom. You really aren't very clever at all; are you?"

Much to my own lack of charity I there and then arose, looked down at him with a contemptuous smirk, and went to intermingle naturally with more congenial company on my own level. I felt great! As for him and his family, sadly, they seemed quite left out. They weren't able to mix. But then, who really wished to mix with a bigoted, marble-mouthed cleric.

Thanks To Yorkshire, I'm A Baptist Minister!

The great day in Bradford arrived for my induction. Yet I just can't remember it. I was presented as a former student of BTI, Glasgow, and Kensit College, London. Yes, I remember the write-ups in the local newspapers, but can recall little of the services conducted there. It all appears quite vague for some reason, except for the building itself. The edifice, although quite small, was truly beautiful within, complete with a delightful pipe organ; pulpit to the other side, and under the choir stalls in the centre a baptistery. What is more I had my own vestry where one prayed to God before preaching to man! Lodgings were soon acquired in the home of a recent widow: a Mrs Helliwell; She lived in a smart semi-detached house, considered suitable for a minister. And it so happened that this traditional, Yorkshire lady was an active worshipper at the 'Congs', an expression used for the Congregational church. The latter was, indeed, a beautiful building, externally as well as internally, and its most recent minister was truly proud to hold his position there. Yes, the Rev. John Harwood was truly a unique personality who knew all there was to know about ecclesiastical stunts. He had a good smattering of psychology, so that at one period he held his own type of clinic but what was even more advantageous for drawing in the numbers was his sense of humour. His notice board was often a treat to behold. Captions such as 'Sunday Morning's Sermon -Over the garden wall', 'Sunday Evening's Sermon - Not on your Nellie!' were bound to arouse curiosity, especially in those who'd been conditioned to view religion as stiff and starchy.

A couple of days after, having settled in at my lodgings, I received, via the landlady, a personal invitation to an 'At Home' at the Congregational manse. I willingly accepted this and it resulted in meeting the Methodist minister, another Congregationalist minister and our host. The meeting was a most affable one in which I learned that the previous Congregationalist minister had also been late of the Glasgow BTI.'

John, though very sympathetic to my background, was equally proud to affirm that he'd graduated from Paton College, Nottingham. Yes, it was the college, which had pioneered psychology as a necessary subject in the ministerial curriculum. Its standard was at one time revered throughout the Nonconformist world.

I can remember two issues that were discussed at the meeting; one materialised and the other didn't. It was suggested by our host that the three of us should be knocking on the same door while a press photographer snapped us. The newspaper caption could then be: 'Three parsons share their visiting'. The Methodist minister was a humble soul and to him such gimmicks were cheap and nasty. The other suggestion was that I should be taught by my host the proper way to visit the hospitals, and this I willingly accepted. If it had been left to myself, I would have gone quietly to individuals who had Baptist connections, left a comforting tract at their bedside, read the Bible to them and offered a prayer. Well, John held different views. He wanted to introduce me to radical methods more acceptable to men of the world. He was in his late thirties or possibly early forties and he knew human nature in the raw, having served at El Alamein. The narrowness of Fundamentalist Bible-thumping was truly obnoxious to this man and those who held such views were often classed as ignoramuses, bigots and killjoys. My predecessor, Pastor Scothom, had been well and truly amongst them. John wanted to broaden my outlook from the start, and consequently mentioned at that first meeting, that in donning the collar I'd joined the rogues' gallery and that he was the biggest rogue of all.

On entering a long, rectangular ward in the Bradford Infirmary, John immediately bellowed out: "You lucky people in bed on a day like this. Don't be embarrassed and don't blush because a couple of parsons have come to cheer you up." I think a series of crummy jokes followed. All I can clearly remember is that some of the patients were even more shocked than I was. Then, returning on the trolley bus to Eccleshill, John uttered in a voice everyone downstairs could hear, "I think we two parsons had better stand up and give our seats to two respectable ladies, Jim!" Such were the methods of this unique minister. "More con men amongst parsons than all the politicians put together!" he would say. I sensed the more he could shock me, the more he loved to pile it on.

I soon contacted several newspapers and before long was commissioned to publish a weekly spiritual article in the Shipley Times. It went under the title, 'Thinker's Corner'. The editor, however, was an ardent Christadelphian. Whenever such articles clashed with the theology of Dr Roberts, the founder of Christadelphianism, then the editor would modify my manuscript. Doctrines such as the virgin birth of Jesus and his visible return were given much space. Consequently, whenever I next bumped into John, I would be severely criticised for such conservative evangelicalism. "Are you going barmy?" he would say. "That's a lot of rubbish you wrote in the Times this week!" He was a Modernist and proud of it.

When John's church became a little low financially stunts were often used. On one occasion I sat for a couple of hours at the side of the main road, sipping cups of tea with him. This, with the eatables, was provided by the sweet ladies of his church. "Would you like to see how one can secure money quickly for the church?" he asked. I replied that I would, so John, complete with his gown and flashy academic hood, walked out to flag down a large Rolls. Switching from his broad Lancashire accent to an equally emphasised upper crust accent, he asked the driver if he'd care to help in the urgent church appeal? I can't remember what words he used. I only know that a bundle of notes, in those days a lofty sum, was willingly handed over. John gave a cultured and forceful, "Thank you very much" and "God graciously bless you!" That driver's face shone as he drove away. "There you are, Jim, he's helped us and is pleased for the opportunity we've given him. We've really made his day. That's how it's done, Laddie!" I was dumbfounded.

My colleague at the Congs was at that time as different from me as chalk from cheese, but I was learning fast from him. If I'd have had such nerve I would have enquired, William Butterworth-style, about the state of the man's soul, and ignored his pocket altogether!

John was, without doubt, a very popular preacher. His fervour came through preparation, anecdotes, stunts, and anything to make a person laugh and see the brighter side to living. It seemed the inspiration behind my own prayers and sermons came after times of despair, loneliness and emptiness that had led me to repeatedly throw myself upon God. And this resulted in His Spirit not only comforting me but, through me, all those to whom I ministered. Without being unkind, the more my colleague put into his sermons the more successful they were. Whereas the less I thought of my own contribution and, in sheer desperation, leaned on God, the more blessing emanated from the little I said. Yes, the Congregational minister brought forth laughter to his congregation while the Baptist minister brought forth tears to his! Yet I couldn't thank him enough, particularly for giving me an insight in to hospital visiting. It so happened that a lay-preacher connected with my church had suffered a nervous breakdown. Arthur Everard was a most sensitive fellow and not a little fastidious. Nevertheless, this immaculate bachelor had been rushed in to Menston psychiatric hospital to undergo urgent treatment. Consequently, the insight received from the Rev. John Harwood would now – hopefully! – be put in to good practice.

Sadly, on arriving at this highly fortified Victorian style complex things appeared far removed from what one expected. A security guard was at the large gates and, having received permission to pass through, I walked along a lengthy drive passed much shrubbery before entering the first of several corridors. There a porter, complete with a multitude of keys on a chain, was waiting to escort me through several doors. Each one he unlocked, and then locked behind us, before we arrived at a ward that smelled a little of stale urine. "This is Arthur Everard!" said a somewhat erratic member of the staff with wild eyes and a pronounced ginger beard". "Never!" I replied as I beheld a dear dishevelled soul fumbling under his blankets with his staring eyes transfixed upon me. "It is the only Mr Everard we have and this is certainly the man you've come to visit!" 'Good God!' I said to myself: 'what appalling deterioration in such a short time. Somehow I just can't believe it'. Indeed, I dropped on my knees, and there on the spot, offered a prayer of ejaculation. He responded by offering his ejaculation; but it was not in prayer! My presence had obviously 'turned the poor man on' and he was not ashamed at what he'd done beneath the blankets. I certainly knew that the fellow I'd come to see was, in modern terminology, 'of the Gay variety', but such a sexual orientation was seldom openly mentioned in those far off days. There had, nevertheless, been a suggestion given in my presence, from one church deacon to another, that their lay-preacher might have had a punch up from another within a Gents convenience and was now in Menston to be 'sorted out'!

I tried to communicate with this poor dishevelled soul but it was no good. He was, again, too engrossed in 'self abuse' as to speak. Then, while endeavouring to read a passage of Scripture, another inmate in the next bed kept crying out: "I want my mammy; I want my mammy!" Consequently, I was swiftly being brought to the brink of tears when another fellow – truly erratic, yet most cultured - approached me. "Sorry!" he said; "there's been a most dreadful blunder. This is not the Arthur Everard you've come to visit. My profound apologies. Do come this way!"

In another ward I met the one I'd come to see, as coherent and cultured as ever. "If I don't get out of this place in the next couple of days Pastor Thompson, I'll end up as crazy as this lot. The members of staff here are as dotty as the patients. But look at that patient over there! They gave him an enema to retrieve more than one pieceof cutlery, along with other things!" The demented fellow was in a bed close by. Well, dear Arthur was known to exaggerate and envelop a story, but what I saw for myself convinced me that if he didn't get out soon he'd end up a perpetual inmate or a suicide. "Some of them are very wise – I'm truly frightened of what they might attempt on me!" he added. "Do you know, Pastor Thompson, two managed to get outside the very gate of the main entrance? That takes terrific skill; but once there, they sat on the side of the main road saying they were now legally free and could not be touched! But, they were soon picked up," he added, "and they are now back surrounded with extra security". Then, looking quite frightingly, he clasped my hand and said: "I tell you Pastor, it's not getting in to this place that's the problem, it's my getting out with a sane mind. Please ask the church members to pray for me." Indeed, I did, and dear Arthur was discharged within several days.

Around this period an invitation was received from a superintendent of the Baptist Union to visit his home in Leeds. Such a Union hadn't helped me to secure a post or even enter a college in the past. Was he different? What did he want of me? 'Well', I thought, 'I'm as good as you', so I deliberately donned my preaching collar and went off in search of his residence. Whether he considered me a young upstart or not, I don't know. He was far from warm and quite condescending in his attitude. If I ceased working in a full-time capacity, referring to myself as a lay pastor rather than a minister, and pursued a course of study by correspondence - discarding the collar temporarily until he gave me permission to the contrary - then in return he would give me Union recognition and with it: financial security. 'Well,' I thought, 'blow you, mate, go and take a running jump.'

Getting up to leave this cleric's house, his attitude suddenly mellowed. "Just a moment, I may still be able to help you!" he said. "---It all depends! Tell me, are you all right for clothes?" My ears pricked up in astonishment as my mind reassessed him: 'Apparently this fellow isn't hard, for underneath there's a kind streak!' Unfortunately, it turned out to the contrary. "What type of clothing are you prepared to offer me?" I asked. "Actually it's underwear I have in mind. How are you for underwear? I can show you a selection upstairs, but it depends on your size!" Well, though it had, indeed, been boisterous weather and one was living frugally, I certainly didn't even want to see his underwear! Leaving this cleric's residence without him even offering to pay my fare I decided, there and then, to stand on my own two feet as a Baptist minister without ever again seeking affiliation to a Baptist Union.

About three miles away from Eccleshill stood the small Shipley suburb of Wrose. I was to learn that a fellow who had attended the Bible Training Institute in Glasgow at the same time as myself lived there. He was the student whose name I had put forward for the pastorate of the small Baptist church in Flint: the student who had suggested that I decline such an offer should it be given, suggesting himself instead as he had undertaken a longer course. Well, the fellow was anxious to meet me again so I looked him up and, as a consequence, he applied for the pastorate of Bethel at Shipley and was successful. Meanwhile, out of curiosity, I decided to visit the mission that he frequented and which, he said, meant so much to him.

This mission was to have such repercussions for my life as could never have been imagined at the time. I was soon speaking at their young peoples' weeknight fellowship, and holding fundamentalist views on the Bible, became quite popular. A contrast to most 'clerics' who denied so much that was contained in Scripture. Full of beans, and possibly of self, I hadn't a scrap of inferiority, for I knew my Bible and religion if little else. What was more, two young ladies approached me towards the end of the first meeting and I gave them a personal invitation to attend my own weeknight service at the Baptist church. One of these young ladies had beautiful features, with eyes that were open and clear, and my mind was working overtime to discover whether or not she was courting. Attractive lasses were often attached and already associating with fellows. I would have found it sinful and wrong to have split up any romance already begun. My calling, I sensed, was to enhance such an association and never to break it.

Later in the same week, and within the hall of my own little church, these two young ladies appeared in response to that invitation. One seemed quite pushing, even at the expense of her friend. I began to feel a strange and growing warmth of affection towards her friend. Indeed, although I knew nothing about her, I felt from the start an affinity of spirit. She appeared so loving and trusting. I sensed, even then, that I wanted to share my life with her for the sole purpose of making her happy. But would she reciprocate? Well, wonder of wonders she did. Katie, for that was her name, was fair eyed, open in features, loving and trusting. That night as I returned to my lodgings, after having walked the two of them partly home, I felt wonderfully at peace with the rest of the world. Her handshake, and a "Goodnight Mr Thompson", had somehow conveyed that she would be pleased to meet me again. Yes, the air felt crisp that night. I was healthy in every limb and I could have skipped the long way back to Eccleshill. Indeed, I'd met the one whose life I was going to share for no less than twenty-four years and, though I did not know it then, we would begin to share it 'for better or for worse' within less than a year!

The days couldn't pass quickly enough now and I wished every hour away until I was in Katie's company. The more I learned of her ways and of her difficulties, the more my love for her seemed to grow. She was merely seventeen. In those days it was hardly respectable to court a girl who was little more than a juvenile. People of the world might consider teenage crushes as innocent and lovely, but narrow-minded, mission hall folk held a strict and rigid code. It reflected the discipline and harshness of a moral restraint, consistent with Divine wrath for those who infringed it. Love, mercy and compassion were very much secondary factors. Indeed, the only love that seemed to count was the theological brand: Jesus's death to atone for the sins of God's predestined elect.

In meeting the one who was to become a future wife, I was also coming into the circle of in-laws who had struggled through much poverty, and years of intensely hard times. It is not surprising, therefore, that such folk often become cautious, deep and sometimes mercenary in their values. That type of Yorkshire person, who says little but weighs up much, sometimes mutters phrases such as, "You'll not get much brass in your job!" Well, how true are these sayings! But, equally, how unacceptable to a young man who was an idealist, and often lived in cloud-cuckoo land. The West Riding type of folk were truly a breed of their own, often clannish, close and, sometimes could be blunt to the point of utter rudeness. But to those of us, who would rush to condemn such aggressiveness, rudeness and bluntness, let us first of all condemn the social injustices of a bygone era, which moulded them. Money meant security. It often had to be more than earned in sweatshops, slaving in rat-infested mills from the early hours of the morning till the darkness of the night. She who was to become my mother-in-law was in certain respects a wonderful woman. She could have excelled academically but was compelled instead to be a bread earner in a mill. An idealist in his early twenties was unable to appreciate such qualities so I considered her to be hard, cruel and, in most ways, unyielding. For reasons I could never learn, she simply took an instant dislike to me and consequently did all she could to bring our romance to a swift end. Yet, outwardly, she was usually most charming.

Lodgings had recently been changed from Mrs Helliwell's to an elderly couple, who were prepared to offer me accommodation at possibly a slight financial loss to themselves. It so happened that dear Mrs Helliwell – a recent young widow – had unwisely agreed to another lodger sharing the same bedroom as myself! Mrs Asquith, a much older lady, treated me as if I were her own son and, before long, she informed me of local gossip concerning myself. One young lass, a sweet schoolgirl of thirteen, had linked my arm while walking her home to meet her Mum and Dad who were prospective worshippers. This was after morning worship. It soon became rumoured by middle-aged to elderly ladies that the Baptist minister ought to be much more circumspect and discreet. Such tittle-tattle came from those whose features implied that they were sour of life. They were outside the fellowship of the church. It never once came from inside where they really knew me.

Mind you, one has to admit that when the choice came between visiting a charming young, cultured and sophisticated lady or an average frumpish worshipper then the former needed a good deal of resistance! Indeed, such was very much the case after having been stopped by a certain Mrs Totty who eagerly introduced herself. This delightful blonde, with fur coat and sparkling rings, had noticed me passing her secluded home on several occasions; and curiosity had resulted in her wondering to what branch of Christendom I belonged. As for herself, she had appreciated a secluded convent education, was happy to discuss religion with me and would be pleased to have me call at her home for morning coffee.

Regrettably, my dear devoted landlady was not too keen for me to reciprocate the glamorous young lady's invitation. "She is not the kind of person you should be visiting", affirmed Mrs Asquith. "She has two young children and a husband a good deal older than herself, and he is very prominent as owner of a large building firm. They are definitely not the type of family you should be associating with", she affirmed. Well, I only know that, speaking for myself, this new acquaintance proved as charming as she looked; and on the one occasion I met her husband I found him gracious, a trifle reserved, yet kindly. Mrs Totty wanted me to know that she admired my form of life and I responded by commending her charming manner. However, one of those few visits to her affluent home was not to be easily forgotten.

A delightful cup of coffee having been placed on the left arm of the chair into which I had pleasantly reclined happened to be next to a child's play pen! Before long, I heard the gurgle of a child and then noticed the mischievous eyes of this toddler gleaming in my direction. Consequently, I smiled towards that little bundle of love, waved and pulled a funny face; and then - as a preliminary precaution of safety - moved my coffee cup well away from what I casually considered to be the extent of his reach. However, hardly had Mrs Totty temporarily vacated the room for more suitable attire than I felt the heat of hot coffee burning through my silver grey suit; and this was followed by viewing the young rascal giggling, and rocking with great glee, as he withdrew his hand back into the pen! Then, as if to add insult to injury, another youngster entered the room as if only to join in viewing the spectacle with equal delight. Consequently, the anticipation of my hostess returning in, possibly, slim, seductive style was utterly dampened. Indeed, when she did return in differing manner, it was with her hands shielding her face from spontaneous laughter.

Pulling herself together, as best as she could - yet not making a very good job of it - she then suggested that I enter her kitchen to temporarily substitute a pair of her husband's trousers - which were exceedingly shorter and broader! - while she sought to dry my own. Feeling quite burnt in the most delicate of parts I swiftly complied and then, while sat in such ill fitting pants within her lounge, began to wonder if my pants which she was pressing in the kitchen with a hot iron were truly clean; and were the pockets intact, as befits a man of the cloth?

The whole experience had so swiftly changed from one of sensual delight to that of secret foreboding; and this was hardly improved when Mrs Totty mentioned that her husband might return at any moment, and she was becoming apprehensive as to how he might respond on seeing a Protestant minister wearing his pants. Well, I only saw dear Mrs Totty once again after that unique and memorable occasion. She apologised most profusely for the 'accident', and wondered if I'd care to go as a guest, with her husband, herself and a lady friend, to the Theatre, However, as I had a prayer meeting to lead on the same evening, prayer had to take precedence over pleasure.

In large letters, on the chapel notice board, were the words: 'Come and hear the grand old gospel', and that's precisely what the folk did hear. Within weeks the congregation had almost doubled. This was to be further accelerated by two ex-Cliff College students holding, at my invitation, an Abundant Life Crusade. This occurred before Billy Graham came to this country for his memorable crusades. One could truly see in the two young fellows fresh from Cliff, Vic and Gerald, possibly more talent than even in Graham himself. These young chaps used publicity and gimmicks to the full, often rehearsing their preaching with appropriate gesticulations thrown in. For myself, it was far too Americanised and riddled with showmanship. Yet, paradoxically, they were in deadly earnest. Not only did they invite folk to come forward and be saved, but, alas, they invited folk to come forward for the supposed second blessing, which was accompanied with speaking in tongues. Consequently they were introducing a Pentecostal practice into a Baptist church. I suppose they were merely going one step ahead of the Baptists in seeking to follow the example of the New Testament Christians. However, mine was a Baptist church, and when the deacons complained, I was compelled to support them. Did not Scripture imply that, by one Spirit, we are all baptised into one body, the Church? 'Had not these young men taken undue liberties while holding this crusade at the pastor's kind invitation? Yes, I sensed they had but, in all fairness to them, the congregation had now trebled so how could I condemn them? With extreme difficulty I tried to reconcile both sides and was shot at from both. I was learning, for the first time, that the role of a leader can be a lonely one.

A Heart Rendering Decision To Make

Nearing the end of a subsequent Crusade Meeting, Katie, having sat with me in a front pew, had been unable to slip out unobtrusively. She had to wait until the meeting was due to close but then at an opportune time, she dived out. Yes, and I soon followed her. Because of such a delay the clock in Windhill struck half past nine and we'd only reached the top of the lane through the wood, which led to her house within it. It stood at the side of a deep quarry. She began to cry and tremble frantically out of fear of what her parents might do and say. The door slammed forcefully as I was left outside. As I made my way past the trees, up the mud path, I prayed desperately that no harm would come to her. She seemed so frail and nervous at times that I was unable to get her out of my mind. Rightly or wrongly I conjured up an image or two of sadistic parents. So worried and obsessed did I become with these thoughts that I confided my fears to the Congregational minister who told me, in no uncertain terms, that I was an absolute fool to get involved in such a situation. These weird conclusions were not to be lessened when a letter arrived two days later, stating that Katie never ever wished to meet me again. 'Typical of them all', I thought. 'She is no different from the rest.' Then, while I was in my church hall, she came rushing in, tears in her eyes, and accompanied by her sister. "I can't stop," she said, "I daren't. They'll just about murder me if they know I've called here. I just want you to know that the letter you received is all false - every bit of it! My mother stood over me and dictated the letter. My sister will verify all I say and that's why I've brought her. Please, do you love me?" Of course I did! We hugged each other and parted. Once more I was walking on air, extra-sensitive to all the beauty of nature around me. Yes, the crispness of the air, the singing of the birds and life was, indeed, wonderful and glorious.

I ought to have been much more discreet, as well as more conscientious, in running the chapel which I dearly loved. But, when one has the choice between meetings with saintly, though critical, deacons on one hand and trotting along with an attractive and truly lovable creature on the other hand, my choice was obvious. Regrettably, pastoral work became more and more secondary until such love, infatuation, or whatever one wishes to call it, took complete priority over sermon preparation, visiting and other activities for which, admittedly, one received only a pittance. 'What could they expect of me considering how little they pay me?' was the way I sought to rationalise my waning zeal for the chapel and idolisation of this girl. It was as if God was with us in such a wonderful way. Indeed, I just knew that He was looking down and smiling upon us whenever we were together.

One Saturday we decided we would go off for the day, and where better, than to see my mother at Newcastle. The distance, in those days, took quite some time; nevertheless, I considered it well worth doing. I can only remember now the terrific row that ensued on our alighting from the return journey. Katie's brother and sister were there, waiting for the coach. They seemed to get tremendous pleasure out of saying that they had no wish to be in her shoes once she got home. Someone had been told of our venture and had split on us. Poor Katie was now literally quaking as well as crying at what might follow when she arrived home. When she did, all I can vaguely remember is seeing her being slapped over the head several times and the door being slammed in my face. I then heard raised voices within and Katie screaming out for mercy. Eventually I retraced my steps up the path and wanted to vomit. One part of me wanted to break down the door, while the other side of my nature made me pray fervently that she might be spared some awful injury.

I could stand the above situation no longer. She was undoubtedly a nervous wreck. So I sought out and confided my fears to a police court missionary. He appeared quite eager to intervene. He visited her parents later that week to assure them that their daughter had absolute freedom to see me whenever she wished. She was well turned seventeen and they could not stop this. Mr Barnard, which was his name, was getting on in years and the outcome did not prove all that favourable for me when Katie's mother sobbed in the presence of this fellow. This was something I wrongly felt she was incapable of doing. He was soon speedily seeking to console her. Consequently, later in the day he assured me that this lady, whom I'd looked upon as hard, cruel and possibly possessed of a sadistic streak, was on the contrary quite a good woman underneath. "Next time you call, and I've told her she must learn to accept you, present her with a bunch of flowers. You'll soon win her over to yourself," he said. Well, his advice was possibly good but I considered it false and equivalent to a bribe. I would, nevertheless most humbly apologise for anything wrong on my part and, indeed, for taking her daughter on a day trip to Newcastle without her consent.

My sincerest apologies were accepted most curtly. It seemed as if a battle of wills would follow. The Lord had increased my confidence tremendously over the years. Well, my future mother-in-law may well have thought the Lord had done the same for her. She was also a believer, indeed, the mission's pianist and an occasional speaker at Bright Hours. But now she was more determined than ever to come between her daughter and myself. Most nights Katie had certain house chores to fulfil on returning home from her work as a clerk at Apperley Bridge. Her pocket money was certainly meagre in comparison to others. I began to buy her gifts, which she was compelled to hide lest they should be confiscated. Apart from that, things appeared to be going quite well; indeed, that I'd walked her daughter home, and that her daughter had not invited me in for a cup of tea before starting out on the return journey, was remarked upon: "Katie must never ever do this to you again." On future occasions when Katie did, she more than once received a crack over the head for suggesting it, once I'd left.

The whole thing seemed most odd, but to add to such an atmosphere was surely the very situation of the house itself. It was an eerie building in a small wood at the foot of a steep ginnel, which was near the edge of a deep and dangerous quarry. Sometimes a shudder would occur as a little more land slipped away from the quarry face and, consequently, the interior of this large house, lit by gas, was strengthened by those bars in the wall, which were quite common in old property. At nighttime the lass had the added ordeal of seeing herself to bed by the light of a candle. Would not such factors make the healthiest of girls a trifle nervous? I viewed it as more weird than any darkened cinema. Yet such a home, strict, disciplinarian and rather bare, was expressive of a love and care of its own which, while it was very deep, could never have been appreciated by me at that time. Indeed, the members of such a family were musically very talented and the daughter I loved was quite a brilliant violinist. What right had I, as an outsider, to intrude into such a close-knit family? I wasn't even a Yorkshireman and my values were quite different to theirs. Was not their daughter their dearest possession? What right had I to intervene? Besides, I was no more than twenty-three.

One particular evening a service we were again attending, thanks to a long-winded preacher, went on well and truly past its time. Katie had to slip out of the chapel to catch the bus and she was obviously highly agitated by this time. I saw the chapel door close behind her and, though sat near the front and listening to this windbag of a preacher, I suddenly followed suit. Surprised side-glances followed from 'old dears' and I said to myself 'Bugger them!' I ran as never before towards the bus stop only to see the trackless (the Bradford name for a trolley bus) moving off. Katie was on the runner board; I considered her to be my life, my future and everything rolled in one. I'd never been able to run properly due to flat feet and hammer toes, but that night I truly ran like Elijah. I caught up with the platform pole and threw myself into the vehicle, gasping deeply for each breath. That night, one unholy row ensued as the clock had again struck either half past nine or ten o'clock. The lass was consequently dragged through the door of the house, having made the journey down the dark, lonely lane to the secluded house. It would, indeed, be more than her life was worth should she ever be late again and, though we sought to avoid it at all costs, the fact is that it did eventually occur and it was, indeed, the last time.

Dilemma, and concern for the one with whom I was so deeply infatuated, had not only been expressed to my clerical colleague and police court missioner but also to my landlady. Mrs Asquith had already informed me about the local gossip concerning such an involvement with what she termed an undesirable family. "The young lass you are associating with," she said, "is the laughing stock of where she works; she's crackers," she affirmed. "I look upon you as if you were my son and I don't want you to be hurt!" It was obvious to me that this well-intentioned soul was completely off the track and must have had someone else in mind. My love for the old landlady temporarily lessened but, on later learning of the kind of trauma Katie was undergoing and realising how deeply in love I was with her, she ended up suggesting that I may well be doing a greater service for God, leaving the church to care for her, than in remaining in it while turning a blind eye to what was continuing. 'Should I really resign from the church in order to marry the one whom I so very much loved?' I asked myself. Had I not striven and, indeed, agonised in prayer for years to acquire such a post as I now possessed? Only a fool would throw it up. But then, if my 'fiancée' (we'd exchanged vows! secretly in Eldwick village church!) was really going through hell, should not the care and welfare of one creature whom I so deeply loved come before the prominent social status I had recently acquired? 'What would Jesus do in such a situation?' Yes, that was the question I ended up wrestling with for an answer. I prayed over it for very many heart-searching hours. Whatever faults I had, I sought to be loyal to God with whom I shared every hour of each day. But then, my God was intensely human, compassionate and not without humour. He was a marked contrast to the caricature put over by theologians in books as dry and drab as themselves.

By this time, not only were people inviting me to speak at various weeknight meetings, it so happened that once a month the local Baptist ministers agreed to a pulpit exchange and, of course, I was warmly included amongst them. On such occasions one could always use a sermon already expounded at one's local church, so the opportunity gave a break from the normal weekly preparation of at least two sermons. It was always a pleasure to address a congregation different to one's own, a change acceptable to pastors and congregations alike. Consequently, there was an opportunity to preach at Trinity, Heaton, Westgate, and Hallfield Chapels, and these were large, stately Nonconformist buildings. Though on several occasions I was welcomed to Heaton Baptists, which was certainly the classiest of them, the opportunity to preach at Hallfield came only once. The latter fellowship was without a pastor of its own and was unable to offer an appropriate exchange; yet Hallfield stands in my memory above all the others.

Outwardly, this chapel was a large and imposing building, though it appeared almost jammed between the two sections of a large departmental store, known as Busby's. But inside, I found it most inspiring in the sense that the pulpit, towards the front, was high and lofty, and above it one was aware of a domed part of ceiling on which stars had been painted on the blue. The service I took was an evening one, the lighting in the church was rather dim and the small congregation of, I dare say, no more than forty was sparse and scattered. Yes, having ascended the lofty heights and temporarily reclining in plush padding, which I seem to remember encircled the inside and the top of this delightful pulpit, I looked down to the devout and dedicated congregation. Why, I really felt that I was truly there to mediate a message from the glorious, vaulted heavens to the humble and expectant worshippers below. Such styles of pulpit as this one impressed me immensely; I always felt that the living Saviour was very close at one's side.

Often, on such occasions, realising it was not discernible to the rest; I would get down on my knees, if not before the very commencement of worship then most certainly during the hymn that would precede the sermon. I would thank my Maker over and over again for the tremendous privilege he had bestowed upon me. With tears of utter intensity I would pour out my heart to Him, asking to be emptied of self and filled with Himself. Whatever my shortcomings, the congregation must never be robbed of any blessing because of the unworthiness and imperfection of their preacher. Such times, I need only add, were followed by mighty periods of blessing on all present. "O' God I love You! Dear Jesus I love you! Holy Spirit I love you!" Such were the kind of words I would reiterate. And then the blessing that followed would often be beyond words. I tell you dear reader that God is a wonderful God; and didn't I know it!

That Jesus should have called me out of a back street cinema world to preach with an eloquence that many with years of academic education abysmally lacked was something I couldn't understand. Why, my days as an apprentice printer as well as a junior postman in Wales seemed hardly a stone's throwaway! If ever a man had cause to be grateful to God, I knew it was I.

There were times when I wept for my sins but more times when I wept for joy.

We Elope, But Oh To Where?

The final most decisive night of my life occurred when we reached the top of that fascinating wood, the trees of which enveloped the dwelling lower down. It was then that, with a chill of horror, we heard the chime of the old school clock deep down in the valley. When you're in love you're oblivious to time. It caused a chill of fear and panic to Katie, and a plea that I escorted her to the very door itself rather than view her from the top of the path. Part of her seemed unwilling to go down for the fear of the consequences yet she knew she had no option. If my memory is to be trusted over the years, I think I waited round the corner until the door had opened then swung closed upon her. Raised voices came from within, and then appalling screams. Feeling very sick I began to retrace my steps alone, and up the mud path of the small wood to the top of the hill. I had hardly reached half way when poor Katie, screaming for all her worth, rushed up towards me, "I've dashed out. They're going to kill me! They really mean to kill me, help me; please help me!" "Don't worry." I said. With an almost divine sense of peace that came over me I said, "Look back for the last time! You will never ever have to face that again. I'll take you away and protect you!" That's precisely what I vowed to God and to that frightened lass that I would do. Loyalty to God, and the obeying of one's conscience, must come before spiritual and social status through the glory of the cloth. "I've got no clothes," she said. "Don't worry," I replied. I believed that, come what may, God would provide for us. The elopement had begun.

To be deeply in love, while one's head was so far into heaven as to be of little practical good, would have been a fair summary of my temperament, and such love is often blind as well as daring. It seldom weighs up the pros and cons, and acts spontaneously and often impetuously. The coolness of that night air comes down through the mist of God-given years. The future prospects were unknown to us. However foolhardy or frivolous as I was to become, there and then I knew that Almighty God was with us. Due to so many years past, the mind is sometimes unreliable. Glimpses into the sequence that followed still come into prominence as clouds of obscurity pass.

Before another patch of mist comes, one or two vivid incidents appear as if they were only yesterday. On reaching my lodgings at Eccleshill, the dear old landlady seemed hardly surprised and she wished us both the very best as we stepped out into the unknown and mysterious future ahead. She had been as a second mother to me in the short time I'd known her, even though she had a delightful son and daughter-in-law of her own. Katie seemed to win her heart instantly and the old lady wished us both all the luck in the world as, with my packed belongings, we said goodbye and I left her for the very last time. We ventured out into the cool night air.

My 'fiancée' was now leaning completely upon me and I, though possessed of a heart of gold, was little better than a broken reed. I could offer her love but, alas, I would hardly ever offer her a steady financial income. "The Lord will provide!" I would say. And somehow, a Divine hand seemed to be with us; for even at so late an hour there was an all-night coach up to Newcastle! Soon we were amongst its passengers, snuggling together and full of expectation.

The hours soon passed. We were both so tired when, in the haze of the early morning, the coach pulled up at the Newcastle Haymarket bus station. Then, to our utter amazement, as our tired and bleary eyes glimpsed at the early morning newspaper placards, we were confronted with the words: 'Bradford minister elopes to Tyneside with runaway fiancée.' For a few moments we felt it was a dream and then we hurried across the road to the newsagents to procure a copy of the morning paper. "We're that couple!" I informed the assistant in amazement. She - or was it a he? - was anxious to learn a little about us, and we were too naive that hour of the morning to realise that the local press would be fast on our heels, almost before we'd left the shop.

We arrived at mother's home in Brunel Terrace. She looked quite flushed, yet she was humorous and not a little amused. "You mustn't come in," she said. "Your fiancée's mother has sent a telegram saying her daughter has come to Newcastle directly against their permission; it may be that they've also contacted the press." Mother then softened and took us in.

Soon Katie was snug in bed in the spare room. "She's a very sensitive girl with a trusting, loving face," she affirmed. "You must see that no harm ever comes to her!" Then she added words I didn't understand: "I suppose they are against you being engaged to their daughter because you're not Yorkshire. You get some funny people in this world, Jim. You need to tread very cautiously." Such words of advice were given with all the love in the world. She seemed to love Katie from the start and she certainly idolised me, her unusual son.

In the afternoon, the question of where we should go presented itself. "You just can't stay here," she remonstrated "Much though I like the two of you, and Katie seems a very nice girl; but you must go somewhere else!" Well, I knew that any possibility of returning to Bradford with Katie was out of the question. Mentally, if not physically, such a return would have done irreparable damage to her. But then a flash of inspiration came to light: there was the fellow whom I'd helped in so many ways at Kensington, London. Arnold, of the National Union of Protestants, was quite fearless and he would surely help out. If he couldn't provide us with reasonable accommodation - as he'd helped Brother Butterworth and me in the past! - then he would know of some devout and sympathetic Christians who would. Katie was nearing her eighteenth year. We'd done nothing at all criminal and, as yet, she was certainly far from being pregnant. We just wanted to be together because we were so madly in love. Indeed, if only her people had allowed us to continue to see each other, and openly be engaged, all would have been most acceptable. As it was, the more they fought to separate us from each other, the more we fought to retain the hours we'd learned to cherish so dearly. All else had become as dross.

Hardly had this one and only morning we'd spent with Mother at Newcastle transpired when a loud and thundering knock, accompanied by a repetitive ringing of the doorbell, reverberated throughout the house. Mother had only answered once and she, on learning it was the press, had refused them access to see us. In sheer desperation a reporter then jumped down from the high, back wall, and a photographer followed him. Soon the back door of the house was just about being forced open on its hinges. They literally started to try and force the door. Then, two cameras were placed near the window for whenever Katie or I approached it. We were certainly not on the phone and the atmosphere became frightening though amusing. Then, all of a sudden, a surge of pity deeply touched Mother: "Poor souls, they're desperate," she said. "It'll be more than their job is worth to go back without a story. Shall we ask them in and give them all a cup of tea?" We couldn't have agreed more, but by the time we'd agreed and answered the door only two now remained - a more gentlemanly type of reporter and his female companion. They sat with Katie, Mother and myself, enjoying afternoon tea from Mother's best china.

Mother opened up to them. She told them I was not the only child: "Colin is Jim's brother and is getting married next week at Wallsend. Jim will have to be present because he is going to be the best man!" The two visitors seemed delighted to hear everything Mother wished to tell them. They hardly lifted their pencils from the well-worn shorthand jotters in their hands. Poor Mother, little did she realise that all this would make front-page coverage in the Newcastle Journal the next morning as well as in the Evening Chronicle the next night. That a week later a photo of my brother's wedding should appear above the caption, 'The Wedding of the Eloped Parson's Brother,' is an irony of guttersnipe journalism. It revealed the depravity to which journalism then stooped for a story. My brother, much shrewder and wiser than I, had sensed the publicity that would occur should I have fulfilled my role as his best man. Yet stepping down at his request had not stopped the event being publicised. An article concerning my absence was the kind of news to which they stooped. And worse still, the sacredness of their wedding was frequented by news hawks and cameramen desirous of acquiring information concerning myself.

Nevertheless, those two visitors from the press to whom Mother had given afternoon tea in our company gave us, in return, a romantic account of our elopement, which was very much in our favour in the late edition of their Evening Chronicle. Meanwhile, the unwelcome reception the press received from Katie's parents down in Yorkshire merely resulted in an account rather slanted against them.. 'Be nice to the press if you want a good write-up, be harsh to them and they'll blacken you to the verge of libel,' was a warning which I began to appreciate with the passing of each week.

Indeed, these were traumatically adventurous times and soon the long distance coach was boarded for a yet longer night journey. This would culminate at Victoria coach station, London. Katie had never been to London before so I longed to make her happy by showing her around the great metropolis. But that night the air was cold, the coach was exceedingly draughty and the seats were hard. I felt weak with cold; indeed, sick to the point of feeling desperately ill. Somehow young Katie seemed to sense it and, making up close to me, she cared for me until I must have drifted off into a deep sleep. Then, awakening to the chilliness of the early morn, and conscious again of the light purr of the coach, I realised from the built-up scenery that London had well and truly been entered.

Complete with one suitcase, we eventually found ourselves at 54 Gloucester Road, Kensington. It was the centre of the National Union of Protestants. Once Arnold Perkins learned of our predicament he was anxious to have us leave his premises quite hastily. "The press would thrive upon your story," he said. On learning that they had been in contact with us already he was quite worried lest they might have traced us to his premises. He sought to give the impression that the NUP was a highly respected association; and that repercussions for such a movement could be disastrous should publicity concerning an eloped minister be connected with it. However, he did allow us to use the premises for a forwarding address until fixed lodgings could be secured.

Life for Arnold, with an ailing wife, had been hard. He was often in and out of jail because of his constant warfare against the wiles of a Catholicism, which appeared to him just as furtive and as devious as any Communism of the period. Yet Ruth worked with him wonderfully to her very end. This was fifty years ago. A time when it was commonly considered a worse sin for a Catholic to enter a Protestant church than enter a Prostitute! This was an age when alert Protestants, such as Arnold, had not forgotten the Vatican's active role in politics during a war which was hardly over. This Church which might well excommunicate a Catholic for marrying a Protestant, yet never publicly excommunicated Hitler or his top henchmen; and later even colluded with some of the latter for their safety! Indeed, a system, which dogmatically affirmed that an unbaptized child could never enter Heaven; yet paradoxically affirmed that an unborn child's life, had to be saved before that of its own mother. And even though the same mother may have countless other children to care for!

Our task that day was to secure clean lodgings and it was to prove a difficult one. One district recommended was Chelsea. It was not the best of districts, though it had its night life then, and passing the old Chelsea Palace appeared quite amusing for there, in big letters, was advertised the play which had been running for some considerable time 'Don't Point, It's Nude.' Katie and I could appreciate humour, yet we would never have entered such a place. It symbolised the coarse, vulgar nightlife of the world, which we'd been well and truly conditioned to oppose. A bit further on we came across a shortish cul-de-sac: it was Upceme Road. At the top of it stood the gas works and, a few houses down; some rooms were advertised as being vacant. The place seemed bright and the curtains were clean, so we applied and were shown a well-furnished bed-sitter, which was suitable for a couple. The landlady, who lived in the basement, was smart and clean looking. She and her husband spoke with distinct southern Irish accents. They wanted us to be happy. Regrettably, we had to share a kitchen with an elderly and cantankerous Irishman who never seemed to be sober - a scoundrel who was out to stir things up whenever Katie wished to use the kitchen.

That night, however, was truly one never to be forgotten because of our full experience of an uninhibited sexual union. Moral restraints took second place under the assumption that God had already brought us together. We didn't need the OK of man to confirm it. After that first night I realised that, if God had made anything better than sex, then He must have kept it for Himself. This was no mere lust or playing on the physical appetites: it was something in which the spiritual and physical were interwoven. They supplemented each other, culminating in a bliss of mental rapture and peace. However, the hours passed only too quickly. The world soon broke in with its glum, harsh and grimy reality. The gas works' buzzer blew outside. The uncouth character from the room next door made his way to the kitchen and refused to clean up the mess he made. Yes, he did his utmost to create an unpleasant undercurrent.

Much time was now to be spent between trailing the streets of the area in order to secure better accommodation, and in scanning the job vacancy columns of the newspapers. Katie had no difficulty in securing work in the accounts department of a very fashionable shop around the Sloane Street area, while I acquired work at a MacFisheries shop, ripping open boxes in the wet cellar. The manager was rough, and yet friendly, but regrettably the assistant down in the cellar didn't enjoy my refined, gentle and polite presence with him there. I, being used to carrying a Bible, detested ripping open fish boxes and recoiled in absolute horror at every profanity used by the person who was working with me. Half a day there was more than I could stomach and in the afternoon I was out once more job hunting. That Katie offered to collect my cards later - plus my half a day's pay! - was credit to her as I regrettably lacked the guts myself. She willingly called and the manager seemed kind, though mystified.

Soon, the ice cream and cake firm of Lyon's, Cadby Hall was approached where thankfully I was offered a job sweeping the floors and being a general dogsbody. The hours were long, but then the money was good so I eagerly accepted the post. It was a job that provided further insight into the depravity of human nature. There were more women than men in this cupcake department, and most women were geared to the side of a conveyor belt putting cakes into boxes. A woman in charge, wearing blue instead of white, kept the pace up for these packers by constantly bawling at them. I associated her task and manner as having affinities with a master on a slave galley. Admittedly, the work was on piece rate terms, but I very much felt the female SS of Hitler's Germany had their counterparts on the Lyon's shop floors. Granted, such slave work was accompanied by lively music blaring through the speakers and, perhaps as an extra incentive, always an exchange of coarse, mucky jokes amongst the women. These were far more coarse than those indulged in by groups of men. It was all very sad as I'd always shown respect to the fairer sex and was now becoming highly disillusioned. I never expected such coarseness from women.

Trailing The Streets Of London

I longed for five-thirty or six p.m. to arrive, as it would be followed by an evening of bliss. Katie would be there at our small-furnished accommodation and I would throw my arms around her. She would have prepared me a lovely tea with the limited money coming in, and we would cuddle up and make love. And how we longed for the weekends that we might do some sightseeing! The latter nearly always included attendance at some new religious gathering. For example, there was the elderly Rev. Dr Waite who ran his own Baptist church and dished out his questionable credentials for a fee, but then he soon gave us the cold shoulder on learning who we were. He was a man of principles! The building was quite smart, but empty apart from half a dozen old ladies who called him the dear, reverend doctor!

A far more impressive and memorable establishment was the Church of the Good Shepherd in the Pimlico region. Here a much more distinguished character had taken over an ex-Nonconformist chapel still partly damaged from the war. He'd made it an enterprising concern through ritualistic and esoteric worship. For Katie the whole atmosphere was too heavy, and appeared sinister. I'd still considered it a tremendous honour to wear a preacher's collar, but the sides-men of this odd denomination were also dressed in clerical garb; one akin to a Nonconformist, one akin to an Anglican and one to a Roman! In fact it appeared as one big clerical dressing-up parade. It had to be seen to be believed! The Organist, who was of smallish stature, proved the first to unnerve timid Katie. Swivelling around, he kept looking across to catch our eye; gave a little smile and a wave. But as this was interspersed with some harsh and heavy organ music, it unnerved Katie even more.

When the actual worship commenced the Most Rev. Dr Nicholson, Archbishop of Karim, appeared attired in all but the kitchen sink! The choir, which entered with him, was mostly of girls in colourful regalia. And - if my memory serves me correctly! - they wore thin veils. 'Was this the Archbishop's harem?' I asked myself Yet I was in the last situation to judge?

The sermon was in the form of answering letters from enquirers and, whatever redeeming features the archbishop had, culture was not paramount, nor his grammar precise. Indeed, one question appeared to have been asked out of sarcasm: 'why did he wear gloves when he took services and what was their significance?' Well, before this prelate had time to elaborate, we both arose from our pews and quite noisily walked out of the premises in disgust. We felt they were making a mockery out of religion! Then, on leaving this ornate church with its over-abundance of sanctuary lamps, candlesticks and thuribles, we spotted the statue of the virgin at the entrance. The water stoup was loosely resting upon its outstretched hands. Consequently we gave the statue a long deserved wash, seeing no harm in that. Then, happily journeyed to our temporary home for a night of sexual ecstasy. We questioned the morals of the ex-West End waiter, the Most Rev. Dr Nicholson while we justified our own.

The miles we traversed in those days must have been astronomical. Limited revenue and high rents did not allow for many heavy bus and tube fares. Yet we enjoyed almost every minute of our time together. To be together was truly paradise! We would travel to Richmond and to Kew Gardens. While visiting the latter, after an unsuccessful appointment concerning the pastorate of a Congregational church, I decided to let my hair down so we romped on the grass, cuddling, kissing and me rolling on top. A park keeper blew his whistle towards us and said, "None of that there here!" I turned over and looked up at him. His face flushed scarlet and he said, "Beg your pardon, Sir;" then he touched his cap.

Some parts of the city were full of excitement. Other parts were eerie. I think of Nottinghill Gate and, more memorably, the start of Waterloo Bridge with its mist, smog, hissing gas lights and still night water down below. But then, even the daytime can be frightening to a timid soul. Katie was three months off eighteen; still slightly nervous and, being so beautiful, one had only to leave her to pay a visit to a toilet and someone would have made a pass or frightened her. The working classes were not the culprits; it was usually the dandy-type complete with a briefcase and a bowler hat!

One religious centre created a lasting impression on us. We had been walking the sunny streets near Hendon when we came across a place, not unlike a convent, with its chapel attached. We stopped and read the words, 'Pillar of Fire!' Immediately my thoughts went back to three years previously; to the term I'd spent at Kensit's College, training to be a Wycliffe preacher. There had been links of fellowship between the two colleges; indeed, the youngest member of the Pillar of Fire, Ginger, had then visited us. This Pillar of Fire was the creation of a woman in America, called Alma White. She was in theology, Methodist, as well as Holiness. Her followers all dressed in dark clerical attire, akin to that of the early Puritans. They lived a communal, self-supportive life, and were strictly vegetarian. We introduced ourselves and they were most friendly. Anticipating an early marriage, we addressed ourselves to them as if we were already man and wife. They welcomed us into a memorable service. None other than Ginger himself arose to play on his fiddle! He led us in an old Sankey type of favourite entitled: 'The dear old Precious Book!' I sensed it brought tears to quite a few eyes, ours included.

Quite a contrasting emotion occurred during the sermon that followed. A somewhat stern, sombre and 'holier than thou' kind of Christian kept eyeing us up and down as he delivered it. Well, preaching certainly wasn't a redeeming feature and, worse still, he had a marked impediment. Consequently, we could have burst our sides in laughter and excused our frivolity by thinking that if he'd appeared to us less self-opinionated we would have been extremely sorry for him.

Immediately after the worship, we were graciously asked to join the community for tea. It was the first vegetarian meal of which we'd ever partaken and, though I'm now a strict vegetarian, I still view it as having been one of the best. The host to 'the Reverend and Mrs Thompson!' extended a most cordial welcome, plus the honour of offering grace. Yes, although I certainly had a qualm of conscience due to their addressing us as man and wife when we were in Scottish colloquilism 'Bidie-in' and in English: 'living over the brush!' I considered the occasion a gracious and blessed one. But, then, need I have had such a pang of guilt? The most human and handsome of their group assured us, in private, that the rest weren't nearly as 'goody goody' as they appeared. "Though we stand for the Holiness doctrine of 'sinless perfection' I can assure you", he said: "things are not underneath what they appear on the surface. I could tell you plenty!" Well, ones brief period as a Pastor had taught me that the outwardly pious – both Reformed as well as Roman - could be inwardly callous, if not cruel.

It was easy for ultra-Protestants of those early 1950s to suspect less virtuous motives behind Catholic practices. Monasteries were often suspected of being breeding grounds for homosexuals. As for convents, we smiled cynically concerning Nuns who thrashed the naked body with a scourge called 'the discipline'. It was a penance frequently prescribed by 'Father' after they'd divulged in great detail most delicate sins to him within a dark cupboard called a confessional! However, gospel hall Protestantism was not without a skeleton or two in its own cupboard. It's what a nervous child could have thought when, to overcome fear of the family dog, her mum locked her in a dark cupboard beneath the stairs alongside of it The intention might have been: 'I'll show you that the dog won't harm you!' Well, perhaps so!

As for matches being lethal in the hands of children, Who would ever doubt it? But for youngsters to learn it, from having to hold them until they burnt their finger ends, is hardly the kind of lesson that would be condoned today. Yet it may well have done the trick remarkably well.

Concerning an effective cure for enuresis being through a forced night excursion to a secluded garden - there to be arrayed in nothing else but the wet sheets themselves, while forced to walk around in circles! - it would surely increase the incontinence rather than ever cure it!

Nevertheless, it is far too glib and easy for one generation to scorn the penitential practices or parental disciplines of an earlier one. Indeed, I still smile when I think of my own mother's reaction when she saw a white lady linked to a Negro gentleman. With horror, she blurted out in wrath: "That woman over there is a brazen hussy; a disgrace to femininity! Just look at her! She needs to be put in the stocks and publicly horsewhipped as an example to others!" Mother was the kindliest of souls; but even she became the victim of ethical hypocrisy.

The members of the Pillar Of Fire, here in Brent Green, professed to living 'a sinless life' through a second work of divine grace. "God has sanctified us wholly and taken away all urge to sin," they said. "There is no room for us to boast. It is His doing and not ours!" Well, I knew it was what John Wesley had once taught as attainable but I sensed they were pulling the wool over their own eyes. Indeed, the youngest member, who longed to return to the States to be reunited with his fiancée, had that day confirmed it.

As a source of income this close knit commune not only ran a private school of some quality, they also housed their own elaborate printing establishment. And then, as a further means towards being fully self-sufficient, they had a spacious allotment cared for by a kind-looking, grey haired gentleman of advancing years who spoke with a soft, gentle American accent. For myself, I considered such features in a cleric to be a portrayal of saintliness, but Katie was shrewder than I. She had also discovered that not only are outward looks often deceptive but, what I perhaps hadn't yet realised; many put on such a face merely to convey a favourable impression to others for their own self-motivating ends.

Yes, the weekends were truly marvellous but, regrettably, those hours flew! Monday mornings constantly loomed up and work appeared so very uncongenial. I sense I'd been well and truly spoilt latterly as a Baptist pastor, in Bradford, and in previous months just looking after myself (well, trying to!) at Harrogate. Caring for the one I loved necessitated slogging for eight hours in a factory environment not too far removed from the tool room once remembered with dread. But now the knowledge that I would be with Katie for the later hours of each day was the greatest incentive of all. I willingly slogged! I would soon be back in Upcerne Road where she would be waiting for me.

On one occasion, returning from work, I learned that she'd gone through a rougher time of it than ever, because of the alcoholic Irishman in the flat next door. It was now imperative that we secure more congenial lodgings. But how did the kitty lie? Alas, it seemed to be lower than ever! Money was needed for clothes as well as food. Poor Katie had only the clothes she was wearing when we'd eloped! But then, a flash of inspiration suddenly occurred: why not sell the story of our elopement to the national press? Celebrities had done this; why shouldn't we? Well, it seemed worth a try.

The first attempt was via public telephone and − if the memory serves me well − directed towards a press agency. One thing was sure: the fellow at the other end of the line felt that my predicament would hardly be newsworthy. "How thick can one become?" I asked Kate. "The man is so dense he doesn't know a top story when offered one on a plate!" More remarkable still, he appeared almost annoyed that I'd wasted his time. Nevertheless, one would not be put off. The News of the World boasted of having the largest circulation in the world. We were always game for a lark, especially to shock the prudish and outwardly respectable - so we soon acted on a mutual decision.

The experience was intense and exciting as we made our way towards Fleet Street. Soon we were entering the premises of that newspaper which is famous in the minds of some and notorious in the mind of others. Our story, I felt convinced, would undoubtedly interest them. Yet, as I was escorted into one room, I felt the atmosphere a trifle gaunt and sinister. Perhaps I was creating such an atmosphere myself! Was I honouring God in offering to sell such a story? Did it possibly savour a little of Judas Iscariot's selling his Lord for thirty pieces of silver? Well, whatever the dilemma, it was too late to back out now! The Editor himself - I'd refused to see anyone below him - walked into the room. He appeared cautious, yet congenial, and was not without a dry sense of humour. A deal was settled there and then, but to confirm this the editor asked our consent that he might ring up Bradford to verify what I'd told him. "You will appreciate how cautious we have to be," he said. "All types of characters have been in this very room. One fellow asked how much it was worth to tell of how he murdered someone, and, incidentally, he actually had!" Well, Bradford soon confirmed my story and this gentleman of an editor opened a drawer. "Here is ten pounds, and, if you promise not to divulge this story to any other newspaper, come back next weekend and we'll give you another ten pounds!" Well, ten pounds was certainly far more than an average weekly wage and we were highly delighted. We left this gracious person but not before furnishing him with our address, lest he wished to contact us.

The next evening, while relaxing in the furnished flatlet at Upcerne Road, the doorbell downstairs rang. The landlady answered and escorted the enquirers (who made out they were our friends) up to our room. One of them was from none other than the Daily Mirror, and the other was from the Daily Sketch. Via the grapevine they had learned of our whereabouts and they were most anxious to learn how things were progressing. They then asked if I'd mind donning my discarded collar for a photograph and, being willing to experience an ego trip, I willingly obliged. There might even be a small write-up to follow! Past pals would read it. How they'd relish seeing a photo of me in the national dailies! Why, my elopement was more romantic than most of the Hollywood romances I'd screened! My fiancée and I were the very stars in a love story that was real. Past friends at the printing establishment in far distant Holywell might read about me! Perhaps those in a Tyneside cinema would as well! It appeared wonderfully exciting! Our visitors' cameras kept flashing in our direction and then, as they left, one shoved five pounds into my hand as an afterthought. Why, we felt over the moon. We expected some unobtrusive article to possibly appear later that week; but much would depend, they said, on how pressed their papers were for news!

The next day was a Wednesday, which I'd taken off from work, as we were anxious to secure more congenial apartments. Well, as we made our way along the main thoroughfare a broad cockney stopped us dead in our tracks. He pointed at us and with a gleeful, jovial accent said: "Daily Mirror, ha! ha! ha!" Well, we eagerly sought out the first newsagent or street hawker in sight and purchased a copy of the same. But then, to our astonishment, we saw that the whole front page of the Daily Sketch had one sole photo of ourselves. The caption reading:

'Marry? Soon As We Can! Well, pride comes before a fall and darkness follows light! A dark cloud was hovering over Upcerne Road as we returned from the gaiety and joy of the afternoon: reality took the place of rapture. The landlady was waiting at the top of the outside steps. Her hands were on her hips and she'd been waiting for our return. With Irish rage and Dublin accent she proudly blurted out: "I would have you know that we are God fearing people here and we run a clean and respectable guest house. You have half an hour in which to pack and leave our premises!" Looking at me in astonished horror she added. "I'd no idea I was harbouring a Protestant minister under our roof. I would have you to know that we are God fearing Catholics here." Lacking in charity I simply added: "But I'll bet you never go to church!", she responded: "I would have you know that I attend every Sunday and saints days as well. Now I'm waiting here until you get your belongings together." "Well, what about the whole week's rent we've paid in advance? " I asked. "You'll not get any of that" she replied, "You gave us the impression that you were married!" "Well, I never said I was, and you never asked me." I replied.

I smirked at this personification of self-approval as her gentler husband looked on in mute pity. Young Katie and I, cases in hand, were again touring the streets of London, not to visit the sights or casually look for better lodgings, but in sheer and absolute desperation to find basic accommodation. All we required was a clean room to share until marriage, via the court, could be granted. And we'd already applied for the latter. The hours of tramping the streets that wet, foggy day seemed intensely long and the darkness began to draw in. Door after door was closed in front of us due probably to our being a young couple, and particularly because the coat Katie was wearing was a slack, open style, the type that in those days was also worn by expectant mothers.

With the passing of those footslogging hours one or two places did offer us accommodation but they were drab, dirty, greasy or even smelly apartments. When some such doors opened, one was confronted by a haze and an odour, while the occasional occupant appeared not a little sinister. I could never have worked eight hours a day while she, timid and fearful, might have been left on her own. It would have been a living nightmare for such a nervous creature. We resumed our footslogging. Different cards advertising apartments to let were browsed through in shop doorways and on side windows. From one district we trudged to another while more rain drenched us.

That night, mounting tension and strain reached its peak: "I can't go on any more! I want to go back," cried Katie, it seems as if I'll have to return home! There is nowhere! No one will have us!" It seemed as if the bottom had dropped out of everything. 'Has God forsaken me?' I asked myself. I wanted to cry but the tears just wouldn't come. "I want to love and protect you," I uttered. "I took you away from the nightmare of your past: we need each other!" Then, as had previously happened in times of extremity, I felt a surge of renewed confidence: "God has brought us together, we need each other; and I can't see you going back to such a frightful situation. You said yourself that they would just about murder you if ever you returned! Let us offer a prayer together, Katie. God will not desert us!" In a fog-dimmed, misty street, in persistent drizzle, the rain dripping from our noses, we prayed from the very depth of our hearts. Yes, it was reflective of the mystic Francis Thompson's words that he'd coined on the embankment:

> *Yea in the night, my Soul, my daughter,*
> *Cry, -- 'clinging Heaven by the hems';*
> *And behold, Christ walking on the water,*
> *Not of Genasereth but of Thames!*

Yes, but for us it wasn't the Thames. It was Fulham Broadway! Christ came to us that night - He answered that prayer and what was more, I knew that he was making allowances for our imperfections which the religiously pious called 'living in sin'. Our very next enquiry was at a pleasant terraced house where a well-built and fairly attractive landlady warmly welcomed us in. She spoke with a German accent and, due to the proximity of the war years; this could have put us off. Yet Mrs Naska welcomed us into a pleasant, clean home, and into an adequate room to the rear. The rent was comparatively reasonable; the district was good and we were wonderfully relieved. A room, occupied by two young ladies involved in theatrical life, was next to ours, while a married couple with a child occupied a room to the front.

Frustrating Work & A Frustrated Landlady

The first few days in our new accommodation had necessitated having time off work, but soon, for financial reasons, it was necessary to return. When, indeed, I did return to work the publicity the national press had afforded us was truly expressed. After having donned my baker's white cap and overalls I entered the cupcake section, complete with the long brush with which to sweep the floors. Everyone present burst into a chorus, which reverberated throughout the whole length of the building: "For he's a jolly good fellow!" It seemed as if the cheering which followed would never end. And one was truly elated as well as grateful to them for it

I was very soon called that morning to the personnel department for they also were aware of the coverage in the national press They appeared highly embarrassed at having given me the meagre post of a sweeper-up on the bakery floor. And, embarrassing for myself, they now wanted me as a costs clerk within the accounts department. I remonstrated with them that maths was far from my best subject. One could hardly have said that secular education had been confined to a primary school, and that marks in the final year for maths were three out of a hundred - the three not for accuracy but for neatness! To that degree I lacked humility and ended up in the accounts office for a very brief spell. There were just two others in that office - a sweet and rather attractive lady who spent most of her time manicuring her nails and a small-built Polish fellow who sought to make my three days most miserable. I wished that each minute, which felt like an hour, could have been spent in the bakery sweeping the floors. Was not such menial work full of compensations? One could slip from there into the far from hygienic toilets and, in a cubicle, sit on a seat, and consume ice cream or cup cakes till they came out of one's ears. The firm allowed one to eat as much as one wished, feeling that employees would soon tire of it, but I never did, even though the environment was most disconcerting. I was opposed to acquiring food in the cafeterias of the factory at an unreduced price so consumed as much during working hours as possible. Indeed, my stomach must have been exceedingly good as those toilets were far from the cleanest of places. Though a large notice stated that the place was a food factory and one was requested to wash the hands after using the WCs and urinals, many ignored that notice. I also felt that large slabs of cooking lard, uncovered and directly outside the gents' urinal, were hardly in the healthiest of places. But who was I to criticise? This was Lyons Bakery and their cakes were in high demand all over Britain.

Though sweeping the floors had normally entailed no mental worries there had been one notable exception. The occasion arose through sweeping one day around the desiccated coconut machine. There were two bins at the side of it. One was for sweepings from the floor and the other was for the grated coconut. Well, having one part of my head in the heavens, and the other with Katie, I dreamily kept depositing the contents of my shovel into the wrong bin. This was not remarked upon for some considerable time; not until a fellow remarked to me, "The topping on those cup cakes sure look an odd colour!" My worse suspicions were beginning to dawn. One or two folk looked across and, being next to a wall, one could hardly look back. Temporary relief occured when a pleasant Charge Hand said, "Let's ignore it; not many will have passed through!" But then a grump of a character began to elaborate on a few bits of hair and grit. "We'll have to shut down!" he blurted, blowing the matter out of all proportion. Later, being strongly reprimanded in the Foreman's office I merely stated that their practice of locating the desiccated coconut bin next to the rubbish bin was hardly a wise policy; and they could hardly deny it. It's decades ago now, but believe it or not, an unpleasant dream sometimes occurs, reminiscent of trays on a conveyor belt approaching. Yes, but for that one incident, sweeping up had been tons better than office work in a costs office. The latter was reminiscent of a maths class way back at Holywell Council school conducted by Gomer Williams.

It was a God-sent relief when a Personnel Officer returned to ask how I was settling in as a Costs Clerk. One could hardly say, 'Let me go back to sweeping up!' Labouring was considered too menial for a man of the cloth. Why? I fail to know. Was not Jesus a Manual Worker? Be that as it may, a compromise was reached. Semi-clerical work was in the offering. It involved checking various gauges used in the manufacture of ice-cream as well as conveying and connecting new drums of paper to the ice-cream wrapping machines. Well, the latter I fully enjoyed while the former was occasionally forgotten. I think I spent too much time reading sections from a pocket Testament; such other worldliness was no doubt a reaction to several marked obscenities uttered in my presence. One fellow, who excelled in an assortment of vulgarities of the cruder kind, was proud to tell me of his after work and weekend activities as a Salvationist. His inconsistencies were due to a desire to be accepted by two types of people and he was not alone. It was easy to see his faults, yet not so easy to see my own! The man was basically a kind, caring fellow.

The foreman of the department was a marked contrast. He stated that he was NOT a believer. In full view of the rest of us he would wink, link a lady charge hand, undo his flies with his other hand and then slip into one or other of the massive fridges with her. That both were married to another merely heightened my disgust of the whole situation. But they were proud to flaunt their liaison. This fellow, who took a dislike towards me, was nevertheless quite apologetic when at a later date my time to terminate employment arrived. "You'll not think much of my way of carrying on, will you? I wonder what memories you'll have of me!" were his final words. I think I told him that I bore him no malice. Who was I in any case, to judge him! It seemed as if he was pleased to leave it that way. Meanwhile, the clocks could never get to knocking off time soon enough. And then I'd rush back to the flat as speedily as my legs would take me, where soon we would eventually enjoy our own time of 'knocking off'.

Upstairs in our lodgings a youngish Geordie had now procured a room for himself. He had a sneaking suspicion of who we were but could never rest until he knew. After much scheming on his part we let the penny drop. He was indeed a furtive character assuring us of his confidence, yet, to court favour with the landlady, told her about us. She soon let the cat out of the bag and was at first extremely sympathetic to our plight. She was also noticeably becoming more congenial and relaxed, and would sing or hum to herself, '0 Johnny, 0 Johnny, how you can love!' With the passing of the days, it seemed as if this mature divorcee wanted to share our leisure periods as well as some of Johnny's. On more than one occasion her face appeared, peering through the fanlight above the door of our room, while we could have been making love. The first time, on our opening the door, she seemed as if she wanted to join in our fun. However, when it happened the second time, we made it clear, non-verbally, that she was intruding on a relationship, which we considered sacrosanct. Well, she now acted as a woman scorned. I'd been far from diplomatic and she now affirmed that her purpose in looking through the fanlight was to make sure that we were not indulging in sex. Hers was a respectable residence and whereas she would turn a blind eye to our sharing the one room, which possessed two separate 'put you ups', sexual immorality would not be tolerated under any circumstances. She then became increasingly hostile and stressed that she held high moral standards, as did her uncle, a cleric, to whom she was indebted. I knew her uncle's church well. It stood in close proximity to the headquarters of the National Union of Protestants and had frequently felt the impact! He was one of the many who'd vowed before God, on ordination day, to uphold the 39 articles of the Church of England, and on the next day broke most of them. Such clerics, via the confessional, set themselves up as moral counsellors and there was never a shortage of penitents from a certain type of spinster ever eager to receive their ministrations, and ghostly counsel.

As the time passed, our landlady was becoming unbearable to all but one under her roof. Indeed, a brick on the outside wall had been cracked by someone trying to hammer a nail into it, probably for hanging out washing. Soon every tenant was quizzed in order to find the culprit. Later a scratch on the table in the hall led to a similar inquisition. It appeared that the dear lady was still deeply unfulfilled!

Katie had by this time secured a post at Cadby Hall in the clerical section. She was bright, intelligent and highly proficient in shorthand and typing. We consequently longed for those brief moments when we could meet each other during short dinner breaks. On Thursdays at teatime we would queue up together at a side entrance of the factory so as to procure misshaped cakes and Telford pies at reduced prices. Then we would almost skip off together, madly in love and anxious to spend the evenings engrossed in pure and noble aspirations. We would read the Bible, say our prayers, and culminate the evening indulging in sex until the sound of the landlady prowling outside our door turned us off.

Several folk at work were not unmindful of our plight to acquire fresh accommodation. One fellow, another Salvationist, had repeatedly mentioned that he and his wife would be more than delighted to have us stay with them should we ever wish to do so. But now, on approaching him for this sole purpose he was fighting shy, putting the onus on his wife, and seeking to evade me. One evening Katie and I visited a house where the lady, quite young and attractive, started to welcome us with open arms into her home. She told us we could, indeed, have the run of her home and would be delighted to put us up. Her heart warmed towards us. Suddenly, her husband appeared. He asked us bluntly what we wanted, rudely eyed us up and down and said, "They're not coming here", whereupon she remonstrated with him, to the point of an apparent tear but it was of no avail. He didn't want any lodgers in his house. Her face looked distraught. She'd been utterly humiliated. "They're not coming here", he repeated, and the dear soul tried to apologise for her partner's ignorance. She was obviously more hurt in having to turn us down than we were in being turned away. We later prayed, as we walked, for God to bless her and give her the strength she needed to live with such a tyrant. Yes, it seemed as if our faith in human nature, as far as landladies were concerned, was partly restored, but it was short lived.

One of us was later informed, during work, of a house divided into furnished apartments, and one was available. This seemed very convenient as it was just past the side entrance of Lyon's where Telford's bakery vans were usually parked. On reaching it, we knocked at the large door. It opened and we met a young Irish couple who said they were from the Free State. The ground floor room into which they invited us was a hovel. They sat on the edge of a dirty old bed, which was conspicuous for its brass knobs and greyish black mattress; the mattress was very badly stained and contained a large hole. The air smelled of stale grease and the atmosphere made me want to scratch. I sensed that, if I'd scrutinised the discoloured walls closer, I would have perceived the movement of vermin. The couple seemed kind, though undoubtedly poor and they were thin and exceedingly pale. Through lack of work in Southern Ireland they had been forced to leave their young children with their in-laws there. The couple were slogging away at Lyons so as to send money back home. They were an exceedingly pitiable couple whose plight stuck in our minds. We could have wept for them, and I believe Katie did, as we realised in comparison how extremely fortunate we were, and how very much they needed help which we weren't in a position to give.

As we walked we often prayed for the blessing of God on those less fortunate than ourselves. We felt spiritually elated in so doing. However, there were one or two who might have questioned whether, in our situation, we could have been used to confer a blessing on anyone. Such was a preacher known as Martyn Lloyd Jones.

Westminster Chapel was a place where the Pastor had attracted attention throughout the evangelical world. He'd used his past secular post as a Harley Street practitioner to advantage. Crowds would fill a mere hall in Aberavon, which was his first pastoral charge; and now he was minister of this prominent, double galleried Congregational church. Yet, like myself in the English Baptist denomination, he was also a non-Union cleric within the world of English Congregationalism.

The man had virtually stepped into the shoes of his predecessor, G. Campbell Morgan, and his congregation was a Mecca for Fundamentalists of a Calvinistic slant. The ex-medic truly packed his congregation almost chock-a-block, with pious folk. He could hardly fail when his theology implied that they were 'saved' and 'eternally secure'. And as for the wrath of God, which his theology equally stressed, this was reserved for the Non-believers who would not - and in fact could not! - do anything to alter their plight. It had all been predetermined by God! Such theology, taken to its logical conclusion, denies the existence of free will and therefore makes nonsense of both virtue and vice.

This strict Preacher, who was usually staid and dour, was hardly likely to appreciate our marked presence amongst his people. We had secured a central pew and wearing my revered collar, which I made a practice of doing on Sundays, my fiancée and I waited for the sermon to begin while we were linked to each other in love. After all, 'God is love!' Well, obviously the man in the pulpit didn't approve: though so narrow in outlook, he must have naughtily scanned the cheaper dailies; for he recognised who we were - even though our photos in London had only appeared in the Mirror and the Sketch. Strong digs occurred in his sermon against young folk who run away from home, making their way to London. When he touched upon a young man, dressed in clerical attire (which he himself never wore), he was hardly likely to expect me to remain inactive. So obviously we arose with some commotion and squeezed along the pew. His tone then mellowed considerably. "I meant no harm," he said: "Just sit down. I meant no harm!" Well, we'd had enough. He knew it and, when he saw that a second request, as well as one from an usher, for us to stay was without effect, he merely said, "Oh, just let them go." Well, I must admit that I looked upon it as one hilarious joke; but several of his followers – as we pushed our way out – apologised for his lack of Christian grace.

Two Men of Influence Track Us Down

On returning to our dreaded lodgings we found Mrs Naska even more agitated than ever. Two smart gentlemen had called round to see us and they would certainly call back. Her curiosity seemed to be eating her away. As for ourselves, we were not a trifle worried lest they had been sent by Katie's parents to compel her to return to Shipley. "I'll never go," she said, "I'd rather die than ever go back there!" Yes, even now she was agitated, timid and nervous. Sadistic fiends delight to torment such people and didn't I know it. Why, within that self same period, an elderly dentist had tantalised her with his instruments. Not until I intervened giving him a severe reprimand did he desist. Katie was petrified and we sought a Dentist worthy of the name elsewhere.

Who could these two strangers possibly be? The possibility of their coming from some legal centre seemed most unlikely. We had already applied to get a special dispensation from the court so as to marry. The grounds were those of cruelty. My mother had actually come down to London to speak up on our behalf, but the hearing had regrettably been turned down because Katie's people resided at Shipley and the London court could, alas, have no jurisdiction over the matter. We'd waited so long only to learn that our petition must be heard in the vicinity where Katie's parents resided. For us to return to the Bradford area in order to fight openly for our rights there was too cruel an ordeal to contemplate. Mother's one and only visit to London had proved fruitless, though her correspondence to us was to be of constant encouragement.

Tea was finished that day. Sure enough the two strange gentlemen made their return visit to see us. We welcomed them into our bed sitter and we waited to learn of their mission and purpose in tracing us. "You have no idea how long it has taken us to discover your whereabouts," they remarked, "and we've come with an offer which we hope will be to our mutual satisfaction." "Who exactly are you, and where are you actually from?" might well have been the gist of my opening words uttered in that far off past. To our surprise and delight, these strangers were journalists from that famous weekly journal: 'Illustrated'. They had 'tracked us down' with a genuine offer and now, without any quibbling, they would give us fifty pounds - a tidy sum in those days - for my exclusive story as to why we had eloped. Then asking about our plans for future marriage they asked if we might consider travelling to Scotland, at their expense, in order that we could marry under Scottish law. Seemingly, a twenty-one year old called Jimmy Goldsmith had recently done this kind of thing. He'd eloped with a young heiress of eighteen-called Isobel Patino. Yes, the 'Illustrated's offer had come in the midst of heightening opposition. We simply knew that God's intervention had once more become manifest at a time of extremity. Time and time again this glorious God would allow us to get to the eleventh hour of desperation, and then He would intervene. With gratitude, we clinched the deal with our guests and, no doubt, we later wept on our knees in gratitude and joy towards God. Meantime, as our welcome guests spoke to us in leaving we could hear the landlady's objectionable movements outside our very door. She had been trying to listen in. Well, we all laughed together and for all we cared she could go and take a running jump.

To enter Cadby Hall, the next morning, and tell them that this would be my last day with them would be a relief indeed. One would be able to say farewell to a sweatshop of iniquity, but happily with some truly worthy exceptions. What is more, the money had been good and all that was required was three hours notice on either side, so this I gladly gave, and I think it was later on the same day that we were interviewed by 'the big man': a Mr Jones who was the editor-in-chief of Illustrated. I know that as we entered an office a young lad was bluntly ordered to bring two chairs upon which we could sit. One of these was a bit rickety. "Go and get a seat with a bottom in it, boy," cried out one of the men, "and be quick about it lad!" As he said it he smiled to us, but I wanted to smile to the lad. Our heart went out to the youngster. He was small and nervous. Then the Editor confirmed everything that had been discussed. Our journey to Scotland would be within the fortnight, but we needed to be ready at very short notice.

At that first interview with the two gentlemen from the Illustrated, we'd learned of their most recent assignment. It had been one of creating an article on the American evangelist, Billy Graham. They suggested our making his acquaintance, as this could be very advantageous for my future in the Christian ministry. "Just a thought!", they said: "It's up to you!" Indeed, they had got to know him considerably well through interviewing him both here and America.

On our second interview, as we were joined by the editor of this leading weekly, we were informed that a meeting had been arranged. Billy would be pleased to see us both. This would be for a short period of time at the close of the rally that very night, in Harringay Arena. "He will be looking out for you," they added. Consequently, we missed no time in preparing ourselves for the great occasion, which would possibly put my future on a sound footing. With thousands of others we pushed our way into the crowded arena and were fortunate to procure seats near to the front. This gave us a first-class view of a gentleman playing his trombone, a member of the team, and we were very much aware of the stage make up, which the occasion necessitated. George Beverley Shey sang deeply and movingly and then, at the right psychological moment, we were told to await the presence of "God's messenger for this hour..." (the announcer's voice dropped to a deeper pitch): "Billy Graham!" Dramatically he appeared in view, Bible in one hand and index finger raised on the other. Soon he was reiterating two phrases, "The Bible says!" and "But, the Bible says!"

Well, although I'd come to meet Dr Graham, or as my more mushy evangelical friends called him, 'Our Billy', I was actually far from impressed. I felt sadly that his presentation of the message was as far removed from some Welsh ministers I'd learned to revere as the moon was from cheese. They avoided publicity (even Martyn Lloyd Jones was far from happy about courting it!), but this man was bathing in it. They came across as very humble; he came across as very proud. They loathed gimmicks but he lavished them. They kept to the background while he sought the limelight. I'd come expecting to witness kind eyes, graceful gestures and a voice of compassion; but I felt I was confronted with the dogmatism and driving force of one who was more suited for a left wing parliamentary election, or a trade union platform. Though the man was undoubtedly handsome I could hardly have said that he appeared holy. Yes, I had my own preconceived theories as to what a man of God should look like and poor Billy Graham was not in such a category. I, of all creatures, donned in a collar so as to be not one whit behind the many other parsons there, was picking fault with this firebrand for God; one whose ministry resulted in the nightly conversion of so many from (to use an evangelical phrase) the 'guttermost to the uttermost!'

The memorable rally terminated and we made our way to a vestibule where a whole host of ministers had accumulated. Several of them looked in our direction. I made it clear that I wished to meet Billy Graham, "Dear brother, don't you realise that almost every minister in London is anxious to meet him too?" "But he has agreed to see us, an appointment has been made," I added. "Then dear brother, if you can possibly push through that crowd then you're much fitter than we are. I fear you'll never do it!" I began to hesitate. Was it really worth the bother? I'd found the event far removed from what I'd expected. Yes, we'd have a go, as it would do no harm. As we grappled our way through the crowd we suddenly became conscious of two clerics at our side. We knew one was such before we'd seen his face. His voice was above that of the others and it sounded as if his speech was hindered by gobstoppers. He was a prominent evangelical who, by his looks of disdain, recognised us both. Then, horror of horrors, as the other fellow turned in our direction he was none other than the austere cleric whom we'd so uncharitably criticised because of his inability to preach well at the Pillar of Fire foundation. He'd appeared as the most Puritanical of that community and we'd been introduced to him as the Reverend and Mrs Thompson. Since then, the press had given us national coverage as two single folk living together in the same lodgings. So, as he came closer, we made ourselves swiftly unobtrusive amongst the crowds and, there and then, decided to make our way homewards. We were to learn later that Billy was asking what had happened to us and our journalist friends were unable to give an answer. A great opportunity had come and we let it slip by. I would often live to regret having failed to keep such an interview.

Our two friends called once more at our lodgings. Everything was now ready. Last minute arrangements had hurriedly been made and our bags were packed. Mrs Naska's curiosity had got the better of her. As we refused to put her in the picture as to whom the two strange gentlemen were she gave us immediate notice to quit. She and Johnny, a lodger, in whom we'd confided at the beginning, waited as we left with our two friends. I turned and looked towards him. He became agitated, his eyes dropped and his face turned away. I sensed I wouldn't have wanted to see my worst enemy in that situation.

Breathtaking Days Culminate in Scotia's Capital

Thanks to our new friends, accommodation was immediately procured in the Shepherd's Bush area. Mrs Evans was from South Wales, but dare I say it? She soon proved to be yet another money grabber during the short period we stayed with her. At first I felt she was an elderly soul with love in her heart. Alas, she was undoubtedly far more mercenary than the two we'd left behind us. Not only was an extra week's rent required in advance, non-refundable should we fail to give her a full week's notice on leaving, but she charged extra for laundry as well. The flats had meters in them, which were so adjusted as to provide a bare minimum of gas and electricity for a substantial amount of money. Katie was later told that she had damaged or scratched some part of the furnishings and an extra pound or two was required to compensate for that. Yet that landlady was not alone. Others of the early fifties would bear her features and the more miserly and mercenary they were, the more shrivelled up their features appeared. The penalty for worshipping filthy lucre was without doubt a heavy one.

While idling these days away – being ready to leave for Scotland at a day's notice - I created a portable rostrum from some steps, strips of metal and a board of wood procured in Shepherd's Bush market. Why, to share each other's lives and to be constantly embracing each other was seemingly heaven come down to earth. To see the glitter and loveliness of Katie's eyes and the beauty of her open face was God's answer to many years of prayer. Indeed, I worshipped the very ground she walked upon and would have died a million deaths for her. Life was young for both of us and we were so deeply in love.

The last night spent in London before we journeyed towards Scotland was eerie. Partly for a lark we had decided to sample sleeping the night in Hyde Park. The weather was warm and the thought of it appeared romantic at first. What was more, the first week's rent had run out and the thought of forking out another in advance on the morrow, when we were due to leave, was the other factor. Indeed, over and above this, the landlady was also pushing for an unjustifiable laundry charge - unjustifiable, as the sheets hadn't once been changed! Yes, this elderly landlady was out to bleed us of every penny. Therefore, welcoming a challenge, I determined to be one step ahead of her.. Consequently, we 'moonlighted' from her premises that night with a conscience as clear as Robin Hood's. But regrettably - on arriving within that massive park - timid Katie felt that, as the dusk fell, eyes were peering on her from many quarters. It was a wonderfully hot night in May, but so nervous did Katie become, that we made our way to one of the main London stations, where we eventually stretched out on one of the hard seats of the waiting room. But then, shady characters, who kept roaming in and out of the dingy and smoke-filled room, hindered our willingness to sleep. We were afraid lest we awoke in the morning to find our entire luggage gone from our side.

Well, the morning arrived, we'd fallen asleep, and our fears had been unfounded. Soon the contrasts would be extreme: Having met up with our journalist friends we were soon receiving VIP treatment, sat back in a car cuddled together, and being chauffeured by a photographer for the feature of which we were to be the two stars. Yet as I sat back my mind was on my God. Less than eighteen months previous, I'd been a cinema operator in the projection booth of the, then, seediest picture palace in the whole of Newcastle. Night after night I'd climbed those spiral iron stairs so as to feed the arcs and run the old projectors beneath that grotty bell tower of the converted chapel. And from those heights, leaning over the rails of an old balcony to the left, I'd seen the remains of the graveyard, which was a play area for children in the early evenings, and for sexual liaisons after dusk. Yes, and just before I'd terminated such a job, promotion seemingly had come my way:

The Picturedrome in Taylor Street, situated near scruffy Byker Bridge, had been allowed to re-open following some major renovations. It had quite remarkably passed the fire tests and I was expected to be the manager there, with a cashier and two ushers under me. Well, I had to be honest I'd have much preferred usherettes! Taylor Street, however, was too rough and ushers would serve the dual role of 'chucker outs'.

Memories such as the above were now flashing through my mind as, reclined within the back seat of the car, we were being driven on 'a journey of a lifetime'. What a blessing that - though the proprietor had pleaded with me to accept the managerial position - I had declined in order to work at a pittance for Evangelist Willie Hudson. How thankful I now was to the latter because he had opened up work for me in Harrogate! The Christian ministry, into which I'd been received, had been the means through which I'd met the one to become my first wife. Such a ministry was one, which sought to find the lost and feed the poor. My God was a wonderful God. He was with both of us on this glorious adventure northwards to dear and bonny Scotland, the land I'd left when no more than a bairn. I'd soon be seeing the Borders again. God seemed to be laughing too. When we indulged in sex out of love, and not lust, we sensed His presence in our union too. In fact, I somehow knew, when He was pleased and would sense those times when He looked sadly towards me.

The first real break on that memorable journey was in Leeds. Indeed, I'd anticipated slipping over from there to Bradford on the Sunday night so as to hold an open-air witness because I was anxious to convey my true reasons for our eloping in response to the conflicting press reports. On the advice of our companions within the car, we called it off at the last minute, even though such an event had been publicised in the notice columns of the Bradford newspaper! Regrettably, a few were to have a wasted turnout on that exceedingly wet Sabbath evening. The prominent Maurice Barnett (later of Central Hall, Westminster) was keen to step in on such a stunt, and it was rumoured that the dear man had turned up to sympathise with us. We spent the evening at the Golden Lion Hotel in Lower Briggate. It was truly a first-class place in those days. However even then a twinge of conscience overtook us because, as the rain came down heavily in a cloudburst past the window   we were reminded of those who had most probably turned up for the open-air meeting at Bradford in order to either cheer or heckle us. There was nothing to do but kneel down and pray: and this we did.

In those days, before the motorways existed, the journey northwards seemed quite a distance. We could have made it, with a little effort, to Edinburgh the next day. However, it was decided to travel in ease and our companions suggested we might like to spend the following night in Newcastle, over which I'd just reminisced. This we did, Katie and I staying at my Mother's. And, as the break coincided with a local holiday, it also provided opportunity to visit the famous Quayside the next morning when various bazaars were in full swing. Indeed, it gave one the opportunity to also preach in the open air, trying out the portable pulpit, or rather the steps, which formed its base!

Soon, however, midday arrived. The journey northwards had to resume. And before long, the car was approaching the beautiful border country! "Well, might it not be an opportunity, on such a spot, to make the elopement more romantic to the general reader by implying you'd hitch-hiked rather than travelled?" asked one of our companions. We stepped out of the car, walked ahead, and faked thumbing a lift for our photographer. Later, however, I was troubled. "Honesty is something we should strictly adhere to if God is to bless us", I said; and they gladly agreed. The remainder of that long journey is vague to recall, but the Scottish capital was finally reached. There our companions would 'book in' at the Caledonian Hotel, which became our regular meeting place. But first of all they booked us in at a truly delightful residence called Piries Hotel and, though our identity was deliberately kept quiet by the thoughtful proprietors, the dining room whispers were passed round, Indeed, a Minister of the United Free Church was pleased to introduce himself to us and wish us 'all the best'. One of the other residents was old Captain Anderson, a broad Scot, who is remembered most vividly, not only for his assertiveness of knowledge, but for the horror he displayed when some English children appeared in imitation kilts! The dear man was justly proud of his heritage; indeed, of his knowledge too. Meanwhile, a sweet young chambermaid wished to make it known that she knew who we were, but the staff knew how to act discreetly. As for the press, they wouldn't have been allowed a look-in.

Our rooms were next to each other though we saw little of them. The weather was fabulous and most days would find us visiting the grand, historic parts of the city or else relaxed and sprawled out on the slopes of Arthur's Seat. Indeed, although we were never really carried away while frolicking on those delightful slopes, the number of field glasses that glittered in our direction would have implied we were. We realised that some seemingly well-respected, middle-aged gentlemen, with an appreciation for voyeurism, were not backwards in coming forwards.

Matters, of course, of first priority were our need to visit the registrar's as well as to apply for the reading of the banns within the established church of the parish in which we were residents. These were transacted without any difficulty, and the resident minister proved helpful. The real problem was in finding a minister who would marry us. One afternoon we visited the massive Episcopal cathedral of St Mary's. Indeed, hardly had we entered the building before we were confronted by a quite erratic, yet delightfully pleasant cleric who, on learning of our need, was eager to arrange a wedding at the earliest opportunity. The man was an Aberdonian by the name of Strachan. He realised who we were and, being so eager to help, one was hardly likely to forget him. Regrettably our journalist friends were not impressed. The cost of such a wedding in a cathedral would undoubtedly be astronomical,' they thought. Alas, how wrong they were! The journalist who dissuaded us was a proud Presbyterian. Hence, the Sunday following found us in the highly fashionable congregation of Palmerston Place Church Of Scotland across the road. The minister of this Presbyterian Kirk was comparatively young and what most impressed me was that he, like myself, was evangelical. Yes, the Rev. Graham Hardy was certainly making a name for himself, and it was quite an experience being in such a packed congregation with academic clerics dotted here and there; and all most welcoming and totally unaffected. A contrast indeed to the established Church in England!

A day or two later, on calling at his manse, the Rev. Graham Hardy stated he would be delighted to go ahead and marry us at his church, and there would be no fee. He'd read about our past difficulties in the national press and would be only too pleased to help us. The date and time of the wedding was fixed and all we needed to do was to turn up. It was to be a quiet wedding and we'd learned to be diplomatic and discreet. At least, we thought we had! Then hotel complications arose with unforeseen repercussions.

Before our days for residential qualification were completed, a large school party had been pre-booked for Piries Hotel. They would only be staying two or three days, but this necessitated our acquiring temporary accommodation elsewhere for such a period and wherever we moved it would have to be within the parish boundaries! We were in the midst of a thriving holiday period, which was extra busy because of the heat wave. There was only one place we could find; it was a good deal less congenial in that it was more of a lodging house with apartments than a private hotel. Yes, 54 Maitland Street was the number of these weird corner premises over a ground floor bank.

A gas jet flickered at the end of a dark passage, which illuminated stairs that went up to a landing. There a stout, middle-aged lady who ushered us inside and introduced us to a thin, gaunt stranger greeted us. He walked with a slight limp and was aided by a stick. The door closed behind us and I remember still that musty, yet spicy smell, which permeated those premises, especially the bathroom. Indeed, it was not unlike the smell I have subsequently experienced in funeral parlours where an embalming has taken place: a heavy, overpowering kind of odour. This, added to the presence of plants, old Scottish furniture and curtains, resulted in an environment, which was a trifle eerie and foreboding. As for the tall, thin gentleman, he was out to impress us. He told us how he felt that he should know us. Hadn't he seen us somewhere before? Well, we soon let the cat out of the bag as to who we were! This merely confirmed what he'd seemingly surmised.

The memory is vague. At this stage the lady of the house either joined us only to leave in a distraught manner, or having been with us, made a speedy departure after having filled up with tears. "Do you know why Mrs Gray is so upset, Mr Thompson?" was the question from the gentleman's lips. "No, tell me why!" might well have been the answer. "Because your fiancée here is very like Mrs. Gray's daughter who experienced a sudden death!" Then words like these followed: "You can help Mrs Gray a great deal by treating her as if she were your own mother. Tell her all your plans for the future. Take it from me, Mr Thompson you can trust Mrs Gray. She is a lady you can trust and you must confide in no one else!" Well, I didn't fail to fall for the bait. We told her as much as we could remember about ourselves and she seemed especially interested in our plans for the future.

The time passed and curiosity made us more conversant with the flat. Regrettably difficulties were encountered. Whenever we left our double room a door nearby would speedily open and we would be asked whether we required anything. Well, we were soon directed to the bathroom! At the end of it there appeared to be an airing cupboard and nosiness led us to open it. Horror of horrors, it revealed a considerable drop and at the foot an accumulation of musty papers from which arose a sickly spicy smell.

Well, we were eager to return to our own neatly furnished room and keep the door closed or possibly locked. Katie, however, had always been nosy. On the first occasion we'd kissed she'd broken it to see who was boarding a bus! Now she was anxious to discover what lay along the dark passage past the bathroom door and round that corner.

So off we crept warily. A door was open and the light was on. There we beheld a dirty, greasy-looking cooker of the old style, but then something quite took us aback. There was an old brass-knobbed type of bed as well, and a mattress which appeared grey rather than white. Hardly had it registered when the door began to swing inwards. We quickly slunk back in fear. To our horror the stout landlady appeared. She was dishevelled, most unkempt and had a wild look in her eyes. Marvellously, she hadn't even noticed our presence as either she disappeared across the passage or we retraced our steps on tiptoe back into our room. Indeed, our bed-sitter was very smart, clean and well furnished. Was she herself so poor as to have to sleep upon a vile bed, possibly void of sheets, within a grotty kitchen? One could feel a twinge of sadness for her. They must have put themselves out for us their present guests. They were possibly trying to create an impression beyond their means! But of more relevance to us, that kitchen was where our breakfast was being cooked and it turned our stomachs to think of it. But what about the tall, thin elderly gentleman with a limp? Where was his room? The only time he seemed to venture out was late evening.

Each time breakfast was subsequently presented to us at our room door we ate the cereals and drank the tea. But, as for the bacon and eggs, with burnt bits added from the frying pan fat, they were ejected from a window. We couldn't offend the one who had presented the breakfast neatly set out on a tray and complete with napkins. There happened to be a ledge, which jutted out from the bank below our room. By the time we vacated those premises quite a line of greasy eggs and rashers of bacon must have accumulated there!

Outdoing Rogues At Their Own Game

Next morning a sudden and unexpected visitor, who had learned of our whereabouts, called to cancel all wedding arrangements. He was none other than the Rev. Graham Hardy who previously had been so kind and helpful to us. He appeared in a very disturbed and hostile mood. Though he was arrayed in a frock coat with lace cuffs, plus buckles on his shoes, his manner was far from genteel. "The wedding is off!" he said, "I refuse to marry you! I expected a quiet wedding and you've plastered it in the national press. What is more, I've got my Kirk elders to consider! What will they think?" The landlady, and the tall thin gentleman with a limp, appeared eager to support us. Then, having closed the door upon him, Mrs Gray turned to us and said: "He'll not be welcomed back here again! He's a Dandy and a turncoat! What kind of a spineless Minister is this who will allow the Kirk elders to rule him? We've shooed him off and he's gone like a frightened hare!"

"Do you realize, Mr Thompson, that someone has 'let the cat out of the bag'?" interjected the thin man with a soft and refined voice.. "Dare I be so bold as to suggest that you tell no one – and I include myself here! - about your future plans?" Tears once again welled up in Mrs Gray's eyes as she made a speedy exit. "The dear lady is extremely upset Mr Thompson. You must excuse her! I told you before: your fiancee is the splitting double of her deceased daughter. She wants you to confide in her. So make her the one exception. Treat her as a second mother. You are a man of the cloth; and she is a lady of impeccable character".

One afternoon, after a visit to the Caledonian Hotel, Katie and I were startled to find a battery of cameramen crossing Princes Street with their attention focused directly upon us. We began rushing along the busy thoroughfare until two policemen appeared as if from nowhere. They told them to get packing and to leave us alone. Indeed, on another occasion a battery of cameramen and hawk eyed reporters chased us along the same prominent street until we found seclusion and privacy in the News Theatre.

When the programme was finished and we were about to vacate the premises, pushing open the swing doors, newspaper photographers rushed towards the entrance. "Poor souls, they must have been waiting outside the whole length of the performance!" said Katie. Thankfully, the manager came speedily to our assistance and recognising who we were, escorted us to an emergency exit. He wished us the best of luck for our future and proved as kind as the Scottish police before him. Indeed, as an ex-cinema employee I felt a real affinity towards him.

Once outside, however, and our freedom along the back street was soon curtailed! Newspapermen knew how to bribe commissionaires and we had only walked a short distance before a car drove towards us and one was pinned against the wall as the vehicle mounted the pavement. The window was lowered by a sole occupant who - knowing that we were under exclusive contract with Illustrated Weekly - asked that he might take us out for the evening to dine at Queensferry. 'Yes, and for no higher a reason than to see to it that no other national paper got any more information than he had!' His name was Maurice Lyndon (possibly of the Scottish Daily Mail). and he proved utterly true to his word: Yes, our host proved a perfect gentleman and it was strange to discover that he was a Jew. Two things we learned that night: he did not believe in Christ; he revealed Him instead! Thank God for passing acquaintances such as that gentleman! They are lights in a dark world. He said he felt we were worthy of the deepest admiration for having eloped under such circumstances and, looking back, one was proud to agree.

Each evening, on returning to our eerie apartment, we would be offered refreshments and quizzed about what had transpired and what was to follow. But now, thanks to our Jewish friend, we'd had it confirmed that the people with whom we were staying were in constant liaison with the various national newspapers and being paid handsomely for any news they could give them about us. Indeed, it was proving more and more difficult to leave those lodgings; and when we did, photographers and journalists were waiting to corner us. One letter came from a newspaper affirming that a good and favourable report would be given should we cooperate. If we didn't, then a bad report would follow! Indeed, once we were put in a very good light because we allowed a snap or two to be taken while viewing rings in a jeweller's shop window. One knew that, frequently, if Reporters returned without a true story a fabrication would be safer for their livelihood than no story at all. Theirs was a thankless task!

A day or so later, another press car cornered us. This time the offer was to take us to the home of a clergyman who, they said, would consider it a privilege to marry us after the minister of Palmerston Place had changed his mind at the eleventh hour. We accepted a lift from the two occupants and soon found ourselves within the vicinity of Buccleuch. The Free Church building there was large and impressive though rather neglected. Congregations had recently dwindled and services had been temporarily transferred to the church hall close by.

Well, traversing an Edinburgh street of past distinction we arrived at the manse where an elderly looking cleric with a heavy stoop opened the door to greet us. Looking up towards us, he ushered us into a dwelling that appeared Georgian both in style and furnishings. We seemed to be confronted by old mirrors and, as if to add to the eeriness of it all, a spiral staircase was nearby. "I appreciate these kind gentlemen bringing you here," were the kind of words our elderly host uttered: "I can appreciate equally the difficulties you must have gone through with your church due to the elopement. You have my sympathies" he added. "I've been through similar. You see, half my church left me when I married my second wife. Allow me to go and fetch her!"

We were intrigued indeed when a lady, looking Katie's age, came into our presence clasping a little bundle of love in her arms. The elderly cleric appeared proud indeed to be the father. Yes, the Rev. Dr Percival Prestcott was, undoubtedly, still full of stamina. "I'll consider it a privilege to marry you in my church" he said. "However, services nowadays are in the hall, so I must ask you and your fiancée to help me to dust the church in preparation for your marriage within it." To this Katie and I there and then agreed, provided it was acceptable to Illustrated Weekly, with whom we were under exclusive contract. Indeed, one of the reporters had informed us of how this Reverend gentleman had once hit the national headlines: offering to marry the Duke of Windsor and Mrs Simpson when divines of the Church of England had adamantly refused. (What was more, in 1955, - a year after our meeting - he would again be in the national press eagerly supporting Princess Margaret's proposed marriage to Townsend when Canterbury and York were strongly against it!) The fact is, the popular press have never been averse to quoting a Dr Prestcott alongside an archbishop, a moderator of the general assembly or a cardinal when a clerical contrast of opinion makes news. After all, who is to say that one parish Cleric is superior to another? As is commonly said to the total credit of the Scottish, 'We're all Jack Thompson's bairns!' Well, be that as it may, before leaving the elaborate manse of Buccleuch Free Church a preaching engagement at short notice had been offered and accepted: I would be guest speaker at the weeknight Bible Study

The memorable evening came round and, Katie and I returned to be ushered into a spacious church hall. And what one remembers most, as I ascended that strange rostrum, was the appearance of the Reverend Doctor's congregation. These 'students of the word' appeared to be furtive rather than open to learn. Indeed, they were far from elderly and rather than look at me with a clear and open countenance were more involved in scribbling down almost every word I imparted. My text that evening was most relevant: 'The greatest of these is Love!' Well, when three or four shuffled along to the end of the benches and then sneaked out before the devotional service had closed, my suspicions began to seriously rise: was the elderly Reverend Doctor engaged in a little fundraising for himself? Next morning proved the affirmative. Prominent dailies had their own write ups of the runaway pastor preaching on love!

Both our journalist and photographer friends from Illustrated were alarmed because of such recent publicity. "It could convey the false impression that you are a couple of gullible fools!" they said. What was even worse, if we didn't honour our contract to be exclusive to Illustrated weekly, we might find ourselves in a sticky, financial mess. To secure the services of a truly reputable parish minister was now top priority, and they would also see what they could do!

As for Katie and I we only tried one other minister. We learned of an academic Episcopalian who had a small Episcopal church not far from St Giles' cathedral. On visiting his flat the fellow - unexpectedly in collar and tie – appeared honoured to make our acquaintance. After or during refreshments we were separately bombarded with questions; the answers to which he eagerly jotted down. "I hope you don't mind my doing this" he said, "but I'm trying to analyse how you tick individually. You see, I may well consider marrying you! - and I really do want to help you both; but I must be sure!. Would you very much object to calling back later in the week after I've studied the notes in depth?" he asked. "Of course not!" we replied as we went happily from his premises.

Well, when we returned, it was discovered that he had taken the liberty to discuss us with the Presbyterian minister: the Reverend Graham Hardy, who had turned us down at the eleventh hour. "I want you to know that he is still very sympathetic towards you both" he said: "He feels quite upset about adverse publicity that followed. But after sharing my notes with him we both feel that you are infatuated with one another rather than actually in love! Consequently, I really can't go ahead and marry you. I do hope you'll understand and not think unkindly of me." Yes, another supercilious cleric had wasted our valuable time!

Once married, we planned to fulfil Christian work together, if not back in Bradford - where I would seek first for reinstatement - then preferably in Wales. However, there might be a real opportunity here in Edinburgh. Consequently, we were soon calling on the superintendent of the City Mission. He lived, I think, in a bungalow. One thing I do know is that he never condemned us once, but gave us a most delightful tea; advised us to get married and to keep in touch so that when a vacancy arose on his staff, we would have first consideration. This kindly gentleman, with true generosity of spirit - being a mere city missioner! - was, not in a position to officiate at our wedding.

Undeterred, we then journeyed to Dalkeith where a Baptist church was without a minister. We arrived at the home of the secretary while a weeknight fellowship for young folk was in full swing. The fellow was not backwards in assuring us of his own 'spiritual gifts', but when I pushed him to present to the church board my offer to be their minister he promised to convene, at short notice, a special meeting where we could all meet and discuss my proposal. Unfortunately, those days passed without any such notification being received. And, when we made the acquaintance of a Baptist minister in an adjoining parish, the truth came out that the man had never had any intention of taking the matter further. "That secretary had no right to string you along with such false hopes", he said. "He has done you a great injustice, and I'll tell him that to his face when next I see him". In retrospect it appeared as if the forcefulness and persuasiveness of my character had been too much for the man to openly oppose. He'd found it easier to lie to my face than oppose such an offer. It's off times easier to be agreeable than momentarily hurtful: to say yes when we should be saying no!

Then, at a time when more doors appeared to be shutting than opening, on meeting our colleagues at The Caledonian Hotel, we learned the greatest news of all; a bona fide parish minister was eager to meet us with the anticipation of officiating at our wedding. His manse was visited and the Reverend Angus McCaskill proved a tonic and an inspiration.. A heavy burden was at last lifted, and now the hours and intervening days could be idled away in further viewing of so many panoramic points of interest. Yes, and sadly, the less panoramic ones too, such as off Leith Walk! Indeed, had not recent headlines been centred round one of those vile tenements where a young girl, made pregnant by her own father, had now knifed him to death? Cobblestones still paved many of the main thoroughfares and up Leith Walk the cable concealed below the track had pulled trams up that steep gradient to the engine house at the top

'viewing, points of interest'

Before that momentous wedding day occurred we frequented several places of worship as many of these were then left open. In Scotland's proud capital, while others enjoyed entertainment and historic buildings, we enjoyed the interiors of different church traditions. One place stood out in a fashion almost as eerie as the Church of The Good Shepherd in London: an Episcopal church off the lower part of the Royal Mile. A large notice had been scribbled announcing Confessions, and It had been misspelled with two Fs!. Having traversed a lot of ascending dark steps along a weird passage, one came into a church of extreme Anglo-Catholic persuasion. We were both highly sensitive and felt the environment was more suitable for a horror film than for loving Jesus. Katie said that such worshippers seemed to prefer darkness rather than light. 'Was it because their deeds were evil?' Then, closer to the day appointed for our marriage, we revisited that massive Episcopal cathedral dedicated to St Mary. Indeed, hardly had we done so than did that little, kind and rather erratic priest from the Aberdeen area come rushing across to say he was most concerned. "Where have you two been? I've been most concerned about you!" he said. "Without any further delays we must get things arranged for your wedding. Do come this way." What we then did was regrettable and utterly despicable. As the kindly, eager priest hurried ahead, taking it that we were following behind, we quietly slipped out of a cathedral door. For we now knew - only too well! - that we had to adhere to the marriage plans already made for us by our proud Presbyterian colleague: George Bruce of Illustrated. Yes, like the church secretary at Dalkeith whose shortcomings I'd criticized, I was no better. Indeed, as a wearer of the cloth I was probably in God's sight far worse for what I'd just done!

Returning to our evening residence the now familiar kind of questions occurred once more, but now I would play the landlady and her partner at their own game! In order to take them off the scent concerning the City church where we were to marry, I stated that we were to be married away on the outskirts. "Well, where exactly?" they asked.. "Well, you will honour a secret if I tell you!" I added. Once again there would be a scuffle and a sound of deep sobs.as Mrs Gray vacated the room. "Oh' Mr Thompson, see what you've done again. She thinks you don't trust her!" would again be the kind of words the thin, gaunt character possibly uttered. But, now we knew how utterly devious both of them were and one would play them at a similar game.

When the wedding was due on the morrow, I implied that plans were being made for us to marry in Dalkeith Baptist Church the day after. (It was partly a naughty way of hitting back at that church's secretary!) Nevertheless, such a 'terminological inexactitude' had its desired effect. When the morning came publicity was already in the newspapers that a Baptist minister at Dalkeith was about to marry us the next day and, of course, there was no such minister there! Fortunately, and as carefully pre-arranged, our colleagues turned up early at our flat where we had secretly packed our bags for leaving on the spot.

Tremendous difficulty resulted as the landlady and her accomplice wished to detain us as long as they possibly could. They'd phoned round and bargained with different newspapers, each desperate to learn of our planned wedding on the 'assumed' morrow. Now three colleagues from Illustrated were at the door, and on hearing the commotion as they sought to enter, we vacated our room with our belongings and squeezed out of the entrance while the loud stout landlady, and the refined thin fellow tried unsuccessfully to detain us.

Due to the foresight of our companions, and so that we could avoid a whole battery of cameramen and reporters at the downstairs entrance on to the street, the bank downstairs had made keys available by which we could descend lower than the level of the ground entrance. Indeed, the old basement beneath the bank – part of which had served as an air raid shelter in the far off war years - was now to be hopefully entered. The basic problem was: would the door in to this old air raid shelter open? We stood along that bleak basement in much suspense as one of our colleagues appeared as if he were 'picking the lock', Or was it that he was trying what appeared to be a whole bunch of keys? But then - as if God wanted us to know that He also was in this adventure with us! - the door began to creak open on its rusty hinges. We fumbled our way along a smelly and disused passage - littered with cobwebs – which eventually came out into the welcome freshness of daylight. Here we ascended steps, crossed a footpath and then found ourselves 'bundled' into a waiting taxi. But as for our third journalist, he had the most unenviable task of confronting the battery of cameramen to say – after several minutes had transpired! – that we'd just vacated the premises by an unforeseen exit. It had all been a matter of vying for time as well as taking them off our scent.

With our heads shielded from sight, the special taxi sped in detour in and out of many a side street of the busy city. However, before minutes had transpired, we looked back to find two press cars on our tail. Indeed, it seemed as if – once again - all odds were against us! But then, as if God were performing a miracle, the lights changed to red as a major crossroads was approached. Our veteran driver made a daring jump across, while a policeman smiled, nodded and forcefully stepped out to see that the cars behind didn't follow suit. This gave us tremendous breathing space. and we soon arrived at the unobtrusive London Road Church of Scotland while possibly our seekers could have ended up in the vicinity of Dalkeith! Yes, they'd been truly foxed!

The Marriage Of The Year

The great moment for our marriage arrived and the service had to be discreet and secretive. The minister was already there, completely robed and ready to meet us. The dear caretaker and his wife were to join us as witnesses, and apart from our friends from Illustrated who'd come to finalise our adventure and take the photographs, the church was, humanly speaking, unoccupied. That the Almighty was with us we had no need to doubt; His presence was deeply felt, and this was largely due to the dignity with which the parish minister conducted such a simple ceremony.

Our friends from Illustrated realised that they were witnessing a unique event. As their publication was later to affirm: 'Never in living memory has it ever been known for a parson to elope!' Yes, they were truly right in affirming that the incident had made me famous as 'the eloping parson!' Well, to the narrow and to the sour I suppose a more appropriate term would have been 'notorious!' Whatever one's interpretation had been while pursuing the daily and evening papers of that year, whether it was one of delight or denouncement, once the event had occurred every paper that mentioned us, had nothing but congratulations to offer. The whole world loves a lover, and we were two lovers so wrapped up in each other as, at times, to be almost oblivious to everything else. The only hint of criticism that we were to find published, expressed the concern of the Rev. Dr Prescott, the fellow who had been working in liaison with cameramen and journalists; the minister in whose church I'd preached on love! To have agreed to a wedding in his establishment would have resulted in a vast congregation, of that I had no doubt, but it would have been a service of utter distraction with a vast accumulation of cameras and shorthand jotters thrown in! His offer, if persued, would have made absolute fools of both of us and this our friends from Illustrated knew only too well.

With the hindsight of the years one learns to appreciate what was not always so obvious at the time: the Reverend Angus McAskill, in marrying us, was inviting possible criticism upon himself. Admittedly, Scottish people on the whole are a far more romantic race than many from south of the border; nevertheless it would be quite unusual if the eldership of a Kirk did not possess amongst it one or two strict and critical members. That a previous minister, the Rev. Graham Hardy, had changed his mind about marrying us after his willingness to do so had hit the front page of the Scotsman is hardly to be wondered at. Yes, he obviously had his elders in mind! However, thankfully, many of these latter are happy to leave such ministerial factors as marriage completely with the wisdom of the one who has been specially equipped and trained for such functions. Indeed, why insist on such high and exasperating training if the leader becomes no more than a puppet? No general practitioner would tolerate his patients stipulating how he went about his job, and a physician of souls is surely no less worthy of a similar respect! Wise elders realise - what so many church councils, vestries and synods fail to appreciate - that every man, truly equipped, should be largely left to his own job! Perhaps more trouble occurs in churches, because of those who think they can do the work of the specialist better than the specialist himself, than in any other profession! Such culprits are usually the last to have folk interfering with how they run their lives.

The kiss that ends ILLUSTRATED'S exclusive picture-story of the year's most controversial marriage—and opens a new future together for the runaways. Angus Macaskill has a smile of encouragement for the pair he has just wed: the girl wife, and the young man whose life is the Church

Many photos were taken on the great day, quite a few during the marriage itself. It was unlikely that the minister knew that these would form a leading article in a future edition of the Illustrated (Wednesday 3rd July 1954)! If he had not sensed a similar possibility before, then he must have lacked the necessary wisdom of a serpent while he retained the innocence of a dove (Matthew 10: 16). I only know that lovable man never asked my fiancée or me why so many photographs had been taken and we hardly had the opportunity to tell him ourselves.

When that renowned edition of the leading national weekly was released, the story of' 'My Runaway Marriage' was not only well illustrated, it was profoundly well written. The words, however, were hardly my own and the literary style conveyed a romanticism far beyond my own literary ability to express.. Nevertheless, what the romantic reader looked for would be found and, alas, that which borders on the fictitious is sometimes more sought for than less emotional fact!

Two things I have learned through my dealings with the press: to believe only half of what I read, the half I accept, and to realise that it is most probably slanted. The first factor is due to a reporter realising that he is better off returning to base with any story rather than none and the second factor is a reflection of the kind of response the reporter receives! After all, such men and women are only human and their job can be at times, to say the least, exceedingly exasperating.

My brother's wedding preceded ours by a couple of months. Yet, because of the very fact that he was related to me (as I have touched on), captions such as, 'The Wedding of the Eloping Parson's Brother' were publicised alongside photos of a wedding, which they'd desired to solemnise in quietness and reverence. Yes, the press at times were ruthless, particularly when we were reluctant at times to cooperate with them! But, on the whole, we fared better in publicity than those who opposed our plans and this, I suppose, because when we could cooperate with them, we certainly did. Indeed, with the passing of those days terminating in our marriage, we learned to enjoy much of their company, and, but for being on contract with an exclusive write-up to Illustrated, we would have told them everything they wanted to know! To two journalists, particularly, we were deeply indebted. We felt that God had sent them to find us from temporary oblivion in London. Through their advice we were now being married in Scotland and here, at this very service, one of them was fulfilling the role of best man, while another one was giving away my bride! They were as much instruments in the hands of God as the delightful minister who pronounced us in public what I sense God had already made us: man and wife! At that period I could no more believe that a minister's words and actions could turn two people into one flesh than that a priest's words and actions could turn a disc of unleavened bread in to the flesh of Jesus! I looked upon our marriage ceremony as akin to a sacrament, but solely in the sense of being a visible acknowledgement of what God Himself, had already done.

The union acknowledged now by the Kirk, and approved of by the land, my bride and I made our way out of the hallowed building almost as secretly and discreetly as when we had arrived. We drove off in the memorable taxi and then switched into a private car to join one of our colleagues and his wife. Taxis were far too conspicuous with so many hawk-eyed newspapermen on our tracks! Soon we left our friend's car, and made our way to acquire respectable accommodation for the night.

In Conclusion

After the marriage of the year was over and the novelty of perusing the congratulatory reports in most of the evening newspapers had been got through, it seemed as if a silent anticlimax followed. We were able to secure accommodation for the night within a quieter part of Edinburgh. When the gentle landlady and her husband were let into the little secret as to who we actually were she did her utmost to make our stay that evening as pleasant as she could, with the limited resources she had available. Her husband could offer us a toast with no more than ordinary beer, though the kindness of the gesture was truly appreciated. She was eager to present us with three plaques of birds with which we might furnish a wall within our future home. Such a simple gesture couldn't fail to touch our hearts.

The wedding night was sexually of little use to us. Whether we indulged or not is not likely to be remembered as we were both physically and mentally exhausted on retiring for the night. Indeed, the only thing that stands out in my memory is the feeling of wonderful peace, which followed months and months of constant struggle. Of one thing I am sure: we knelt in gratitude to Almighty God to whom we both belonged and dedicated our lives to be used for His Glory.

Next morning, before we left that home for the great Waverley Station, the landlady asked us one important favour: might she make it public, by a plaque or by some other means, that hers was the house, and within it was the room, where the renowned runaway pastor and his bride had spent their wedding night? She had no need to ask; the privilege was ours to give! We shook hands and, myself in a collar and tie, we made our way casually and unobtrusively towards the city centre, our purpose to board the delightful southbound express Queen of Scots.

Indeed, it was even more delightful when we discovered that, as part of a wedding present, we were being ushered into a comfortable Pullman coach and soon, with a lump in our throats, we were waving goodbye to our journalist friends whom we might never see again. The train steamed its way out of Waverley station. One or two photographers flashed their cameras from outside our window. Then, as we picked up the morning paper for something to read, we read the headline: 'Married At Last!' We clasped hands and commended our future to God. Yes, we were travelling out into the vast unknown. The immediate destination would be Yorkshire. Because our consciences were clear we intended to meet any opponents we knew face to face. Little did I know then that the journey into the future would be spiritually more exciting, more humorous and, alas, more fraught with tragedies than all I had previously passed through.

The train, early on, plunged momentarily into darkness on two brief occasions. It was possibly a loose connection. Though far from superstitious I noticed it but I said nothing. Was this an omen? One occasion was a little longer than the other, but the light eventually returned. Dear reader, it always does! Perhaps some day I'll write about my further escapades. Till then, God bless and keep you in His care.

Acknowledgements

The author conveys deep appreciation to his wife Doreen, for having typed the whole original manuscript from scraps of disjointed material, and for having made order out of chaos. Without her utter dedication it would hardly have ever materialized into a book.

Gratitude is also expressed to Jill Russell of Aberdeen and John Harrison of Portnockie for constructive literary criticism of the earlier, embryonic edition of this work, approved and accepted for publication by the, then, leading Scottish publisher: Lochar; and bearing the title: Virtues & Vices Of A Spiritual Tramp.

For photographs of Holywell and district, appreciation is expressed to Philip Mason of the Flintshire Archives Department, Hawarden. Nr Chester   For further illustrations he is, again, indebted to his wife Doreen; also to some, long deceased; and others sadly untraceable. He has also been mindful of Ted's invaluable expertise and Hanna's care.

Subsequent Notes On The Author

Following on from the period recorded in this book, the author very much found himself back at square one, and fulfilling the lowliest of tasks. To quote but one instance: exchanging clean towels for old from a tricycle. Yes, and allocated to do it in the district where he'd been the proud young Minister! Nevertheless, varied preaching and pastoral opportunities come along; and these are only turned down when offer of a remunerated four-year slog in a top liberal seminary presents itself. Varied experiences as a Congregational minister follow from this; only to be superseded, via a memorable term in Oxford, for the Anglican priesthood.

Following a curacy in a mining parish, posts move from an affluent rural 'North End' living - conducive to blood 'sports'; to that of bells and smells in an Anglo Catholic downtown suburb - with a hospital chaplaincy attached. Yet two things constantly trouble James: the utter bigotry and intolerance that frequently existed between rival branches of churchmanship; and the 'exclusive to human' concept of salvation and redemption they sadly shared in common.

Thankfully, Vatican 2 was not without some good effect; major branches of Christendom began to realize that they had more in common than in what divided them. Sadly, the author was not unaware of the fact that such impetus had been triggered, primarily, through dwindling numbers in the pews! Nevertheless, Catholics, at long last, began to accept the hymnody of Protestants. Protestants, at long last, shared occasional services with Catholics; yet - quite unforgivably, for the author! - the needs of the larger creation were excluded from every Trinitarian Denomination in the world

James became moved with moral indignation as he witnessed the churches disgusting apathy towards the plight of factory-farmed animals; even their commendation of vivisection and barbarities, such as bullfights in Spain. "One can throw a goat from a church tower with the blessing of the priest;" he said, "and an archbishop 'graces' a bullfight. But woe betide those who practice contraception in even the poorest of places!" He evolved, theologically, to affirm Christendom's grossly inadequate concept of God's love; having a whole host of Scriptural 'ammunition' with which to prove it.

Clashing at such a time with this enlightenment, the author undergoes the horrors of desertion and divorce, while a financial crisis loomed in his parish! He'd previously known what it was to have lost one child; yes, and to have another who is severely retarded. The author knew how Anglicanism at that period frowned upon divorce and remarriage – even though one did not initiate it and fought desperately hard to stop it happening! Indeed, he knew that – in the eyes of his 'superiors' - to be 'gay' may well have been much more acceptable.

When about to marry his second wife, Doreen, in 1983, James was advised: "Why don't you take her in as your housekeeper Father? One appreciates that you've been used to a sex life; but you'll appreciate that marriage, itself, must be out of the question!" He has seen the blatant hypocrisy of several who hear the confessions of others. Yes, and of many who preach as hot gospel evangelists, carrying a well-worn Bible with them! This writer has 'seen it all'

James pioneered animal blessing services in Yorkshire and Grampian. Indeed, he later compiled a hymnbook specifically for them. To the consternation of some within the church – but to the jubilation of others both inside and outside! – he's acclaimed 'the animal padre'. A title received when a senior hospital chaplain in Aberdeen: and confirmed by TV appearances that followed! He then addressed Retreats for, what is now, 'Catholic Concern For Animals'; a group close to his heart.

His last leading church was dubbed Noah's Ark; and he, himself, referred to as Father Noah. Eyebrows lifted when, on the Moray Firth, he consecrated a pet cemetery. Yes, and later officiated at a most stately funeral for a faithful hound.

Now turned 75, he still enjoys a busy life, with his second wife, Doreen, in the beloved Wales of his youth. From here his calling has led him to Germany, Eire, Spain, Italy and France, to bless sanctuaries and try and open the eyes of the churches to the myopic and tunnelled vision approach they hold of Christ. The one who called himself the Good Shepherd; has 'got the whole world in his hands'; and told us to proclaim His gospel to 'every creature.'

Two Publications By The Author Are Displayed On Pages Following
These prices include postage and packing.

Ty Coch Publishing,
Peacehaven, Fron Park Road, Holywell. Clwyd CH8 7UY
Tel: 01352-712368

HOW TO BOUNCE THROUGH LIFE

WITH VIM, VIGOUR & VITALITY

JAMES THOMPSON
Hypno-therapist, Psychotherapist, Bible Expositor, Animals' Padre

£7.50

First Published 1996. A 126 Page 'Self Help' On Keeping Positive

£3.89

First Published 1996. 21Thoughts For Urgent Christian Consideration

Many articles relating to the author are available on the website. Simply type in, *via Google*, **James Thompson Animal padre UK**.

He may also be contacted via: **Christians Against All Animal Abuse**